M000085024

# THE WARFIGHTER'S SOUL

## ENGAGING IN THE BATTLE FOR THE WARRIOR'S SOUL

### GREG WARK & RAY RODRIGUEZ

BroadStreet
PUBLISHING

BroadStreet Publishing® Group, LLC
Savage, Minnesota, USA
BroadStreetPublishing.com

The Warfighter's Soul: Engaging in the Battle for the Warrior's Soul
Copyright © 2022 D. Gregory Wark and Ray Rodriguez

978-1-4245-6020-2 (softcover)
978-1-4245-6021-9 (e-book)

All rights reserved. No part of this book may be reproduced in any form, except for brief quotations in printed reviews, without permission in writing from the publisher.

All Scripture quotations are taken from the New King James Version® (NKJV). Copyright © 1982 by Thomas Nelson. Used by permission. All rights reserved.

Stock or custom editions of BroadStreet Publishing titles may be purchased in bulk for educational, business, ministry, fundraising, or sales promotional use. For information, please email orders@broadstreetpublishing.com.

Cover and interior by Garborg Design Works | garborgdesign.com

Printed in the China

22 23 24 25 26 5 4 3 2 1

*For all men and women who serve and have served in the US military. Your selfless act of serving the country's citizenry is unrepayable, short of taking a post.*

# CONTENTS

Preface . . . . . . . . . . . . . . . . . . . . . . . . . . . . . 5

Introduction . . . . . . . . . . . . . . . . . . . . . . . . . 10

1 Inspiration . . . . . . . . . . . . . . . . . . . . . . . . . 14

Part I The Warfighter's Soul . . . . . . . . . . . . . . . 19

2 The Oath and Power of Words . . . . . . . . . . . . 22

3 Invisible Wounds . . . . . . . . . . . . . . . . . . . . . 32

4 Warfighter Faith . . . . . . . . . . . . . . . . . . . . . 55

5 Society's Unpaid Debt . . . . . . . . . . . . . . . . . 63

Part II Detection . . . . . . . . . . . . . . . . . . . . . . 76

6 Signs and Syndromes . . . . . . . . . . . . . . . . . . 79

Part III Relief and Recovery . . . . . . . . . . . . . . . 89

7 Psychological First Aid . . . . . . . . . . . . . . . . . 92

8 Speaking a New Language . . . . . . . . . . . . . . . 102

9 The Power of a Listener . . . . . . . . . . . . . . . . . 110

Part IV Application . . . . . . . . . . . . . . . . . . . . 117

10 Building Memorials . . . . . . . . . . . . . . . . . . . 119

11 Changing the Pattern . . . . . . . . . . . . . . . . . 127

12 Taking Life Back . . . . . . . . . . . . . . . . . . . . 138

Part V The Cause . . . . . . . . . . . . . . . . . . . . . . 150

13 Elements and the Battleground . . . . . . . . . . . 154

14 Morals, the Law, UCMJ, and ROEs . . . . . . . . . 161

15 Causation . . . . . . . . . . . . . . . . . . . . . . . . . 165

16 Soul at Risk . . . . . . . . . . . . . . . . . . . . . . . . 188

17 A Renovated Life . . . . . . . . . . . . . . . . . . . . 198

Acknowledgments . . . . . . . . . . . . . . . . . . . . . . 203

Endnotes . . . . . . . . . . . . . . . . . . . . . . . . . . . 205

Bibliography . . . . . . . . . . . . . . . . . . . . . . . . . 223

About the Authors . . . . . . . . . . . . . . . . . . . . . 239

# PREFACE

The flag...is a visible symbol of the ideal aspirations of
the American people. It is the one focus in which all
unite in reverential devotion. We differ in religion; we
differ in politics; we engage in disputes as to the true
meaning of the Constitution, and even challenge the
wisdom of some of its provisions; we inject self-interest
and greed into most of the ordinary transactions of
daily life, but through the sanctifying folds of the flag,
the collective intelligence of the nation rises superior to
the wisdom of its parts, and thus ensures the perpetuity
of the Republic.[1]

—Major General Arthur MacArthur

To declare war is the most sobering decision a nation's leaders will ever
make. Because nothing tests a society more than war. Its debate brings
out every kind of emotion, every belief stance, every political position,
and every life's philosophy. Nothing can polarize a people and then unify
them more then war. War's "justness," therefore, is a relevant discussion
for debate for a nation right up until the time the decision is made. But
once the decision is made, a nation's moral responsibility is to unify
around those who are called to prosecute it. The nation who sends men
and women to battle must come to the place where those who are fighting the war *never* have to question their support and respect.

Several years ago, I met with an Iraq veteran and a veteran of the
war in Afghanistan for breakfast. Our conversation focused on their
experiences, many painful, as one story of deployment and war seemed to

spark the other vet to tell of his experiences. Neither vet cared what those around thought as they laughed, teared up, spoke profanities, and ate. Both shared the common torture of losing their childhood best friend.

After a while, an older man walked past our table in the direction of the restroom. The next time we saw him he seemed confused, and we later found out from his caretaker that it was due to dementia. As he approached, we noticed he was wearing a World War II veteran hat. When he came close to our table, both the soldiers stood to their feet introducing themselves as veterans and reached out to shake his hand and thank him for his service. Surprised but joyful, the older man began to share his experiences with the two fellow veterans with absolute clarity and no signs of dementia. Knowing he was speaking to brothers, he spoke like he was as a young warfighter again. Our new friend spoke about landing several times on a foreign beach to face the enemy in combat. We fixated on him, and time stood still as he teared up along with the rest of us, remembering his fellow brothers and the loss of his best friend. It was as though his friends had died just yesterday, an experience all three men and I shared. Our new friend was ninety-two years old and truly a hero.

Over the years, I have been privileged to sit around fires with those who served and listen for hours as men and women told their own stories. I noted how hard it is to serve our country. Our men and women give so much, and the memories they live with never go away. While they may heal a bit, the pain is always there.

Warfare has been part of the human experience since the very beginning of our species. I don't think it's a stretch to say that humanity is somewhat predisposed to it. "Since the United States was founded in 1776, she has been at war during 214 out of her 235 calendar years of existence. In other words, there were only 21 calendar years in which the U.S. was not engaged in a war."[2] While the exact number of years without war remains debatable, we can agree that war has been a significant part of this country's existence.[3] Most boys from early childhood have a dream of fighting and defeating an "enemy." As a child, I would often make a bow and arrow out of green limbs and play cowboys and Indians with several of my boyhood friends. We would divide into teams and go

# PREFACE

to the orange groves of Fullerton, California, and pelt each other with oranges until only one man remained standing. In our later years, we would joke that this was the true birth of paintball.

However, this book isn't about war; it is about the effects of war on the warfighters. Unlike the make-believe warfighting games of one's youth, adult military members take a stand and volunteer to go into the abyss of battle aware of the risks. Still, most are unaware of the consequences war can have on the stability of their soul. Over the past decade, an unimaginable tragedy has begun to unfold that seems to be ignored or shrugged off for the most part. I don't think it's because people don't want to do something. I just think it's because there are few real answers. This tragedy is happening to the best of us, the selfless and honorable segment of our population. They don't speak of their suffering, their dark experiences, or the depth of their sacrifice. I call this people group warfighters. You might call them veterans.

The idea that an average of twenty-two veterans commit suicide per day originates from a 2012 suicide data report on veterans at risk of suicide.[4] After the Department of Veterans Affairs took a passionate stance to reduce veteran suicide in 2007, research into the issue began. Using data collected from twenty-one states, the researchers reported, "Among cases where history of US military service was reported, Veterans comprised approximately 22.2% of all suicides reported during the project period. If this prevalence estimate is assumed to be constant across all US states, an estimated 22 Veterans will have died from suicide each day in the calendar year 2010."[5] An estimate to be sure, but since its publication, that number of twenty-two veteran suicides per day has become the moniker or calling cry for action to prevent veteran suicide. In the VA's "2020 National Veteran Suicide Prevention Annual Report," it estimated that in 2018, a total of 6,435 US Veterans had committed suicide.[6] That number averages out to approximately 17.6 suicides per day. This statistic does not imply that things are getting better, only that reporting has improved, resulting in more accurate numbers. Yet the twenty-two per day moniker continues.

Too many of our veterans continue to make the agonizing decision to end their own lives each day. They may be veterans from Vietnam or

7

any war since. Furthermore, the suicide rate of active-duty personnel has continued to climb.[7] For example, a 2019 report by CNN news indicated that 2018 saw a 300% rise in the suicides of Special Forces personnel.[8] Additionally, this problem is not limited to just the US military. In a 2020 article on mental health in the military, The British Forces Broadcasting Service reported a five-year increase in suicide amongst its military.[9] These reports show that during the wars in Afghanistan and Iraq, the rate of suicide has skyrocketed. While the Pentagon has worked diligently to erase the stigma attached to suicide, the rate among warfighters remains high. This unbelievable statistic hit us unprepared as a nation and must be faced with determination and tenacity to stop it.

When warfighters' time in active service ends, many other aspects of their lives end with it: their time away from home, their pay, time with their military brothers, the grime and smell of war. However, their personally endured tortures do not so easily wash away. Tortures resulting from participating in the conduct of war, regardless of their MOS (military occupational specialty). Torturous memories endlessly replaying out of sight from even their closest family and friends.

As such, it's our turn to have their backs. It is our turn to tend to their wounds. It's our turn to sit by their sides while they heal. And it's our turn to hold them up as they rehabilitate from their physical, mental, and moral injuries. Today, science is making great strides in mind mapping and the promotion of knowledge that heals the warrior, but little time is spent on healing methods for the soul. A soldier unprepared for the anguish of war is as vulnerable as a soldier sent into battle without armor. Due to the stressors of military life, veterans are often left with life-altering ailments that make life after service seem unbearable. For too many, the results are a high degree of homelessness, an ever-growing suicide rate, devastating divorce statistics, post-traumatic stress, traumatic brain injury, and more.

The seriousness of the issue of veteran suicide deserves a life-and-death approach if we are to win the battle for the souls of our warfighters. We aren't seeking passive answers or ways to numb the pain. I approach this issue with the belief that the way to save the lives of those who stand at the precipice of life and death is through the discovery of multiple truths.

# PREFACE

We will enter this darkness with the determination that truth-seekers must carry. And no matter how long it takes or hard we must fight, we will find it. My dream is to wake up a struggling and confused nation to focus on a blight we can fix. To make hope go viral among our warfighters and their families. It's our turn to sacrifice for their freedom. It's our time to go all in, to find answers, and call those suffering out of the shadows and into the clean, healing air.

When writing this book, Ray and I made a conscious choice to address the warfighter, but we are aware that it isn't only that part of the military who struggle with suicidal ideations. It is because of this that we wrote programs that will greatly help all military personnel regardless of role.

*Greg Wark*

# INTRODUCTION

If suicide started in a cave, it would be found in the
darkest part of the cave, ending with a final drop into
a bottomless abyss. The cave entrance is not hidden
in some distant jungle. It is as visible as an exit ramp
on any roadway. Enter here, states the sign, and I'll
save you from all your troubles. We all see the sign. It
does not hide itself nor lurk in the shadows. When the
roadway of one's life becomes a monotonous treadmill,
this sign sits at a fork in the road, like all the other
signposts. Some signs list criteria, a set of qualifications
and requirements one must have or be willing to
achieve prior to entering. The suicide exit sign does
not. To the burdened traveler, its message rings out,
I'll save you from your troubles, sometimes followed
by a whisper. The whisper lulls the listener with the
words, and others will no longer be burdened by you.
Tired of their troubles, the weary travelers venture in.
Some look around and are detoured by the darkness
returning for another day of chaos. Yet, there are those
so burdened by the traffic on their roadway, desperate
for a better life and unable to find it, who continue
farther and farther into the cave in the hope that in
there, they will find their future.

—So goes the description found in the mind of one soul rescued from the cave

This allegory describes the lure and promise of suicide. Having worked

10

with countless individuals struggling to find their way in life, it is easy to see how such a place might draw them in. When the excitement of life and the fight to achieve it has left, anyone, be it a farmer, business-person, scientist, or soldier, is at risk of entering an intense struggle for survival. Imagine a drowning man fighting for one more breath. He will eventually surrender to his death without a rescue. This book concerns that rescue.

We propose to lead you along two paths: one for the sufferer and one for the rescuer.

To the sufferer, a potential member of the "Lost twenty-two," don't ring out just yet. Wait one more day and then another. This text offers knowledge, understanding, and training for that very purpose. You will gain knowledge and understanding about the environment in which you find yourself, and you will learn how to tread in such waters. As the real-life stories found here demonstrate, it is possible to lighten your pack (your burdens, if you will) just enough to remain afloat while waiting for rescue to arrive. You will also find basic skills for rescuing yourself by finding that solid ground on which to launch a brighter future.

To the rescuer, consider these as first responder tactics. Injuries requiring physicians, wounds requiring surgeons, and diseases requiring medication must be left to skilled professionals. Your goal here is to help inspire the sufferer, to help them find purpose and continue living. In this book, you can learn some first aid skills and tactics that will help you identify those in trouble and learn how to start the conversation that could lead them to the help they need.

To our fellow service members, we are connected. Connected in cause and connected in our military culture. We are brothers to the end. Let that end be long in coming.

An ancient author on military strategies, Sun Tzu, instructed his officers to know one's battleground. Knowing one's battleground makes victory possible; not knowing it assures defeat. Defeating suicidal thoughts requires knowing where the battle is being played out. We begin the process of Sun Tzu's "taking whole" approach by guiding our readers through getting to know the battleground of the soul and the battle for the soul against invisible demons.[10]

This book consists of five parts. Part One discusses the warfighter's soul. When young people join the military, they and their souls are separated from the rest of society. They are trained and indoctrinated into a different culture. This book describes how the transition from a civilian culture to one in the military and back again can negatively affect the veteran as well as some methods for overcoming these transitions. It further considers the debt society owes to the military, how it might be paid, and the subsequent penalties for non-payment.

Part Two addresses detection. Beyond depression and stress, what other signs might a rescuer notice in a person considering suicide? In this section, the use of the term *syndrome* relates to signs we've categorized and not necessarily to specific syndromes articulated in psychology manuals. Nonetheless, they do reflect conditions that we find indicate a potential for suicidal thought.

Part Three concerns relief and recovery. Confronting stress and trauma can be a daunting task. Images, smells, and sounds of combat become ingrained in the warfighter's mind. It requires a lot of work and time to lighten their influence. It is not for the faint at heart. But doing some of the work—even a small part—can bring a small amount of light into another's darkness. Using a crawl, walk, run technique for reversing and/or redirecting a sufferer's current course toward destruction could allow them to slowly gain control over their situation.

The opening segment speaks to the current work and efforts regarding first response and the need for immediate help. Next, we discuss the first step and methods for starting a conversation. Much like addictions, the first step to solving the problem is to admit it exists. As a rescuer, you will likely need to initiate that conversation. Learning to listen and identify the separate issues that burden a person makes it possible for you to help. Thoughts of suicide consist of multiple problems bound together and loaded on the back of the sufferer. Here, you learn to first open yourself up to listening to some very ugly stories. Were they not so, there would be no trauma. You will learn to listen for the sufferer's sake while at the same time avoiding your instinct to make impulsive judgments about the event. You learn about potential pitfalls, such as telling the traumatized person what they should or should not have done or articulating what you would have done.

Part Four introduces methods the sufferer can apply right away. These tactics have worked successfully for several years. Be sure to read "Framing the Issue" at the beginning of Part Four. It will help you understand one of the major concerns of being a rescuer: recognizing when you may or may not be able to help save a life from venturing into the suicidal cave.

Part Five attempts to answer the more esoteric questions of why a person would commit suicide. Do not look for easy answers here or anywhere else. There are none. However, understanding why one person might be more susceptible to suicide's lures than the next is possible. Isolating and identifying the problem(s) becomes easier when you know the parts and functions of the broken device, in this case, the soul.

The first chapter in this section identifies an arguable yet workable list of elements and definitions describing the soul. We lay a foundational perspective in approaching the elements of the human soul, not as definitive but only to provide a common point of reference on the subject. The second chapter in Part Five attempts to establish the working mechanisms within the soul and the rules by which they function. The next chapter speaks to the law. All laws result from our human struggle with our most general philosophical questions: *Who am I, and why am I here?* From there, the questions grow to include others, for example, groups and societies. Laws, rules, orders, and morals are constructs developed by individuals and groups to maintain order while we continue our effort to answer these basic questions.

Next, we explore *causation*,[11] a legal term identifying the cause of a problem. It attempts to answer the question of why someone would choose to commit suicide. While trauma is a prominent cause of stress, there are so many other causes as well, some small and some, well, traumatic.[12] Demystifying the interplay of stress-causing agents and one's personal guidelines for one's existence offers a unique view into how, given enough disruptions, the entire system might collapse into a judgment of guilty and a sentence of death.

# 1

# INSPIRATION

Thus, do we memorialize those who, having ceased
living with us, now live within us. Thus, do we
consecrate ourselves, the living, to carry on the struggle
they began. Too much blood has gone into this soil for
us to let it lie barren. Too much pain and heartache
have fertilized the earth on which we stand. We here
solemnly swear this shall not be in vain. Out of this, and
from the suffering and sorrow of those who mourn this,
will come—we promise—the birth of a new freedom for
all humanity everywhere. And let us say...amen.[13]

—Rabbi Roland Gittelsohn

In March 1945, following a five-week, heavily contested battle on the
island of Iwo Jima, the United States military established three cemeteries,
one for each of the three Marine divisions that had fought on the island.
For the 5th Marine Division, Chaplain and Rabbi Roland Gittelsohn gave
a stirring dedication. We cannot in good conscience separate the loss of
those who inspired Gittelsohn's words from those veterans who leave the
battleground alive and yet leave part of themselves behind. Of those, we
have lost and continue to lose too many to suicide. Their loss signals an

ongoing war on a different, more personal battlefield. The struggle with suicide is as real as combat on a physical battlefield. It engages in the battlefield of one's mind, and it is furious and unrelenting.

When patrolling soldiers come under overwhelming fire from an enemy, they send a battlefield radio signal known as TIC (troops in contact). This designation requests that a QRF (quick reaction force) immediately deploy to their location. Its purpose—to overwhelm and kill the enemy by superior numbers and firepower. This action intends to subdue the enemy and mitigate loss of life to the patrol. Many veterans today are signaling a TIC here at home. However, instead of "troops in contact," the call echoes "veterans in contact." This urgent and silent VIC, unfortunately, often goes unheard and unmet by an adequate QRF. Today's suffering veterans need specialized and prepared QRF. One capable of overwhelming and destroying an enemy not made of flesh and blood. Building such a QRF and teaching and training veterans new battlefield tactics aimed at surviving this enemy is the motivating force behind the writing of this book.

Warfighters communicate in brutal, clear, and concise messages. Messages devoid of fluff. Time and clarity are essential. Orders are carried out exactly as specified. Failure to do so may result in grave consequences. This language is difficult to hear by a society ruled by political correctness, sensitivity to harsh environments, and lack of direction. In this environment, many VIC messages go unheard. They need a reaction force armed with wisdom founded on purpose and direction and that is unafraid of engaging. A force capable of bringing peace of mind. A peace that calms the mind and then sets it on a fresh course with clear direction and purpose. A peace armed with hope and perseverance. Peace is obtained through victory!

The terrible price paid for not speaking out is the death of vital wisdom. Soon followed by human lives. When wisdom is silenced, the dark side of mankind speaks up and grows louder. And this dark side never shuts up. It screams its devious and convoluted deceptions from the mountain tops. Void of wisdom, man is left to believe what he hears the most. Lies, deceptions, and misdirection, all glazed with carefully selected facts, make up the enemies' destructive weapons, and all are effective whether they come from leaders with ulterior motives or from a close friend who may be described as a wolf in sheep's clothing. Lies have a capacity for multiplication, and the more often they are heard, the more believable they become. Wisdom's weapon of choice against such lies is truth. Truth burns through facades, smashes falsehood, washes away the murky waters of compromise, and launches all good things in those who embrace it.

It is often the case in those contemplating suicide that the mind has embraced something other than the truth. The confusion builds as the sufferer questions the actions or inaction on the battlefield. Over time, truth becomes unreachable, resulting in hopelessness and despair. Mitigating this outcome requires a response force capable of bringing a calming atmosphere of truth.

More and more, well-dressed lies make truth not only unpopular but also disdained. Boldness in speaking the truth is looked down upon, and compromise of the truth is viewed as progressive. A common counterattack against the idea of truth includes questions such as, "Okay, but whose truth?" Or "Who or what gets to decide what is truth?" From this point, the conversation tends to become just another skirmish of wit and will. When wit wanes, opinion fills the gap, and it is endless. I (Greg) am not suggesting that we can all agree on what constitutes truth. But truth isn't about opinions; it's about realities. When dealing with suicidal tendencies, reality is deeply personal. Sometimes, we can determine whether someone may be experiencing these tendencies by asking personal questions, such as:

- Hey, are you okay?
- You seem to be somewhere else right now.
- What is going on inside you?
- Tell me what you are thinking.

Truth is exposed through the uncomfortable process of prodding.

Two of my favorite movie stars are Matt Damon and Robin Williams. Damon plays Will Hunting, a savant in mathematics who works as a maintenance man at a prestigious university. When the head of the mathematics department places a challenge on the board outside a class, Will Hunting solves it. Once the professor realizes it has been solved, he begins searching for the "student" with these exceptional abilities. After no success, he places another problem on the board hoping to expose the genius. By chance, he sees Will Hunting writing on the board and attempts to chase him down. Over time, the movie reveals Will Hunting to be a deeply disturbed person needing a psychologist (played by Robin Williams) to find help. Toward the end of the movie, there is a moment when the psychologist corners Will Hunting and tells him, "It's okay." Will responds with a passive, "Yeah, I know." Then the psychologist repeats himself, "It's okay." Again, Will responds, "I know." This scene repeats itself five times, and each time, Will becomes more emotional and ultimately breaks down and begins crying. Will had become adept at hiding the truth not only from himself but also everyone else. The problem is that when we cover the truth, the mind and soul begin to erode, and destructive behavior begins to be revealed. In *Good Will Hunting*, the best of who Will Hunting was to become was only possible when truth set him free.

If you are the one standing at that precipice of life or death, there are a few things I want to ask of you. I'm aware you feel alone and hopeless and that taking your own life looks like the only answer. I am aware you are suffering big time with the voices and images replaying repeatedly in your mind. But I want to ask you to do what you have done countless times before as a warfighter: Will you accept a new mission? This mission is to read this book, apply this truth, and kill the enemy. Your enemy is the will to take your own life. This very well may be the greatest and most powerful enemy you have ever faced, but if you stay with me, you will soon gain the weapons not only to kill your enemy but also to find the enemies of your band of brothers and lead them to kill their enemies as well.

You are used to brutal communication, so what I am about to write is nothing new. I ask you to suck it up a little longer, accept this mission, and complete it. And one more thing. I would like to lead you to a new oath. But as you take this one, I want what comes out of your mouth to be more than words. I want you to find a place you feel best and most at peace and meditate on these words. Then, when you are ready, say this as many times as you need for you to absorb its ramifications.

*"I will not permit myself to define my life's value or lack thereof. I will not give the events that have invaded my soul the right to define my life's value or lack thereof.*

*Lastly, I will not allow the dark voices in my head permission to define my life's value or lack thereof."*

Absorbing this truth into your soul is the first step toward rediscovering happiness, meaning, and purpose. The person you are today is about to meet the new person of all your tomorrows.

# PART I

# THE WARFICHTER'S SOUL

Some might describe the human soul as a container filled with things learned, things hoped for, beliefs—some tested, some proven, many just accepted. People have claimed that the soul contains the essence of the person. All else is only flesh and bone. The ability to peer into a person's soul, if possible, involves some knowledge of its structure and components and an understanding of how these parts work together. Humanity has been chasing this formula on many fronts throughout history. From Plato and Aristotle to Saul Kripke and Julia Kristeva, philosophers have searched and theorized in hope of understanding all things universal, natural, metaphysical, and mental. Psychology has sought to understand the mind's mechanics, what, how, and why one thinks and behaves.

Theologians struggle with the concept of human existence. Where did we begin? Why are we here? Medical science, in particular neurology, looks at the brain's structure and operation for its own perspective about understanding humans. Physicians and psychiatrists concentrate on identifying ailments and, most importantly, finding remedies for those ailments. Each of these disciplines adds to our knowledge of the particulars and complexities contained in a person's mind. In all our discoveries, where does the soul reside? What does the soul consist of? While questions such as these remain largely speculative, researchers from each of these fields offer many trustworthy insights, ideas, and methods for better understanding the soul. In this light, we also hope to establish a common point of reference concerning the soul, the spirit, and the conscience for the purpose of this forthcoming conversation.

As you read this book, please keep in mind, perspectives vary extensively about the soul and the spirituality element. A person's beliefs and belief systems are individual. Societies may hold common identities and rules establishing them as defined groups, but the individual inevitably puts his or her personal touch to each. Some apply their personal touch with broad strokes and some with small fine lines. Some apply group rules strictly while others apply them loosely. As a comical and yet realistic example, in the movie *Pirates of the Caribbean: The Curse of the Black Pearl*, there is a scene in which Elizabeth Swan (disguising her surname as Turner at that moment) demands, "Wait! You must take me to shore. According to the Code of the Order of the brethren—" Captain Barbossa then replies, "First, your return to shore was not part of our negotiations nor our agreement, so I must do nothing. And secondly, you must be a pirate for the pirate's code to apply, and you're not. And thirdly, the code is more what you'd call 'guidelines' than actual rules."[14]

Here, we find three relevant points applicable to all individual interpretations of societal rules and our ability to use common definitions as you read this book. The first requires an agreed-upon rule. Is there a soul or not? The most common perspectives identify the soul as being the human part(s) that are not body parts nor chemical reactions nor neurotransmissions nor anything physical. The second point means you must be part of the group for the conversation and rules to apply. We will be discussing subjects that may not apply to everyone. If a comment or belief does not apply to you, feel free to skip over it, ignore it, or just not accept it. The third point, and possibly the most important, concerns interpretation and devotion to the rules. You may find a considerable amount of helpful information here. Use what works for you as you see fit and skip the rest. Whether we are trying to clarify definitions, establish rules, or generate laws, there is always room for debate. To one, the rules are laws. To the other, they may only be "guidelines," as Captain Barbossa points out. This varying application of rules or opinions makes any group/society extremely dynamic and fluid. Adding clarity helps, but every situation, no matter how similar, will add its own level of uniqueness.

A person's view on life, their personality, and their individuality all rest on their interpretation of the world around them and on the choices they make from the options given to them. People commonly share points of view to better understand the world and each other. In part, the basis of all human dialogue balances on being able to offer perspectives and ideas in return for agreement, confirmation, or correction. It may be said that conversation provides the substance by which societies are built. Without it, separation, distrust, fear of one another, and isolation would result. Considering these multiple views, we ask our readers to lend us their understanding and allow us some consideration of perspective as we continue through the subject of suicide. It will serve as good practice as you encounter those struggling with their challenge of continuing with life.

We hope all our readers, whether educated in the universities, the streets, the farm, or any combination thereof, would be able to understand and use this material to better their lives and the lives of others they encounter. More specifically, we will provide our readers with a "go pack" set of tools so they will be able to help in eliminating veteran and active military suicide. A large part of this pack requires an understanding of military culture and elements of the soul unique to members in the military. What makes them different? How can a nonmilitary person relate to their struggles? These are some of the questions addressed here. We also investigate the issue of orders and rules. Conflicting orders or rules can be extremely problematic. Rules, laws, ethics, and morals all play a part in maintaining order in society, a group, a military operation, and even thoughts in one's mind. With so many directives and guides crashing into each other in a soldier's mind, one can begin to imagine the stress developing, let alone the instantaneous changing internal and external environment that occurs when the shooting starts.

# 2

# THE OATH AND POWER OF WORDS

Unfortunately, in today's world we must be reminded
that the power of an oath derives from the fact that
in it we ask God to bear witness to the promises we
make with the implicit expectation that He will hold us
accountable because we honor them.

—James L. Buckley

Among my (Greg's) earliest memories were my father's speeches at the
dinner table. My father used the quality time of our nightly dinner to
impart, build, and establish his values to his children. One of those values was understanding the power of words. He taught us that a man
who doesn't keep his word is not a man at all. He made it clear that if we
promised something to another individual, no matter what the cost, we
were to keep that promise. To do otherwise was to engender the greatest
shame not only to ourselves but also on our family. And it was one thing
for us to bring shame to ourselves, but it was altogether another to tar-
nish the family name.

We learned to think before making a promise or a commitment. And he tested us almost every day as he laid out our chores both before and after school. The acceptance of those duties was essentially a promise from us to him, and if we failed to fulfill that commitment, our father considered it a broken promise that would be met with swift action at the end of a razor strap. This arrangement taught us that words have meaning and carry with them consequences. It also taught us that all words were not created equal.

He often talked about the different types of promises we would make throughout our lives, teaching us that often in life, promises are tested, and how we reacted to those tests determined what kind of a person we would become. He taught us that if we gave our word to another, that meant we first had considered its gravity and, therefore, had no excuse to back out. As I grew older, having this foundation allowed me to recognize the differing levels of words and the importance of knowing their weight. The promise to our future spouses, bosses, business partners, teachers, and friends were not just idle words. Our success in life was predicated upon the weight we gave to our commitments.

An *oath* is a set of words that, when spoken, are among the highest levels of commitment a person can make. Therefore, all government offices, from the president of the United States to the leadership of all three branches of government, are led by those who have taken an oath of office. The oath is more than a commitment to a person. It represents a commitment to the ideals that make a nation great and allow it to function in unison, as the Constitution intended. The solemnity of the moment when someone takes an oath underscores its value. Once the person swears the oath, there is no backing out. To do so is met with the greatest shame and dire consequences. This swearing-in commits the oath-taker to defend the Constitution of the United States. While the oath of office is different for a military officer, the result is the same: it fundamentally transforms those who take it. It's more than a promise or a commitment. An oath binds the soul of those swearing it to a path in life and actions until the time for the enlistment or commission is over.

For the warfighter, the oath represents a beginning. When individuals take the oath of military service, those making this solemn promise knowingly give up certain freedoms and their safety, both in training and war. They knowingly place their families in a high-stress environment and follow that path to its conclusion. And their reward? A life of training, putting in long hours learning to be a warrior, and honing their skills through repetition. It is the ultimate life of discipline and duty. Warfighters become blended into one with those with whom they serve. They share everything all while giving up privacy, luxuries, and more. It is a life that not only requires the sacrifice of the oath-taker but also of their families, who must do without their warfighter's presence for many months at a time. These families face the fears of knowing their loved ones are in combat zones around the world. They also face the fear of knowing full well that their loved one may receive the call to make the supreme sacrifice: giving up their lives in the defense of their country and its people.

## Career

From our earliest years of life, most of us learn what we could be someday. Our parents dream for us as they see our talents grow and as we participate in sports, martial arts, dance, or drama, music, or mathematics. No good mom or dad would do anything less. Several months ago, our seven-year-old granddaughter, Marlea, came to me and asked if I could help her build a business. I hid my shock and pride and said, "Of course, baby." So, I took out some paper and handed her a handful of colored pencils. Mistakenly, I then began to speak to her about being a veterinarian since she loves horses and other animals so much. She gave me a long considering look and then blurted out her plan to open a bakery specializing in themed cupcakes. Once again, I hid my shock and pride, and after an hour, we had ten pages of notes and pictures she drew of her unique cupcakes. She even had the bakery name, *Marlea and Mia's Cupcake Creations*. (Mia is her best friend.) The interesting thing to me was that at such a young age, she had a dream, one I could crush with my opinion or bolster by my encouragement.

Many in life choose their career path based upon family tradition, financial incentives, the direction of school counselors, or the demands of the culture around them. This is what makes society work. We need politicians, doctors, lawmakers, lawyers, pastors, factory workers, artists, janitors, contractors, and construction workers. And each of these comes with challenges akin to the industry, but virtually all of them promise some certainty. Each of these comes with a job description that communicates what the employer expects and how the employee will be compensated.

But most jobs or careers don't come with absolute certainty of danger. They don't come with the assurance of difficult times in foreign countries and many months away from home and family. This is true only for a select group of people who choose a life that protects America's freedom, its ideals, and its people. This choice promises physical, mental, emotional, and financial hardship. When considering a career, warfighters look beyond themselves and take up a life for others. I'm not speaking of social workers, preachers, or politicians. I am speaking of the soldiers, sailors, airmen, marines, and coastguardsmen who voluntarily step up and willingly say, "Here I am. Use me."

A soldier's fitness report determines a great deal. These fitness reports are like a credit report. They determine a person's worthiness for progress. The problem comes when a soldier has issues mentally or emotionally that, if spoken, becomes a negative mark in the FITREP (fitness report). To avoid this negative mark, the soldier stays quiet and suffers in silence. The United States military is the best in the world at protecting its citizens and fighting our enemies. No nation can compete with the might of this nation. The problem comes when the war is over. It may be over in terms of fighting human enemies, but when that ends, a new war begins, and this one can be just as lethal as the previous war. There is no band of brothers in this one. No one to talk to or unwind with. Too often warriors fight this war alone, and this truism is underscored by what we see today in the massive loss of life in veteran suicides. Our inability to care for our warriors is the Achilles' heel of our nation. Presently, we are losing this fight. We need to own this tragedy and take action now.

## The Department of Veterans Affairs

Abraham Lincoln decreed that the US Department of Veterans Affairs was to "care for him who shall have borne the battle and for his widow

25

and his orphan."[15] Anyone who has dealt with the VA knows it's a broken system. Even Bernie Sanders, with whom I staunchly disagree ninety-nine percent of the time, said, "While serious people can have legitimate differences about when our country should go to war, there should never be a debate whether we fulfill the promises made to the men and women who served this country in the military. As a nation, we have a moral obligation to provide the best quality care to those who have put their lives on the line to defend us."[16]

True care for our veterans is not going to come about by throwing money into an already broken system. The budget of the VA is in the billions. I wonder what the private sector could do for our veterans with just a fraction of $270 billion slated for 2022. Because of the stresses related to military life, veterans often find themselves with life-altering ailments that make their post-service lives challenging at best and unbearable at worst. The results are high rates of post-traumatic stress, traumatic brain injury, divorce, homelessness, suicide, and more. I am not okay with this, and every recipient of the liberty they provide shouldn't be either. Way too many veterans choose each day to take their own lives. In fact, "Veterans accounted for 14 percent of all adult suicide deaths in the US in 2016, even though only 8 percent of the country's population has served in the military."[17]

I am told by many veterans that the statistic is much higher. During the years I have worked with military members, I have unfortunately been front and center to several suicide attempts. I have learned that when a person contemplates suicide, many dominoes have already fallen that have brought them to this point. Depression, alcohol abuse, anxiety, drug abuse, loss of purpose, and a lack of community are each a domino, and when they start to pile onto each other, the choice to take one's own life without consideration of the carnage it leaves for loved ones can become a tragic reality. It isn't these symptoms that bring a warrior to contemplate suicide; it's the trauma that causes them.

The problem with this unprecedented issue is there are too few who are sensitive enough to pick up these symptoms in those who need help. The suicide epidemic among veterans is not just the problem of Veterans Affairs. A few well-placed psychologists and therapists and chaplains cannot fix this problem. It won't help to do seminars for those who are suicidal because those considering suicide aren't looking for seminars. While each of these has its place, the rise in the suicide rates today demands a new approach. One that produces real answers followed up by a proven plan of action. The tragedy of veteran suicide is a problem for all of us. These are the men and women who have laid down their lives and given up their innocence for the fight to secure safety and freedom for our nation. To hold the position that others will take care of this disaster affecting humanity is to abandon personal responsibility for those who have given the most.

# Advice from a Warfighter Father

I have never had the honor of serving my country in military service, but it wasn't for a lack of trying. After graduating high school, I had fully intended to follow in my father's, grandfather's, and great-grandfather's footsteps and join the army. I still clearly remember that day. Having already spoken to a recruiter and been briefed on how the process would go, I made my decision. I woke up early to a beautiful California morning and walked into the kitchen where my brothers and sister were. I was dressed in shorts and flip flops holding a duffel bag over my shoulder. I then said goodbye and that I wouldn't see them for a while. When they asked me where I was going, I told them, "To enlist," and then I walked out the door. At the time I drove an old Datsun pickup that I had to hot wire to start. Once inside my truck, I bent down, touched the two wires together, then placed it in first gear only to look up to see my father standing in front of the truck. He slowly walked around to my window and asked me to step out. When I did, he did something that rarely happened. He gave me a prolonged hug.

My dad wasn't that verbose. He was quiet most of the time, but when he did speak, it was worth listening to. I don't know why I hadn't included my father in my decision to join the army. I suppose I just thought it was a no-brainer after considering his life path. And since he was a Korean War combat veteran and a sergeant in the army, he knew what military life was like in the worst of times, so his opinion on my enlistment had to matter.

Standing there outside my truck, he questioned my plans to join the army, which surprised me. I began to remind him of his service, but before I could say much, he interrupted me. He said "Son, the war in Vietnam ended three months ago. We are not at war, and the way I see it, we won't be for another decade. I don't want you to spend your life doing drills and going places where you cannot make a difference." Then he leaned in close and asked me to consider attending college. I was dumbfounded! Throughout my life, he had never once spoken of college either to me or my brothers and sisters. My father only had a tenth-grade education and at the time was a foundry worker for a factory in Long Beach, California.

As I began to consider the change to my plans, it didn't take long for me to come up with some big obstacles. We were a lower-middle-class family, and I wondered how I was going to pay for college. One thing I never considered was anyone else but myself paying for it. My father raised us to believe that nothing in life was free, so if we had money or objects, it was because we went out and earned them. When I posed that question to Dad, I fully expected him to tell me to get a job and figure it out. But surprisingly, he was ready with a solution.

My mother had died several years earlier when I was fourteen after suffering for several years. As a result, all four children were paid Social Security benefits each month. It was enough to pay not only for my tuition but also for my living needs. My father then offered to pay for my college by giving me the monthly Social Security benefits. The next day I began to look for a college that had the best programs for a dream I'd had since childhood.

## The Sierra Nevada Mountains

My family loved camping, specifically in the Sierra Nevada mountains at a place called Twin Lakes or Mono Village. It was high in the mountains with two lakes, waterfalls, glaciers, horses, and hiking, and a spectacular hike through the John Meir trail. To this day I am never happier than when I am surrounded by the wild, and it was and still is where I'm most at home. It was because of this love of the mountains that I decided to work toward a degree in wildlife management and enrolled in Lassen

College in Susanville, California. Fast forward to 1994, and I have graduated from college and earned two post-graduate degrees. But wildlife management went by the wayside when I met organic chemistry and we didn't get along. Instead, I earned my degrees in theology and ministry.

Upon finishing my education, my wife, Amber, and I decided to plant a church in North San Diego. Planting a church is kind of like building a house. The difference is you can't physically see each day what you have accomplished. You just must trust that what you speak on will produce fruit in the lives of fragile souls. Most people think that the only real measure of success in church planting is the number of people who attend. And while I won't argue that this isn't true in some cases, it really shouldn't be as high on the list as it is. There are many cults and false religions that draw massive followings. For me the determiner of success was growth in the lives I touched. If lives aren't becoming better for those entrusted into my care, then I should be fired just like in any other business or position in life.

I was never very comfortable in the role of senior pastor. Through education and internships, we learned how to pastor people, plant a church, and all the in-betweens, but there was always an inner sense that my role was ultimately going to be very different. Living in San Diego with a population of over 1.4 million people, we were successful in drawing people together and ultimately built a sanctuary in San Marcos directly across from San Marcos State University. We leased and then purchased a building and began to renovate it, eventually producing a beautiful church and sanctuary. But something happened directly following the Sunday we held our first service in our new building. After the service had ended, I walked up the stairs to my new office, sat down on my new chair at my new desk, and kicked up my feet. Exhausted, I closed my eyes and let out a long sigh. Thankful for the new building and how well the services went, I began to bask in our success. A moment or two went by, and I heard these words: *Don't get comfortable.*

# A New Mission

Exactly two weeks after I heard those words, the stage was being set to rock my world. It was a Friday afternoon, and I received a call from my good friend Bill Lykins, an airline pilot who also owned a production company called Sandstone Pictures. Bill called that day and told me he was going to be filming at the Basic Underwater Demolition Training Center all day and asked if I would like to go with him. I thought about it for a minute and accepted his offer. During my drive to Naval Base Coronado, I realized that I had no idea what they did on this unique naval base. It is situated on the idyllic Coronado Island in the San Diego Bay. The only connection I had with the island was with the historic Coronado Hotel, where my wife, Amber, and I had stayed several times celebrating our anniversaries. The beaches there are beautiful with the white sands stretching for miles.

Bill told me to meet him along with his crew at a park about one mile from the gate leading us to our destination. When I arrived and parked, two US Navy vans were waiting to take us on base. But before we departed, a SEAL instructor made it clear that we would be on government property and should act exactly as instructed. He was dressed in his instructor uniform, and I almost saluted him when he laid out the orders. One thing he said stood out, "The minute we roll past the guard shack, you are no longer in a democracy. Just remember that!" The worst part about it is that I chose to sit next to him in the van. Looking back, I am not sure I breathed for the ten minutes it took for us to get to the guard shack.

When we arrived at the door to the BUD/S center, it was impossible not to see the words written on the building: "The only easy day was yesterday." This is the code of those who would be SEALs. But upon walking past those words into the building, I felt as though they had been branded on my soul. My life was about to be forever changed that day as a path I never contemplated would be illuminated. Not an easy path and certainly not one chosen by many.

As we were led into this unique world, most of the staff who came with us began the work of setting up for the production. I wasn't there to do anything but observe. Our first stop was PT, or physical training. I cannot recall how many men were there but at least one hundred, each dressed in a PT uniform consisting of a brown T-shirt, khaki shorts, and boots. They stood in perfect order, and literally, everything happened at the shout of those in command. The day would involve a four-mile beach run and a four-mile swim in the chilly Pacific Ocean back to the compound. Then each of them would run the famous "O," the obstacle course, reputed to be one of the most difficult obstacle courses anywhere. One of the obstacles is a three-story structure without walls. The SEAL or BUD/S student must climb each level by hand and then take a descending rope back to the bottom. And the term for those who fall off the line is *sand dart*. Brutal!

During the run, I was in the back of a truck with the very intimidating instructor we first met in the van outside. Once the run ended and we were back to the compound, I got out of the truck and took a walk alone through the BUD/S compound. I was headed to the lobby when I came across a large group of students wearing white t-shirts being hosed down by instructors while doing flutter kicks and sit-ups. I remember standing there for about twenty minutes watching the instructors torture, I mean, *train* them. It was at that point I realized a new mission was being presented to me. To serve these individuals and those like them and to help them learn how to live successfully outside of their professional lives. This event was the beginning of what I would spend the next three decades of my life doing. Looking back, I wouldn't have changed anything.

# 3

# INVISIBLE WOUNDS

All people have regrets. Warriors are no exceptions.
One would hope it was possible to distinguish between
events caused by one's carelessness or lack of ability
and those caused by circumstances or forces beyond
one's control. But in practice, there is no difference. All
forms of regret sear equally into the mind and soul.
All forms leave scars of equal bitterness. And always,
beneath the scar, lurks the thought and fear that there
was something else that could have been done. Some
action, or inaction, that would have changed things for
the better. Such questions can sometimes be learned
from. All too often, they merely add to the scar tissue. A
warrior must learn to set those regrets aside as best he
can. Knowing full well that they will never be far away.[18]

—Timothy Zahn

## Foxholes Illuminating the Soul

It has been said that there are no atheists in a foxhole. I'm sure this
isn't true although it underscores a very important issue. When in the

proverbial "foxhole," the warfighter is more in touch with his soul than at any other time. The thought of what could come is visceral and, in the adrenaline-filled environment of battle, awareness of the ethereal is very real. In my experience, I have never spoken to a warfighter who has been in combat who didn't believe there was something that existed after this life is over. There is a substance of some form within our being, unaccountable by science, that speaks of such an eternal place.

The soul consists of many parts all beyond the physical mass of the brain, and yet it is a part of that mass. Beliefs cannot be seen or touched by the five human senses, and yet beliefs are held in the soul along with our individual spiritual traits and conscience. When we act out on those beliefs, the soul is the primary active part of the human being. The soul is fragile and can be wounded. Since the conscience abides in the soul, how one takes care of the conscience determines the health and well-being of the soul. A person is not strong simply because of an acute awareness of one's strengths. A person is strong because of the awareness of both strengths and weaknesses. To know one's vulnerabilities is to know where to place protections. To know one's strengths is to know where to put weapons. Working with men and women as a mentor and counselor has left me with no doubt: the soul is as real as the skin on our hands. The only difference for me is that skin has an expiration date whereas the soul continues to exist into perpetuity.

## Thieves Seeking to Own Your Soul

Throughout history, there has been an unseen war directed at every human being. It is the war for ownership of the soul. Through religion, occultism, mind control, monarchies, political structures, belief systems, cult leaders, satanism, psychedelics, or a mixture of any of these, the war for souls is relentless. It is possible for entire cultures of people to have their souls controlled/owned and not be aware of it. This was the case in the dark ages when the collapse of the Roman Empire and the loss of political structure left a vacuum, allowing for the rise of churches and religions to take control. Men claiming to be the embodiment of God and his law would only need to utter the words, "God wills it," for men to rise to the edict of war.[19] These "spiritual" leaders ruled over men's souls and found ways to justify damning those who wouldn't submit. During the crusades, so-called heretics were punished or killed for not submitting. A priest or bishop would hand down sentences, many times for made-up crimes.[20]

A modern-day example of this was seen in the rise of Nazism, where a narcissistic warmonger named Adolf Hitler convinced a great part of the German people to accept the Third Reich and Nazi party propaganda.[21] After many years of struggling to rise to power, Hitler and his circle of "thugs" finally took control of Germany and subsequently started a world war. When the Jews refused to turn over ownership of their souls to him, Hitler initiated his "final solution"—the annihilation of the Jewish race. His orders succeeded in the murder of over six million Jews. This genocide reveals the depths to which men will go to own the soul or attempt to destroy it for lack of submission. In twenty-first century, North Korean dictator Kim Jon Ung has such control over the people that they literally fall at his feet. A body language study shows he elicits great fear by all his people. This man has taken the control of the people's souls, as did his father and grandfather. There are many more examples, but the very fact that over the centuries this much attention is given to the attempts to own the soul reveals that the soul may be the most valuable asset in human existence. It has been fought over more than any treasure, position, or property. When men are forced to believe and do what they don't want to, they lose the ownership of soul. It can only be taken back through a rebellion of the soul over whoever or whatever has co-opted it.

## Every Subject's Soul Is His Own

Every subject's duty is the king's; but *every subject's soul is his own.* Therefore should every soldier in the wars do as every sick man in his bed, wash every mote out of his conscience: and dying so, death is to him advantage; or not dying, the time was blessedly lost wherein such preparation was gained: and in him that escapes, it were not sin to think that, making God so free an offer, He let him outlive that day to see His greatness and to teach others how they should prepare.[22]

—Shakespeare, *Henry V*, emphasis added

The soul doesn't belong to a king, a family, a race, a religion, or the universe. The soul belongs to the person it inhabits. It may indeed be the only thing over which any of us have actual and complete ownership. The excerpt above is Shakespeare's history of the response King Henry V gave to a group of his soldiers before the English and French battle at Agincourt. While encamped before the battle, some soldiers were discussing the impending fight, fearful that their small number would be no match for the French. They were riddled with exhaustion from the long journey and the previous battle at Harfleur, as well as sick with disease and suffering from dysentery. The view of this situation from the soldier's perspective must have been devastating. Only months before they were busy tending their shops or farms. Now, a large force of well-rested and trained soldiers prepared to slaughter them.

The English and French had been at constant war for nearly eighty years by this time. It is estimated the English were outnumbered at the very least two to one and perhaps as much as six to one. This night, one of the soldiers challenged Henry's responsibility over their souls should they die in battle. He thought, *If I been ordered to kill and probably be killed, then the king who ordered me here is responsible for what happens to me in eternity.* The soldier, not realizing the king's presence, as he was disguised at the time, said of their impending death, "If the war is not for a good cause, then the king has to answer for their departed souls" [paraphrase mine]. Henry aptly corrects the man saying, "Every man, whether the soldier in battle or sick person in bed, is responsible for even the 'mote,' smallest, piece of their own conscience" [paraphrase mine]. You and you alone own and are responsible for your soul. This six-hundred-year-old conversation holds true today. Every human ever born has the same conditions set upon them at birth: the right to determine the transrational connection with their soul and eternity.

In my experience, the great difficulties confronting the issue of the soul are not narratives regarding the soul's structure but in helping the person walk the all-important journey leading to a final decision on the future of one's soul. When a person dies, the body decays and returns to the earth. Physicality and the restrictions of human flesh removed, what remains becomes a single status, what many describe as spirit. What we decide to call it is unimportant as long as we acknowledge the fact that man is not the totality of his body and mind. He will someday live beyond death, his soul intact, and his soul's future will land him where he prepared for while on earth. The soul carries within it the conscience that is the ability to determine the difference between right and wrong. But it is not as black and white as that definition seems. There is a load of grey between right and wrong. And from what I have been told thousands of times working with warfighters over three decades, things are much greyer in war than in any other experience in life. This is important to know to understand why there are so many psychological and emotional difficulties in those who have fought in war.

## Unknown Caller

It was a late Friday evening during the First Gulf War when my phone rang. I was sitting on my deck on our farm enjoying the stars and the serenity when an unknown caller ID showed up on my smartphone. For most people, answering an unknown caller is not usually wise, but for me, I answer every time. The reason is that those who are overseas fighting in America's wars mostly call under that designation. I answered the call, and someone with whom I have spent a great amount of time was on the line. He was a member of an elite special operations unit and was in a leadership position on the team. He said, "Doctor Greg, I need your advice about something that is really messing with me inside." I knew this man as a seasoned warrior, so for him to call me had to be urgent. He had been on at least six combat deployments that I knew of and wasn't new to the experiences of war. But for some reason that night something happened that was eating at him. I would love to tell you the specifics of the story, but they aren't mine to tell. All I can say is that what happened did so in the grey of battle, and an after-action study revealed that the decision that he made was not the right one. The fact that it haunted him revealed the sensitivity of the voice of his conscience or soul. We spent over an hour talking (thank God for SAT phones), but his willingness to call me kept him from being left guilt-ridden over the matter. Instead, we used the experience to help him learn what to do when placed in similar situations in the future. We restructured the memory or experience so it became a building block in the soul rather than a destructive force.

## Unconverted Trauma

Recently, I counseled a soldier who told me of an event where he was part of a unit where many of his comrades died. Since his traumatic event had not been converted into a proper recognizable and understandable context within his memory, on every anniversary of that terrible day, he would become depressed, angry, and suicidal. It has been many years since the event, but he continues to revisit it year after year after year. Many would call this post-traumatic stress disorder. I call it simply *unconverted trauma*.

The best way to explain unconverted trauma is to use the hand. A traumatic event produces a subconscious obstruction, something like a hand with the fingers spread in front of the eyes. If that trauma remains unconverted, the sufferer will unknowingly view everything through this obstruction, thus causing stress. If this condition remains long enough, the mind will adapt to the obstruction, making the current real image or event seem invisible. With a warfighter, the possibility of having multiple unconverted traumas (obstructing hands in the way) is likely, which is why post-traumatic stress is such a significant problem.

A trauma properly converted becomes part of a person's memory. A memory, even if it is still painful, once converted, has the potential to be a springboard to new ideas, an inspirational story, a source of strength, the imputes for a new outlook on life, or the initiator of a practice that helps others who share the same experience. Conversely, a trauma unconverted becomes a festering soul sore that over time will produce memory ulcers and anguish in the soul. Acting out of this pain, the soul will seek something to stop it. Alcoholism, abuse of loved ones, drug addiction, detachment syndrome, sleeplessness, depression, loneliness, and suicidal thoughts are all are signs and actions of unaddressed trauma residing in the soul. Exacerbating the problem, the medical community often treats the sufferer with cocktails of drugs or by placing the individual in an institution. In some cases, these actions are warranted, but they should never be primary responses. These are unacceptable for a warfighter who has given so much to an unprepared nation and now is getting back little in terms of true answers and support. There must be a better way for warfighters.

## Converting Trauma

Jim is a very close friend who served in a unique Naval unit. To say he was a legend is an understatement. He was involved in most major conflicts and wars over the past twenty-five years and later spent years as a contractor in war zones. During the shutdown in 2020 due to the COVID outbreak, he asked me to help facilitate writing his biography, which to him was previously unthinkable. In his unit, speaking of their activity was discouraged and could result in a Captain's Mast. (In the Navy, this is a relatively informal forum for handling minor misconduct.) Despite this tradition, many of the men who served with him pressed him to write his story. Once he accepted, we planned a series of sessions to record his life and legacy. Jim had never spoken of his operations to anyone. I would be the first to hear the intricate details and be front and center to the painful emotions accompanying the stories. When we began the project, I wasn't aware my friend had been contemplating suicide for some time. I would later find out how dangerously close he was to ending his life. Speaking his story to me inadvertently allowed him to process his trauma and might have saved his life.

The first step in converting trauma is to acknowledge that the event was a trauma. While this step may seem at first to be easy, it is not, especially in a warfighter. Combat training involves a hardening of the mind to the sights, smells, and sounds of battle. It also makes the taking of an enemy's life rudimentary and turns it into a just-doing-my-job scenario. And while this is necessary, trauma most often happens surrounding the actual battle. It could include the death of a fellow warfighter, the death of innocent children, of a combatant just killed, or an encounter with a grieving, shrieking loved one. It could involve guilt over a decision made in the grey of battle or contrived guilt over not being in the proximity to help a fallen brother-in-arms. I once helped a soldier restructure a memory where he killed an entire family of enemy combatants, but his trauma didn't happen until he kicked down a door and was met by a weeping old woman, the matriarch of those he just killed. To clear the house, he needed to act decisively and quickly, so he pushed her down and cleared the house. In the years since that event, he suffered from guilt not for the killing of the enemy but for pushing that old woman down. As we spoke of it, he would break down, and it became clear, at least to me, that this event was a trauma. For him to get over it, he needed to admit to himself the weight of the event and realize it was creating stress. Doing so caused him to focus on that moment, revisit it in detail, and enter step two in the restructuring process.

The second step in the restructuring process is to talk about the event in detail. Since the feelings of a traumatic event are painful, most likely the sufferer would brush the thoughts aside when they would come up, thus avoiding the pain. But the pain cannot go away by brushing the event aside. The pain can only be mitigated by confronting the event and communicating the deep feelings surrounding it. This involved recounting the sounds, sights, and smells of the event, recounting each action or inaction leading to the event. It also involves taking into consideration the connection the event might have to past circumstances in life. For instance, part of the process of restructuring my friend's trauma with the old woman was the acknowledgment that she reminded him of his grandmother. He had unwittingly connected the old woman in Iraq to his beloved grandmother and imposed guilt on himself due to the connection.

By talking about the event in detail, there is no limit imposed on what is discussed. The listener must be adept not only at listening to what is said but also at hearing what is not said. Often those who suffer trauma communicate nonverbally more than they do verbally. The listener must facilitate and encourage discussion regardless of the emotions that the trauma elicits. Once the event is communicated and the full impact of the event is revealed, one can move on to the third step in the restructuring process.

The third step in the restructuring process is to forgive. There are not enough words in any language to communicate the power of forgiveness. Whether it is to forgive another or oneself, the freedom that comes through such an act is miraculous. It is important to note that forgiveness is effective in dealing with acts that are done to us, through us, and even those that are ethereal. Forgiving oneself for an act, real or imagined, is not an easy process. Often those who were required to take lives in combat feel they have committed the unforgivable. And this mindset is extremely dangerous when it is subconscious because the sufferers don't know they have given themselves this life sentence. And even if the events that lead to the sentence are true, all men from all circumstances have an equal right to forgiveness. And while those harmed may never forgive them, finding forgiveness for themselves is an essential step toward freedom.

The fourth step in the restructuring process is to take control of the event and declare freedom. When trauma is left unconverted in the mind, it takes control over those who suffer. Because they look at life through the lenses of their traumatic event, life is distorted, and stress will rule the consciousness. The act of speaking to the event allows one to stand outside of the event instead of dealing with it internally. And while we acknowledge that this is somewhat of an ethereal process, it is nonetheless deeply effective. The declaration shows the event that it no longer has the right to define who one is or what one does.

Once the memory is restructured, the hand is removed from the eyes, thus eliminating the cause of the traumatic stress. This therapy, along with others written in this book, is a tool that will bring back hope and freedom to those who engage it.

# What to Expect

Once the restructuring has taken place and the vision begins to clear, the stress will abate, and the mind and soul will begin to heal themselves. During this process, hope and purpose come back, and the outlook of the now healthy individual changes for the better.

I have read many books written by former warfighters, and in every single one of them, toward the end of the book, the author tells the story of what has come from all the suffering. Some started nonprofits for other veterans. Others found a voice and began to travel and speak about their new outlook. And then others started a business, using their skillset as a tool. Overall, the all-important purpose that is lost in trauma is restored, and the dawning of a new fruitful day begins.

# Caution

A vital component to the success of this process is for the listener to understand how to help the restructuring process. Those suffering with trauma need a listener who doesn't insert him or herself into the process. One's opinions and emotions need to be held at bay to not elicit frustration. The listener needs to be empathetic and completely present to the moment and to avoid unnecessary distraction. Also, the listeners must tell themselves that if they are the ones the sufferer chose to talk to then, they are qualified, regardless of how they feel about themselves. It is important to note that anyone who chooses to learn how to help others with traumatic issues can learn the means to help regardless of their education.

# Reintegration

There is no bond as strong as the bond that is developed among warfighters. It is lifelong and difficult to break even in death. Nothing the Department of Defense offers comes close to preparing warfighters for the experience or ugliness that war injects into the soul at unrelenting speed. Nor do they prepare for the mental rewrites and readjustments they'll be required to make—in a moment's notice—to the rules scribbled in their moral codes. Also lacking is a method for reintegrating this calamity of changes to one's soul back into a civilian life that now seems as distant as any foreign country.

I am close friends with a former high-ranking enlisted special operator who served in the Navy for over twenty years. He was respected and revered for his professionalism and calm while under duress. Toward the end of his military career, he had a training accident that resulted in several years in the hospital, dozens of surgeries, and the guarantee of a painful future. Having known him as an operator at the top of his game and as a patient with most of his lower body in pieces, I was able to see how hard warfighters can fall. Once separated from the Navy and placed into the civilian world, he soon spiraled downward into depression and thoughts of ending his own life. His reintegration was turning out to be a disaster. I watched this man among men, a hero, brother, and mentor turn into a lost soul. Losing brotherhood, he went from being a special operations asset to a civilian liability. And the way he was wired, he would not put up with it.

While he was in the hospital, he was never alone as his brothers refused to leave him alone with his thoughts. But as the months passed, his physical condition improved enough for him to be released. While this may seem to be good news to most, his brothers feared what he would do when he was alone. One of the great difficulties of being hurt that bad is the pain management. Hospitals at that time didn't think much about prescribing some very addictive drips and pills. And when these are taken for many months, the addiction is all-consuming.

Soon, my friend attempted to take his own life. His physical pain, while great, was nothing compared to his bleeding soul. If it weren't for the premonition of one of his brothers, who was able to stop his attempt, he would not be among us today.

If you are a veteran, I'm sure you are shaking your head up and down because this is not a surprise to you. Either you have felt this way yourself or you know dozens who have. That fact reveals the great need to change the way we prepare our warfighters for war and prepare them again for their reintegration on their return. Their entangled souls must be set free.

## Thoughts and Theories on the Soul

The principal objective of this chapter is to introduce the reader not only to the complexity of the subject matter but also to its void. Much of the referencing here, including Dr. Lanza's article, is not intended to offer conclusive evidence of the soul's substance or properties but rather perspectives on the soul. Further, in my writing on the subject, I include a perspective from faith, spiritual influences, and the idea of perpetuity. The intent is not proving one reference over another but to show that any one person's philosophical view of their own personal existence can be and is shaped by a multiple of influences and a variety of conclusions as well as personal choices for what each person accepts as truth.

Every person is a philosopher to one degree or another. A philosopher seeks to know. In the world of academia there are many branches of philosophy. Take the philosophy of knowledge, for example. In this search, the philosopher seeks to know how and why people know things. However, he finds his limitations both in his physical senses and mental capacity, leaving him or her struggling with needing assurance. They need to know that they know. The layperson resolves this by trusting their senses or the reports of others. Trust is a key element in being able to move out of this eternal loop of needing more reassurance. Think Missouri, the "Show me state." Their skepticism is settled once they have seen the proof. Trusting another's knowledge, whether in book form, a news article, or verbally, puts the receiver accepting or rejecting the information given as truth. Walter Cronkite, a news reporter in the 1960s and 70s, engendered such trust. Many viewers and commentators referred to him as the most trusted man in America. It would be a difficult task to find anyone today who has earned the same level of trust, given the large number of reporters and the ability for almost anyone to spread opinion as fact so quickly over the internet.

To the traumatized individual, doubt and skepticism strike hard. Learning to trust is a major challenge. Trusting the reliability of one's own senses equally so. Further, an element within the philosophy of knowledge, reliabilism, posits a need to prove what one's been told or what one senses is true. *Did I actually see the cat, or did I only imagine it?* Our saving grace on this dilemma is faith, a substance without properties (of a physical nature). Without faith, I only have a void surrounding my little bit of knowledge. Moses in Exodus 3, after meeting with God, had no point of reference on how to describe God to the Israelites. He asked God for his name, and God replied, "I AM WHO I AM." To me this is the definition of faith, trust without knowledge or confirmable facts. Moses chose to believe without fully knowing and moved on.

Following are some thoughts and theories on the soul. They are not intended as conclusive, only for reference. For those whose life focus has become disoriented by trauma, a leap of faith may seem impossible. Society displays many roads from which to choose. Looking for your own narrow road, a way of life if you will, isn't easy. However, with a little help from others, you'll discover your path and purpose little by little. These functions in life, blended with your beliefs and faith, are part of the building blocks that make up your heart and soul.

In a 2011 article in *Psychology Today*, Robert Lanza, MD, addresses the soul as a theory of scientific reality. His theory, supported in quantum mechanics and Heisenberg's uncertainty principle,[23] reveals a strong possibility of the soul as an independently existing element. According to Lanza:

> Many scientists dismiss the implications of these experiments because until recently, this observer-dependent behavior was thought to be confined to the subatomic world. However, researchers around the world are challenging this. In fact, a team of physicists (Gerlich et al, *Nature Communications* 2:263, 2011) showed that quantum weirdness also occurs in the human-scale world. They studied huge compounds composed of up to 430 atoms, and confirmed that this strange quantum behavior extends into the larger world we live in. Importantly, this has a direct bearing on the question of whether humans and other living creatures have souls. As Kant pointed out over two hundred years ago, everything we experience—including all the colors, sensations, and objects we perceive—are nothing but representations in our mind. Space and time are simply the mind's tools for putting it all together. Now, to the amusement of idealists, scientists are beginning dimly to recognize that those rules make existence itself possible. Indeed, the experiments above suggest that objects only exist with real properties if they are observed. The results not only defy

our classical intuition but suggest that a part of the mind—the soul—is immortal and exists outside of space and time.[24]

For readers currently suffering from "glassy eye" syndrome thinking about quantum weirdness, just imagine a researcher looks in the mirror and says, "Look, I see my reflection." The reflection then says, "No, you're the reflection." Reality seems so simple for most of us. Unfortunately, for the traumatized person, logic and reasoning can become disconnected from their thoughts. The human senses of touch, sight, smell, sound, and taste feed representational information to the brain for processing. The brain learns to trust the information provided the information remains constant. This constancy provides a steadfast platform from which we may launch into new information and ideas. Steadfastness, a term we mentally hold dear as we attempt to make sense of the world around us, provides those strong footholds from which we can launch to our next challenge or venture. For example, the chair in which one sits is steadfast. It has never turned into a chicken. But how would you process it if suddenly the chair did turn into a chicken? This example may seem silly, but trauma can affect a person's steadfast reality of life in much the same manner.

Author and philosopher Edward J. Furton explains: "The soul has an 'intellective memory' that survives death and can also have new thoughts." He adds:

> These are interesting philosophical inquiries, but they also have some measure of empirical support from a remarkable phenomenon within the field of medicine. Some patients who are dead by standard medical criteria report after resuscitation that they were aware of efforts to revive their bodies and are able to describe specific events that occurred during their death state.[25]

Along with science and philosophy, theology offers a glimpse into this possibility. In the Old Testament's book of Daniel, the story of Shadrack, Meshach, and Abednego explains that King Nebuchadnezzar had the three men thrown into the fire pit in execution for refusing to bow down to a golden image. Afterward, the king saw four men in the fire, and none were burning. He immediately rescued the three.[26] Just an ancient story, maybe, but then again perhaps science is on to something already accepted by many through faith.

## Faith and the Spirit(s)

The farther one threads into general concepts and elements of the mind, the more one must continue with a sense of faith. Faith, it has been said, "is the substance of things hoped for, the evidence of things not seen."[27] Its literal definition intends strong confidence and commitment. In this same confident sense, men and women commit themselves to serve in the military through a confession of faith. The oaths for both enlisted members and commissioned officers contain a "faithful allegiance" requirement to the Constitution of the United States.

> I, _____, do solemnly swear (or affirm) that I will support and defend the Constitution of the United States against all enemies, foreign and domestic; that I will bear true faith and allegiance to the same; that I take this obligation freely, without any mental reservation or purpose of evasion; and that I will well and faithfully discharge the duties of the office on which I am about to enter. So, help me God.[28]

> I, _____, do solemnly swear (or affirm) that I will support and defend the Constitution of the United States against all enemies, foreign and domestic; that I will bear true faith and allegiance to the same; and that I will obey the orders of the President of the United States and the orders of the officers appointed over me, according to regulations and the Uniform Code of Military Justice. So, help me God.[29]

For anyone, having served in the military, this commitment, if not recognized upon stating the oath, soon becomes very real in conflict. The commitment of offering life and limb in defense of the nation's values and well-being, as espoused in the Constitution, demands a heavy price. An understanding of faith goes a long way when trying to understand one's spirit.

To some, the concept of a spirit is confusing. To others, it is a religious creation, and even to others, it is nonexistent. Some go to great lengths to prove that there are actual "spirits" or disembodied entities doomed to walk the world, haunting whomever they choose. In Plato's *The Republic*, he writes a dialog amongst some friends, including Socrates. The discussion is a philosophical one in which Socrates poses the question: How can a person debate on a subject unless there is more than one position taken? Debate, discussion, or argument is the central point in this question. His second point is that this cannot be done with only one point of view; otherwise, that one point is the decision. We debate within ourselves when decisions need to be made and there are multiple points of view. When one must weigh these various perspectives, each with its own reason(s), resulting decision(s), and goal(s), one individual, a single soul, has to make the final decision.

How many times have you found yourself unable to decide which way to go or what to do next? *Should I go to college or not? Does she love me or not? Should I shoot or not?* Socrates explains that for different sides of an argument to be taken up inside a single person, there must be more than one part of a person to take those different positions. He further explains that if this were not true, then every person would always be able to decide what to say and do because there would be no opposing sides and no argument to make. Socrates concludes that a person's soul must have more than one part.

In Eric Brown's explanation of Socrates' position, he writes, "According to the *Republic*, every human soul has three parts: reason, spirit, and appetite. (This is a claim about the embodied soul. In Book Ten, Socrates argues that the soul is immortal [608c–611a] and says that the disembodied soul might be simple [611a–612a], though he declines to insist on this [612a])"[30] This discussion continues using these three parts of the soul to explain the internal conflict a person has when faced with making decisions. In normal situations, one balances benefits and cost, risk, and reward, truths and falsehoods, one opinion from another. Once a decision is made, the whole person, the soul, becomes responsible for it. Before deciding, many influences (i.e., parts) play a role in driving the decision home. Here, to explain our internal debating process, Socrates suggests dividing the soul into the following parts: reason, spirit, and appetite. Further, he suggests that each part has its own set of beliefs, emotions, and desires. Meaning, belief in the ideas and thoughts they are promoting; an emotional passion for their thoughts; and each having a desire or goal they are trying to achieve.

Imagine three people named Reason, Spirit, and Appetite standing in a room trying to decide something. Eric Brown might best describe these three individuals when he writes, "Socrates uses his theory of the tripartite soul to explain a variety of psychological constitutions. In the most basic implementation of this strategy, Socrates distinguishes people ruled by reason, those ruled by spirit, and those ruled by appetite (580d–581e, esp. 581c): the first love wisdom and truth, the second love victory and honor, and the third profit and money."[31]

The purpose of Socrates' dialog is to show a probability of multiple internal and conflicting influences. In general, people do not hold internal conferences and set up a meeting in their heads to discuss plans although they do go through various levels of internal debate, discussion, and conflict-resolution type processes with every decision they make. The soul, therefore, appears to consist of a complex combination of parts, influences, and choices.

## Choices and Intervening Spiritual Influences

If a person is the sum of his or her choices, then where do options come from? Are the options available to you as complete or as a partial list? Are the rules by which you choose to live your life your own, or were they shared with you by someone else? Many years ago, a Marine staff sergeant shared a lesson his father told him, "It is best when building relationships to remember people's good qualities and not remember their bad ones." A good rule to be sure, although requiring a list of exceptions. One that comes to mind is, "You should forgive a repentant thief but don't trust him with your wallet."

While the staff sergeant may attribute this lesson to his father, the chances are that his father heard it from someone else. Who heard it from whom first becomes guesswork at certain points. Plus, how the lesson is remembered (and memory is not infallible) can influence the lessons we learn and the choices we make. Stories from parents, mentors, teachers, friends—the list can go on and on—all touch us in some form or another. As a result, every person and/or event that has influenced a memory has recorded a part of their spirit along with the memory. Once there, they hold an influence over the new owner. Good influences should be welcomed. Bad influences should be avoided, for they tend to be the most outspoken and demanding. Later in the book, you'll learn tactics for silencing the "bad" spirits.

# Perpetuity

By faith, many believe in the existence of heaven. Some call it paradise. In a sense of respect and honor for their fallen, warriors call out for a reunion in Valhalla, a place of honor and celebration. If the soul does not travel to such grand and pleasurable places, where does it go, and by what criteria is this decided?

The concept of human's eternal existence has been a subject eliciting a vast array of responses for thousands of years. Throughout time, philosophers, scientists, clerics, psychologists, physicists, archeologists, and world religions have attempted to put this ethereal concept into words. Unfortunately, attempts to prove a human's existence into perpetuity has always fallen short. Mankind's existence beyond this life is not limited to logic, reason, substances, or the space-time continuum. The only possible way to accept the concept of an afterlife is simply to believe and have faith in what our internal instinct is already convinced of. We are born with instincts that drive our lives. One of those instincts is a deep leaning toward the awareness of the afterlife. This is the reason why men, since the beginning of time, have desired and sought communication with beings or gods whom they believe inhabit the afterlife.

Much evil has been visited upon man due to the positions and beliefs human beings have supposedly received from these ethereal beings. Conversely, much good has also come, which proves the case of the existence of good and evil. The brutality of the evil that man has visited upon his species, along with the incredibly good, at least indicate the inclusion of transrational beings intruding themselves into the affairs of men. This also indicates the presence of spirits only capable of evil and spirits only capable of good. Suffice it to say, all men are destined not only to die but also to live in a new state into perpetuity.

## Conscience, the Voice of the Soul

The conscience can be wounded and thus become calloused. When the soul becomes calloused, if the injury isn't addressed soon, dangerous times will come. A cursory view of mass murderers like Jeffery Dahmer reveals a black and calloused soul. The same applies to school shooters. In an ABC piece written by Meghan Keneally on April 19, 2019, Keneally wrote:

> "The people who conduct school shootings tend to be disaffected mentally unwell individuals searching for a sense of social connection and life meaning. They go online, they look at past attacks, and in a perverse way, they connect with not only past incidents but also past attackers," [John] Cohen [former official with the Department of Homeland Security] said, adding that "the story of the Columbine shooters is a story that resonates with a group of kids that are experiencing similar situations."[32]

I would take this a step beyond "the need for social connection and life meaning." A person who puts together a plan to murder the innocent and then carries out the attack must be extremely calloused. The same can be said of some suicide bombers who strap a bomb to their bodies to be blown up among innocent, unsuspecting crowds. I would venture to say, a calloused individual may be found at the core of every evil deed carried out in the history of mankind, whether directly or indirectly.

# Callousness at Its Extreme

As the father of five children and grandfather to thirteen grandchildren, nothing terrifies me more than a child sex trafficker or those who would use a child for such heinous sexual acts. In my travels, I have seen the effects of this horrible crime firsthand. In Eastern Europe, Cambodia, and in the United States, child sex trafficking is becoming more and more of a blight on society. This has come to the surface recently due to the arrest of billionaire pedophile Jeffrey Epstein.[33] Epstein was convicted of sexually abusing a child and charged with sex trafficking dozens of other minors in New York and Florida before his death in 2019.

This proclivity is not just on the dark web. Those whose calloused souls are akin to Epstein also walk our streets, attend our churches and synagogues, and show up at public events seeking victims. The Ark of Hope for Children organization reports, "Child trafficking victims, whether for labor, sex, or organ trafficking, come from all backgrounds and include both boys and girls…Trafficked children can be lured to the US through the promise of school or work and promised the opportunity to send money back to their families."[34]

In most cases, the souls of those who prey on children are made calloused from long term addiction to pornography and other insatiable lusts. Because lust is insatiable, those who view pornography are led from one stage of addiction to another deeper and darker stage. This happens until the addicted contemplates the unimaginable. Callousness forms when one denies the prodding of his or her conscience to turn away from lusts. Eventually, the addict cannot sense the conscience at all.

When the conscience begins to signal something is wrong and it is not taken seriously and restructured, a soul wound occurs. And like a wound to the flesh, a callous on the soul will remain unless it is properly treated. This is at the root of post-traumatic stress issues. There are no drugs available to treat a calloused conscience. Since the conscience is inanimate, this type of injury can only be treated by inanimate means. More on that later.

# The Warfighter's Soul

When soldiers enter basic training or boot camp, they're taken through a series of orchestrated programs designed to make them more reactive thinkers. They go through various maneuvers that push them beyond their personal thoughts or physical abilities. The human body is often far more capable than an individual might think. Ask any professional bodybuilder or athlete in any physically strenuous sport, and they will tell you their truth—their personal understanding, all stifled by their personal limitations and ignorance of the subject. Basic training helps new members with this reality. The military also develops mental fitness in its recruits, however only in a limited fashion. During bootcamp, recruits are challenged beyond their norm to accept and persevere through stressful situations. Practice, lots of practice, in physical and mental scenarios causes a development commonly known as muscle memory. Practice becomes instinctive; instinct saves time and, in a combat situation, saves lives. This memory isn't stored in the muscles. Although, as any sports trainer knows, neglecting to train any single muscle causes significant and potentially harmful stress on the other muscles, depending on the activity.

Neuroscientists have found that memories relating to skill and memory of facts, such as learning the skill, are stored in different parts of memory. Think of this as the difference between teaching and doing. One can teach riding a bike; the other can win bike races. The two do not necessarily go together. Another type of memory, known as episodic memory, stores memories of life events.

Memory issues around traumatic stress result, in part, because different parts of the brain are more engaged in stressful situations. For example, the part of your brain that reacts to stress kicks into high gear during a traumatic situation. As a result, that area draws energy from other areas of the brain, making those other areas less effective.[35] So if a warfighter goes through a traumatic experience, the memory-making areas of the brain may not be as engaged as the stress-reaction areas of the brain, meaning that memories around a traumatic event may be hazy or even nonexistent.

Because warfighters must be able to react well under stress and pressure, boot camp instructors tend to put recruits under pressure immediately, such as by screaming at the top of their lungs at the young recruits. This level of stress development begins to build the recruit's ability to manage through events that will generate much higher levels of stress and train their brains to work from muscle memory when they have no accompanying levels of facts or skills memories to work from. Facts and skills offer a balancing effect to shocking events, much like knowing how a magic trick works removes the mystery when watching a magician perform it. As a result, when people do not have the appropriate facts or skills to work with in a traumatic situation, the brain may try to compensate in ways that are not always accurate.

For example, the shocking story of Private John Lyttle's experience with dead bodies occurred days after the initial landing and assault on Iwo Jima. John describes in vivid detail the scene of walking amongst bloated and decaying corpses.[36] For anyone who has never experienced a dead body close, finding one in this condition can be horrifying. There is an inescapable smell. Many describe it as being foul, but the aroma also carries hints of what can only be described as sweet. The brain furiously attempts to match up known facts and scenarios with this image to make sense of what it is experiencing.

Neuroscientists view this as shifting levels of energy in the brain. "When one part of your brain is engaged, the other parts of your brain may not have as much energy to handle their own vital tasks," says Dr. Kerry Ressler, chief scientific officer at McLean Hospital and professor of psychiatry at Harvard Medical School.[37] In this effort, if no matching data is found, the brain will fill the gaps with data it does have. It may pull up pictures of family or friends and imagine them in this bloated condition. This outcome, in effect, strains the brain, the body, and, in a more permanent fashion, the soul. The soul begins desperately to search for an escape. It is conditioned for survival. The brain appears to be pulling its resources into survival mode from memory mode.[38] To John Lyttle, the shock may not have been as drastic because he may have had relatable memories from which to draw. He was raised in Ojai, California, known as a farm and ranch community. This may have offered him an opportunity to experience the death and bloating of large animals. That memory alone would suffice as a better comparison when his brain began searching for an explanation for what he saw on Iwo Jima that day.

The military trains men and women to respond to orders instinctively and without question out of necessity. They are trained in offensive and defensive tactics. Organizational skills are heightened. These experiences prepare them for extreme conditions as any military member may be called on to put his life in danger at any moment. Physically and mentally, they prepare for the difficult tasks that lies ahead. As explained here, mental, or cognitive training may require a higher level of understanding of one's entire soul, not just how and what one thinks but also why one thinks.

The soul, as an arbiter of a person's physical activities, psychological experiences, and memory stores, inherently also works as a protector of those parts, constantly making judgments of good and bad, right and wrong, and so on. Likewise, the essence of the warfighter works as a protector of his team.

In battle, our warfighters are not only engaging an enemy with physical and emotional thought and action. They're also engaging the enemy with their souls, and it is in this context that the soul finds its deepest wounds and greatest joys. The culture of a warfighter is unique from almost any other. A warfighter is part of a team where each member walks together through the same experiences. And while they are each wired differently as human beings, there exists a cohesiveness critical to success. Each member is linked by the bonds of brotherhood and trust, which are never more important than on the battlefield. While on a mission, they work together, each member in the link of men having his own battle responsibility. They train as a team, holding one another responsible to be the best at his job. This is because it is mission-critical that each link in the chain of men perform under the stress of actual combat in the same manner as they trained. When the mission is complete, each warfighter has the team with which to debrief and deal with the traumatic experiences encountered in war.

# 4

# WARFIGHTER FAITH

*When it comes your time to die, be not like those
whose hearts are filled with fear of death, so that when
their time comes, they weep and pray for a little more
time to live their lives over again in a different way.
Sing your death song and die like a hero going home.*

—Tecumseh

To me, there are two ways we all die: a good death and a bad death.
There is nothing in between. All warfighters deserve to die a good death.
They have earned that right because they laid down their freedom and
selflessly stepped forward to defend a people even if the cost is their own
life. The lives we live should be in preparation for the moment when
our time comes to depart into the eternal realm. My mentor, Dr. Edwin
Lewis Cole, taught me that we are stewards of everything and owners of
nothing. This includes our life. All of us have a choice of how we meet
death. I wish all of us could choose the things that make up our lives, but
we have little to do with them. Good and terrible things happen to us all,
and the conundrum of life is that good people aren't spared. To live so
that we meet a good death should be our greatest goal. A good death is
to meet life and whatever is thrown at us head-on, with a determination

to leave behind a strong legacy, a legacy for those still living that brings them courage—courage and a willingness to do the same.

With fear and trembling, I say the following. Suicide is not a good death. And while I have great compassion for those who chose this path, it leaves a legacy of hopelessness to those who are left behind. They're left with a memory of sorrow and mourning.

My wife and I lost our thirty-seven-year-old son two years ago, and there isn't a day we don't mourn for him. What makes it even more painful for all of us left behind is that he died of a drug overdose. His death wasn't a good one for his four sons, his wife, his mom and dad, nor his siblings. The hard part is he loved his children and was the kind of person who would never want to cause his boys pain. But since his death, his children have suffered emotionally and psychologically, even to the point of hospitalization. His sons are left to carry the weight of his death throughout their lives. Our son Adam's legacy doesn't speak about the wonderful things he did but of one deeply selfish act. I say this to underscore the fact that it is how we die that almost always defines how we will be remembered.

A good death guarantees hope and courage to future generations for decades to come. How we die will define how we are remembered regardless of all the good and bad we may have done. This is exactly why it is so important that we refuse any thought of taking our own life, even if we think that means living a life of suffering until help comes to bring freedom or our natural death arrives. I know this may sound heartless, but suicide leaves a type of curse, carnage left behind for the living to clean up. I liken the difficulty of living under suicidal thoughts with the life of a prisoner of war. Every day is filled with unimaginable suffering and torture. But the torture doesn't take from the POW the desire to live regardless of the suffering because the warfighter maintains hope of being freed. When those who are suffering choose to live with the pain instead of taking their own life, they are essentially creating a hope for themselves and granting their loved ones freedom from a life of sorrow. Those who love you, your children, parents, and friends, would rather watch you suffer in the hope that you get better than to see you die by suicide. Suicide is not just the taking of one's own life, but it is also the taking of the lives of those who love the sufferer. From my own experience, suicide leaves behind a permanent, unremovable stamp on the hearts of the living. Nothing can make this memory feel better, and time alone will not heal it. The only hope for those left with this stamp is to convert it and use the experience to motivate themselves toward a good death. And to never do to their loved ones what has been done to them.

> Be ashamed to die until you have won
> some victory for humanity.
> —Horace Mann

# A New Normal

Often in life things happen to us, either randomly or due to our choices, that change the way we view our normal. Some think of normal as a routine or an event we act out or attend continually. Others think of normal as the boring and uneventful path of life that will never change. As I ponder this concept, I have concluded that there is no single "normal" for mankind. There are simply periods of time that offer new normal at random stages of our lives. As such, each of us may have hundreds of "normal" periods throughout our lifetime. Some of these will be mountaintop experiences while others will be found in hellish pits. All humans face this reality. When these periods are marked as "good" or "bad," for too many, bad periods occur way too often. It is precisely due to this comparison that I want to bring up the vital and all-important issue of faith. Regardless of what you may think of faith or how you define it, in most cases, faith gives those who embrace it a means to find what all of us are seeking at one time or another: some sort of respite or escape from the grind of this world.

As children most lay their faith on the care provided by their parents. Daily meals appear as if by magic. Clothes are cleaned, and a home is provided. That's not to say all children are cared for equally across every family but only to show an early type of faith. Faith is a trust stronger than a belief or a hope. As the children, now adults, move out of the home, their faith first turns to themselves, their abilities, knowledge, talents, and skills that have carried them this far and are trustworthy. But that faith is no faith at all. You know your abilities and limitations. Believing that you can count on yourself to somehow save you miraculously from your troubles is no faith at all. You need more. Faith follows belief, a strong belief in an unevidenced reality of something or someone greater than yourself. Even the most highly trained, highly capable, and highly intelligent warfighters will at some point run into a situation they will be unable to overcome. At that moment, faith alone remains. Without it, only hopelessness is left. Here, the individual either reverts into hopelessness or perseveres with a hope for success, support, or rescue. One's soul continues to operate, and the mind continues to function.

Beside their inspirational and aspirational benefits, these belief, faith, and hope attributes of the human soul trigger physical activities that allow the mind and body to continue functioning as well. In a 2016 *National Geographic* article, Erik Vance explains how medical science and psychology no longer ignore the healing effects of belief systems and faith.[39] The article's focus does not comment on any particular system but rather on what happens within the human body that allows it to heal.

> Normal pain sensations begin at an injury and travel in a split second up through the spine to a network of brain areas that recognize the sensation as pain. A placebo response travels in the opposite direction, beginning in the brain. An expectation of healing in the prefrontal cortex sends signals to parts of the brain stem, which creates opioids and releases them down to the spinal cord. We don't imagine we're not in pain. We self-medicate, literally, by expecting the relief we've been conditioned to receive.

Further in the article, Christopher Spevak, a pain and addiction doctor at the Walter Reed National Military Medical Center, explains his process for treating veterans of Iraq and Afghanistan. He first asks his patients about the good memories they have from their childhood. He then finds a relevant item with a taste or smell associated with their good memory. He asks his patients to take the item along with the pre-scribed painkiller. Overtime, he reduces the medication providing only the aroma or tasty substance to the patient. His conclusion, "We have triple amputees, quadruple amputees, who are on no opioids, yet we have older Vietnam vets who've been on high doses of morphine for low back pain for the past 30 years."[40] Another interviewee, Tor Wager, a professor at the University of Colorado Boulder and director of a neuroscience lab, added, "The right belief and the right experience work together, and that's the recipe."

According to a 2017 study entitled "Spirituality and Mental Well-being in Combat Veterans: A Systematic Review," published by Oxford University Press in its journal on Military Medicine: "Spirituality is often the first and most used coping method when facing a health crisis, trauma, or stress." The article continues, "Finally, deployment to combat zones and participation in direct combat activities (i.e., killing) can have spiritual and morally injurious components that seem to transcend and include traditional psychological injuries, with emotions of guilt, shame, and forgiveness."[41]

# Faith

Faith can be viewed as two different types: one institutional and the other personal. The two types are distinct and yet quite similar on many levels. First, the most common understanding of faith is an alignment with and trust in one of five major religions, Judaism, Islam, Hinduism, Buddhism, or Christianity. Each of these has multiple subcategories and off-shoots. Members of these institutional belief systems or religions are accepted into "the faith" with the understanding that they will conduct their lives in a manner reflecting at least that of the religious community.

The second type of faith is a base level belief in an unevidenced theory regarding the existence of one's life, a faith none of the five human senses can fully grasp as evident. It is something one believes and hopes for but provides no human means of measurement. It is deeply personal, highly trusted, and as real as one's next breath. It is not subject to con-sensus by others and cannot be controlled by a society's inclinations nor their pro and con evidence. It has been my great honor to help thousands of warfighters, many of whom have suffered from suicidal leanings, find faith. Once the sufferer comes to terms with this deeply personal faith, its transformative effects are, without any shred of doubt, life-altering.

## The Power of Faith

There are many types of wounds a warfighter might suffer during their time in and after service. While the physical wounds are sometimes grave, significant studies have revealed the psychological wounds can be much more debilitating. But some wounds are so deep that therapy cannot get to them. However, no therapy can go as deep as faith. In these cases, faith is the deepest possible form of interaction and support for the soul.

The presence of chaplains in the military underscores a recognition of the positive role faith has in those who serve. Principally, the warfighter must accept the very real possibility of taking another's life, a capability instilled in them in boot camp. Warfighters are not free to decide for themselves whether to accept an order to place their own lives in danger or to take the life of the enemy. Unless the order is considered illegal, orders are to be carried out regardless of the cost. For this reason, chaplains representing all five major religions have been part of the warfighters' world since the nation's inception.

To the warfighter, it is often very difficult to merge faith with their duty. Due to the nature of the work, a warfighter often assumes that faith in God is inconsistent with the behavior of war. I remember one time speaking at a club meeting to a group of midshipmen at the United States Naval Academy. When the question-and-answer time came up, one young lady stood and asked the following question, "Doesn't the sixth commandment specifically say, 'Thou shall not kill'?" It was a real question and one that many called to defend their nation wrestled with. There is something in the human psyche that abhors the idea of taking another human life. For this to be acceptable, one must have gone through the complete reset of "normal" human psychology. When the midshipman asked her question, a grim silence fell on all in attendance. They were all wondering the same thing.

With all their eyes on me, I answered with the knowledge I had accumulated due to my struggle with the same question. I said, "The sixth commandment doesn't say we shall not kill. It says we shall not murder." There is a huge difference between the two. Wars have been fought since man's beginning. And God himself ordered many of those. Nations must defend their people against unjust aggression by an enemy. In these cases, warfighters have a moral responsibility to rise and defend the innocent and bring justice to the aggressor. More on point to the midshipman's question, a very real problem with killing occurs when those who are called to kill blur the difference between killing and murder. This is a very real issue for those who go off to war and who face death every day. Over time, those with a genetic antisocial predisposition combined with a consistent exposure to this environmental hardening can merge into a killer.[42]

The entrance of faith in these times allows the warfighter to move outside of the human realm, which is where most, if not all, the pain resides. It is in this realm that those lines that have been blurred can become clear again. It is also where hardened hearts can become once again soft along with the conscience. One factor that is vital to the warfighter is the understanding that finding faith is not an event as much as it is a journey that will ebb and flow for a lifetime. While one may find faith in a moment, it will change to meet the needs of those who believe. The important thing is to let faith do what it does best—find its way into the places it knows best and work outside of our awareness. Finding faith is as simple as our acceptance in a belief. We don't need to fight to have it. We don't need to understand all the facets of it. We don't need to be "perfect" to be worthy of it. We can be angry with God and still have faith. We may have done terrible things in our life and still have it. Faith will not judge you, lie to you, condemn you, or hold up impossible rules to have it. Faith waits patiently for anyone who desires it. Faith waits for a surrender.

## Our Hope

All we have put into this book has been influenced by our faith in God. In these chapters we seek to provide the answers faith and our experience have taught us over many years. Our purpose is to give a chance to those who are suffering from the plague of suicide. And while this book is written to the warfighter specifically, we hope that these answers will save thousands, whether warfighters or not. We wish we could have been there for the thousands who have suffered so greatly and ultimately had given in to suicide. Our hearts are broken that they died alone, heroes with no hope and without brothers and sisters to help them into eternity. But our faith gives us hope that belief in what isn't seen along with the other answers we have delineated in this book will invade a society of brave brothers and sisters who have and will continue to give the greatest sacrifice so that humanity can be free.

# 5

# SOCIETY'S UNPAID DEBT

Each year, the U.S. military recruits some 175,000 young
Americans. At the heart of its pitch is a sacred promise to
take care of those who serve—what President Abraham
Lincoln described in his second inaugural address as the
national duty "to care for him who shall have borne the
battle and for his widow and his orphan."[43]

—Phillip Carter

In 1998 journalist Tom Brokaw wrote his book *The Greatest Generation*.
The book's title has since become a commonly recognized moniker for
that group of people who survived the Great Depression, helped win
the war against Nazi Germany, and defeated the Japanese in the Pacific.
As Mr. Brokaw explains, "I came here on the fortieth anniversary and
began to meet the veterans and realized we had not heard their stories
once the war ended. Who were they? What had they become? And as I
began to do more research on that, I realized how much we owed them
in every conceivable way in our country."[44] They are a generation of survivors, champions of freedom, and nation builders. On this last point,
Mr. Brokaw goes on to say, "[They] survived the depression, won the war,
came home and built the country that we have today."[45]

I believe Brokaw is spot on with his analysis, and there are many things to learn from our history as a nation. Societies have proven over the centuries a propensity to forget what previous generations have taught. The greatest generation taught what a nation could do when it stood as one, each doing a part for the overall good. It showed what a unified nation was capable of when facing down tyrants, dictators, and people who follow ideologies that allow the innocent to be brutalized and oppressed. As one, our nation and its warfighters took on communism, socialism, and imperialism and won. This capacity to work as one is due to ideologies learned in school or taught to us by our parents. It seemed our nation knew what the oppressors believed, how they abused their people, and why it was wrong when compared to true liberty and freedom. We knew we were on the right side of morality, and when we were asked to stand up to this tyranny, there was no resistance to enlist to fight it. Young men stood in long lines to join the fight because they felt it was their duty to help those who were being victimized. To them, the sacrifice was worth it, and this mindset carried them to the battlefields around the world to fight and die if necessary. Bolstered by a nation that stood in solidarity behind them, our warfighters and those who supported them found the courage necessary to take on insurmountable odds and win the freedom of the oppressed. They were called the greatest generation because they represented what it takes to win over evil, a unified resolve, and an undaunted determination to win.

As wartime ended and a nation began to heal, our society began to do what constructive societies do with success: build. Focused on the economy, infrastructure, and education, our nation grew. But not everything about this evolution was good. Particularly, ideologies on war and our feelings toward those who fight America's wars changed in a negative sense. There grew a distaste for war, and as a result, the opinions toward it also changed. Consider the difference in attitude beginning with the war in Korea and then in Vietnam. Our nation seemed to have lost its support for its warfighters.

By the time the US entered the war in Vietnam, the purpose for joining became confused in the eyes of the public. The nation demonstrated an antithetical position and had developed a visceral attitude toward not only war but the warfighter as well. The warfighter had become a tool of war rather than the once recognizable hero for defending the oppressed. Our nation seemed to have turned its back on those who fought. Even if a war is unpopular or unjust, it is never acceptable to attach onto our warfighters our distaste for what politicians have led us into. To do so is to invite a national curse. The nation, as Tom Brokaw recognized, owes it warfighters a debt "in every conceivable way."

# Vietnam

Prosperity, security, and perhaps a sense of invincibility may have caused the national character to forget what it took to be strong. The birth of the "hippy culture" may have been a symbol, a signpost indicating a turn in the national character. A turn from unity in purpose to one wrought with individual desires. In such an environment, the Vietnam War became a symbol of distraction from these self-centered pursuits. These events brought about a vastly different attitude toward our warfighters. Society turned on its best, and instead of supporting the men and women who were fighting a war thousands of miles from home, our American culture instead held the warfighter as representative of the nation's evils. "Peace, not war," became their battle cry. "It's your fault we're in this stupid war," still rings in the ears of many Vietnam veterans today. With guilt fired at them from the crowds, the verdict of "baby killers and murderers" came thundering from the societal judge. When arriving home, our warfighters were treated like lepers in first century Rome, doomed to their own secluded colonies. They were shunned, ignored, and spit upon. How these already traumatized warriors were treated exacerbated their trauma, sending many into a spiral of self-destructive behavior.

I have a dear friend who did three tours in Vietnam as a special forces soldier. He once told me that when he came home after his last tour, he was treated so poorly that once he had arrived home, he saddled a horse and disappeared into the wilderness for over eight months. During his time in the wilderness, he faced and overcame many demons, including the loss of a nation's gratitude. He in turn become an inventor, an entrepreneur, and a successful businessman. He will admit that his motivation was revengeful in part. He wanted to show the nation, who was so ashamed of his sacrifice, that they didn't win.

## The Price Paid

Many believe our nation paid a high price for this change in character. Where World War II had ushered in prosperity, Vietnam delivered economic distress. For a decade after the Vietnam War ended, our society suffered economic recession and high interest rates. In a 1973 *New York Times* article, the author, addressing the economic legacy of the war, wrote, "On the international side, the war had a direct role in creating the massive deficit in the United States balance of payments. This in turn ultimately led to the devaluation of the dollar and the end of the Bretton Woods system."[46]

Financial loss was not all that was lost. Add to this the growing drug epidemic and an increased spread of sexually transmitted diseases brought on by the sexual revolution. That's not to say these problems did not exist before but to show a pattern of increase resulting from the shifting national character and values.

The growing popular, or "pop," culture caused many of its youth to begin questioning long-held beliefs. As a result, America's youth began searching for answers in cults, Eastern religions, and other ideologies outside commonly held belief systems and mantras. Musicians began to produce songs with words designed to engender rebellion against any form of government. Police became "pigs," and cult leaders like Charles Manson became heroes. Where universities were once the arbiters of good character and values, psychology professor Timothy Leary promoted LSD, mushrooms, psilocybin, and hallucinogens to gain higher awareness. Mentors became drug pushers. It has been said that Timothy Leary found his god in LSD. In some alternate form of sagacity, these "different" cultural change ideas came clashing together at a music event Woodstock, NY, in 1969.[47]

Part peaceful music festival and perhaps, in part, an underreported or unrecognized explosion into a new social identity, half a million young people came together to get high, have free sex, and listen to music (some joyous, some toxic) all while energizing their rebellion of the current social limits to a fever pitch. This new diverse identity had unified itself as a unity of disunity. The hatred for anything institutional made it easy to attack our military and its members. Fortunately, this different view on life continued to change with their children and subsequent generations.

The baby boomer generation gave way to Generation X. Born between 1965 and 1979, Generation X were the cynical latchkey kids who noticed the destructiveness of "free whatever" and began to modify their perspectives. The Xennials, known as the analog to digital generation, found themselves entangle with the growth of technology. Now, the digitally savvy millennials seem to have reversed course in part on their view of national character as well as the benefits of military service.[48] While the nation healed and prospered, it also changed its attitude toward those who join the military. Society has never regained the bond between soldier and civilian born in the greatest generation, but it certainly appears to be headed in the right direction.

# The Price of Forgetting

Knowing where you stand makes knowing where you belong easier to determine and makes it easier to identify those who stand with you. Texans, all Texans, stand together, unified against all newcomers, or so goes the popular thought. While true in some respects, common traits and common causes do bring people together, but differences, clearly identifiable differences, divide people into separate groups. Historically, in war, flags, banners, the Colors, uniforms, and people groups made it easy to spot the enemy. Much of the unity our nation has lost since the greatest generation may be due to an inability to specifically identify friend from foe. Enemy troops no longer take to the battlefield in identifiable uniforms. Men, women, and children are found tossing hand grenades at our troops.

On the home front, where communism, fascism, Nazism, and socialism once stood clearly on the other side of the line regarding national governance, now large portions of Americans are embracing a variety of governing forms, including some of those listed above. For example, the societies who suffered through the Great Depression and two world wars lived in a time when socialism meant something vastly different than what is presently being taught in our schools, colleges, and universities. When Bernie Sanders made socialism part of his failed presidential campaign in 2016, anyone over the age of forty was shocked. This group of citizens grew up witnessing the horrors of a socialist societies. The Soviet Union, China, Cuba, and North Korea adopted this ideology, and the result was mass poverty for most and great riches and power for a few.

Communism differs from socialism in that a communist government owes and controls all property and economic resources. Socialism purports that all citizens share these resources equally, as allocated by a democratically elected government.[49] Socialism's claim to provide equal shares for all and a democratically elected government may sound altruistic, but in historical practice, it only works on a small scale. On a national scale, it has proven to quickly devolve into communism soon after inception.[50]

With the exception of Israel, and only when they were a small and young nation, from 1948 to 1973, there is not a single successful example of socialism working for the betterment of those who serve under it.[51] Each nation that adopts this system collapses into communism or a darker form of dictatorship. The political arm of socialism, in effect, guarantees the rise of despots and power-hungry, maniacal leadership that has little regard or compassion for its people. One of the best examples of this is the nation of North Korea. Under the leadership of Kim Jong-un, the people of North Korea have little to no freedoms. They live in poverty and suffering and are required to worship their "dear leader."

How then could any of the elections, with no less than four democratic candidates in recent history, make socialism a promise if elected? From this historical perspective, much of the blame may lie at the feet of those who have refused to teach this nation's history. Over the past two decades, there seems to be a greater interest in rewriting history to match a current ideology rather than to study history as a guard against repeating mistakes. This loss of fundamental understanding of historical wisdom is a case study revealing how easily societies forget valuable lessons. How we treat those who defend our nation is vital to our prosperity. If we give honor to those who sacrifice the most, we will continue to enjoy all the fruits of our democracy. But if society acts as though the warfighter's dedication is not majorly responsible for our corporate and individual success, then we are accepting the erosion of our national foundation and a loss of all we as a nation hold dear.

During the Second World War, our nation not only sent men and women to war but the nation's home front also reorganized itself into becoming a directly connected part of the war effort. Americans fought for our freedom by working in factories developing whatever was needed for our warfighters to succeed. War bonds were purchased to pay for the war, and when our men and women came home, they were greeted with the open arms of a jubilant and thankful nation.

## The Military's Role in Society

Today's military, unlike the forces during the two world wars, Korea, and Vietnam, is an all-volunteer military.[52] As a result, it is seen by many on the outside, and even some on the inside, as a career choice just like any other job. This mindset fails to recognize the difference in level of commitment between a nine-to-five job and enlistment in the military. While the designation "warfighter" checks all the boxes signifying a career choice, it is not like any other job. No other job requires an oath of enlistment. No other job comes with a mandatory term of enlistment. No other job comes with orders the employee is legally required to obey. No other job comes with the stress of deployments into areas of the world where the competition (enemy) is under orders to kill you.

This enhanced level of commitment to the security of the nation is paid for all. In a sense, it separates those inside the fence line (military base, post, facility, or perimeter) from those outside the fence (civilians). However, disconnecting warfighters, stigmatizing them as "different" from the society it protects, creates a dangerous precedent. Stigma is defined as "a mark of disgrace or infamy; a stain or reproach, as on one's reputation." Our society does a good job of saddling suicide with stigma. To make sense of it, perhaps, we label the person who ended his or her life: *He was selfish. She was crazy.* This is a terrible injustice because those who attach the stigma only do so to make sense of what happened for themselves. When an individual is suffering with thoughts of suicide, stigma only pushes them toward suicide. Seeing those who have taken their lives stigmatized communicates nothing good to those who are still alive.

I recently met with a promising army captain who was invited to our office to learn about our security company. After some time, he prodded me asking about my life and experiences. When I told him about this book, he changed his expression completely. At first, he was confident, looked me in the eye and talked, laughed, and told me about his goals. But when learning about my involvement in veteran suicide, his visage changed. He spoke quietly to me, his eyes looked downward, and at times watered up. Once he felt safe with me, he began to tell me his story.

As a young officer he was often tasked with carrying out the orders of the officers over him. But toward the end of his deployment, his colonel asked him to deploy a drone over an area where there was known Taliban leadership. During the process of gathering intelligence, it was discovered that a school was near. It would be impossible not to harm anyone he followed those orders. When the junior officer briefed his colonel, he was told that it was his decision but that his CO wanted it done. In a military world, that means the mission was going to happen. He really had no choice in the matter. The young officer ordered the hit and later found out that two children were killed. After some discussion with him, it became clear that this event deeply troubled him. During our conversation, he admitted to great guilt and talked about being continuously drunk for over four months after returning from his deployment. After he unloaded, I made it clear that, while I understood his guilt and the stigma attached to him as a killer, help was near. We spent the rest of our time together restructuring the event and destroying his self-imposed stigma.

It needs to be understood that a man in this condition can be easily pushed over the edge by unwitting attachments. This is underscored by the stigma attached to the Vietnam veterans who came home to chants of "baby killer." Vietnam veterans may be the most stigmatized warfighters in American history. And this didn't happen only through words. They were spit upon and denied jobs when their applications revealed their service. Stigma is a killer.

Society needs its warriors, and warriors need their society. Only in such a symbiotic relationship can a nation remain strong and prosperous.

In 2018 I met with a former Army Ranger who later became a CIA agent. We spent several hours talking about his unique life and career, and I asked him a pointed question. I asked, "After all your years of service to this nation, have you felt much gratitude?" His response was quick and heated. He said, "I don't need...gratitude because I didn't do what I did for others. I did it for myself. I don't seek nor want anyone's 'thank you for your service,' and they can keep their gratitude." I must admit to being taken aback, and after a few moments of gathering myself, I asked if he was just messing with me or if he truly believed what he had just said. (I have had my share of people like him screwing with my head in the past, so I needed to check that box before I accepted his diatribe.) He looked back at me with a smirk and then said, "Let's just change the subject."

My friend's response, if real, revealed a deep wound I am worried may exist in many of those who have fought in the many years of war since September 11, 2001. For most, however, duty, honor, and love of family and country compel them to risk their lives by serving in the military. In both cases, society needs its warriors, and warriors need the society they protect to welcome them, care for them, and assure them that they continue to be part of the total national fabric.

> As a Navy SEAL Platoon Commander on my fourth-combat deployment to Iraq and Afghanistan, I often called on my close family and friends back home for prayer. On multiple occasions, my own life was closely threatened, and I quickly came to realize the absolute power and necessity of prayer. Every prayer said made a difference and saved a life. One night in May, it was my own life! I wrote home to my prayer warriors for immediate prayer: "I just don't want to run out of miracles! The situation here is much, much different than it has ever been before...Pretty much like I'd imagine being in

hell! I'd only ask that you please continue to pray for my platoon and me...specifically for strength, courage, and bold, decisive leadership. I ask that the Lord guide my hand, my eyes, and judgment while leading my men into battle. That he would give my team the wisdom and patience to outthink, out maneuver, and continue to destroy the terrorists we hunt every night. I'd pray that our actions continue to bring quick and certain death to the enemy! Pray that the Lord forge an impenetrable barrier, that his heavenly angels would shroud us with his protection to shield us from the enemy." We are absolutely in a war of good versus evil. We fight evil men every night, and they do everything to test our resolve and our righteousness.[53]

# A History of Care: The Greeks

For most warfighters and a large part of military brats, crying is a sign of weakness. Presumably, ancient Greek warriors equally believed that it wasn't safe to break down in tears, not a good idea during battle. However, as Bryan Doerries reminds us, these ancient warriors recognized that the emotions associated with war couldn't be bottled up indefinitely. Doerries began an effort to bring the importance of decompression and reconciliation to the forefront by introducing our military to Greek tragedies.

Doerries' own story begins with a 2007 *Washington Post* article he read describing the negligent care of returning combat veterans at the nation's premier military hospital, named after Walter Reed, a late nineteenth century army physician. Returning wounded veterans of Iraq and Afghanistan wars found themselves recovering in rooms with torn walls, damaged ceilings exposing the room above, and mold.[54] He points out that Walter Reed is "the crown jewel of military medicine," but the strain of sustained war has taken its toll on its structures.[55] But as a theater director and amateur classicist, *What can I do?* he asked himself.

In answer to this question, Doerries found himself bringing the drama of Greek tragedies and the potential healing qualities to the attention of military leaders. As strange as this effort may seem on first brush, Doerries appears to have found a goldmine of revelation hidden in these dark stories.

Ancient Athenian warriors gathered to cheer their victories, weep for those they lost, and remind themselves that war is not all glory. Tragedy appears in many forms, affecting warriors regardless of their roles. One play, *Ajax*, written by an elder Athenian general named Sophocles, tells the story of Ajax, a fellow warrior of Achilles in Homer's *Iliad*. In the 2004 movie *Troy*, starring Brad Pitt as Achilles, Ajax was the towering warrior played by Tyler Mane.[56] True to Hollywood script writing, Ajax is killed in a blaze of glory, having killed countless Trojans and suffering multiple wounds. The movie portrays the antithesis of Homer's written account in the Iliad, Sophocles' play, and Doerries' point. Following Achilles' death, pride gets the better of Ajax, and he commits suicide. "Ajax is deeply offended at the award of the prize of valor (the dead Achilles' armor) not to himself but to Odysseus. Ajax thereupon attempts to assassinate Odysseus and the contest's judges, the Greek commanders Agamemnon and Menelaus, but is frustrated by the intervention of the goddess Athena. He cannot bear his humiliation and throws himself on his own sword."[57] Not exactly a glorious ending, but to Doerries' point, it portrays war in realistic fashion: tragedy flows with guts and glory in every war. Post-traumatic stress is modern in name only; its symptoms have plagued warfighters throughout history. Doerries seems to have touched a nerve in a positive way. As he began presenting his Greek tragedies to military members, veterans, and their families to grand and tear-filled reviews, silenced voices began to speak. Doerries states:

> After a performance of *Ajax* at a California Marine Corps base, a muscular gunnery sergeant stood in front of more than a hundred members of his unit and haltingly began to tell his story. "I had no intention of speaking today," he said. "But I lost every

member of my vehicle from Afghanistan. And I lost them all *after* we got back to suicide." On any other day, he might not have shared his emotions in front of subordinates and peers. But he had just listened to professional actors bring Sophocles' ancient words to life…After another recent performance of *Ajax*, a soldier stood up and said, "I knew Ajax was thinking about killing himself when he deceived his family and troops and walked away from his tent brandishing a weapon. But I don't think Ajax *knew* he was going to kill himself until he was alone on the dune with his gods." The operative word is alone. As a society, despite our best intentions, we have left too many veterans alone on dunes.[58]

To Doerries' point, creating safe spaces where veterans can share their stories with their families, friends, and an understanding public is a good start in helping them reintegrate into society and, at the same time, to diminish the guilt and shame they may be carrying with them.

Our citizens must take responsibility for those who fight for our freedom. This means that while doing our own thing, seeking our careers, and raising our families, we must always remind ourselves that what we have and who we are came at a price. We need our warfighters, and they need us. There are many ways to support them. A great example is in the life and actions of actor Gary Sinise. You might recognize him as the actor who played Lieutenant Dan in the movie *Forest Gump*.[59] His acting career has undoubtedly made him prosperous, allowing him to live a very comfortable life. But that was not enough for Gary. He decided to give back to those who paved the way for his success. He started the Gary Sinise Foundation with a mission to serve our nation by honoring our defenders, veterans, first responders, their families, and those in need. Gary also authored a book, *New York Times* bestseller *Grateful America*. This foundation has built over seventy smart homes for wounded veterans, given over five hundred thousand meals to our nation's defenders, given over three hundred emergency grants, and much more (these numbers are current as of the time of this writing, but they continue to increase).[60] He has become a partner to those who served, and I don't think it's a stretch to say that his happiness and prosperity are a direct result of this partnership. We echo his sentiment, "While we can never do enough to show gratitude to our nation's defenders, we can always do a little more."[61]

# PART II

# DETECTION

In writing this section, we recognize that no exact science nor list of symptoms exists that would allow us to perfectly identify a person in jeopardy of taking his or her own life. However, over the course of several combined decades in counseling with men and women veterans and active-duty military, we have found the following signs and syndromes to be quite telling when someone is in extreme distress and in need of care. Please bear in mind that every person is unique and should be treated with respect. Unless you are a licensed medical professional, they are neither your patient nor someone to be studied.

When our son died, my wife and I didn't understand much about addiction and what happens to an individual when he takes this path. It has helped us greatly since to study the effects addiction has on the brain and all its components. My wife, Amber, and I attended a group weekend at a rehabilitation center in Murfreesboro, Tennessee. During this weekend, we were educated by experts on all the aspects of addiction. Several things stood out to me after that weekend. First, an addict's brain changes almost completely due to drugs. On this subject, Dr. Roger P. Watts writes the following:

Addiction is a brain disease, not a mind disease. Addiction effects [sic] the physical organ we call the brain, and it is the broken brain that has difficulty coping with the lack of alcohol or other drugs when a person stops using them. We call this difficulty the hallmark of chemical dependency or addiction. It is important to know that this addiction in the physical brain has certain side effects that affect the mind. The mind is the repository of our hopes, dreams, thoughts, ideas, morals, ethics, principles, the reason for living, and willpower. Using drugs and alcohol causes these qualities of life to be suspended as the physical needs of the brain override the needs of the mind…the brain gets hijacked by the alcohol or other drugs.[62]

This essentially means that those who suffer from addiction are not themselves while under the influence of their chosen substance. This is exactly why they give up on themselves, their hygiene, and any values they once held dear. Therefore, they can steal from loved ones with seemingly no guilt. Therefore, a person, once so beautiful, can become gaunt, full of sores, living only for the next high. And even after an addict becomes drug-free, it takes over a year for the brain's physiology to be restored.

I believe something similar happens to those who have suffered combat-related trauma. There is no doubt combat is traumatic, but what effect do these events have on the physiology of the brain? Traumatic stress demands an increased amount of stress hormones to activate in the brain. When the brain responds to stress in later events, it may trigger the same higher doses of these hormones. Dr. J. Douglas Bremner gives us a glimpse in the following:

Brain areas implicated in the stress response include the amygdala, hippocampus, and prefrontal cortex. Traumatic stress can be associated with lasting changes in these brain areas. Traumatic stress is associated with increased cortisol and norepinephrine responses to subsequent stressors.[63]

Cortisol, norepinephrine, and adrenaline are three major hormones produced by the adrenal glands when a person is experiencing a stressful situation requiring a fight or flight response to the situation.[64]

I have known warfighters both before and after they entered combat. And without exception, I have noticed the eyes change once they have experienced the rigors of combat. I have never said anything to any of them, but the change is unmistakable and underscores the saying that the eyes are the mirror of the soul. This physiological change betrays a change in the mind. And while what they did is in most cases honorable, they will never return to the person they were before. To many, combat experiences can bring out courage, strength, and great actions on the battlefield. But the opposite can also be true. It can leave the brain both physically and emotionally wounded, which can lead to deadly considerations.

# 6

# SIGNS AND SYNDROMES

The epic story of tomorrow can't be written
if it ends today.
—Unknown

It is impossible to stop a person from taking their own life if that is what they are determined to do. I have had to come to terms with that fact no matter how difficult it is for me. Having admitted this, I believe that a new awareness outside of professional awareness and programs is essential if we are to change the statistics of warfighter suicide. Because of the work we have done in this area, I am often asked how I know when a friend is in danger of taking their own life. And each time I am asked, I make a sigh of relief. I do this because the very fact that the question is asked means another set of eyes and hands has joined the fight. The tragic truth is there are too few willing to engage and care for those suffering with thoughts of suicide.

## Top Five Signs of Suicidal Ideation

It is important to note that there are differences between the symptoms of suicidal ideations in warfighters listed here and those in civilian life. While I care deeply for anyone suffering from suicidal thoughts or, more directly, the stress and events driving suicidal thoughts, the focus here is directed at syndromes suffered by those who are serving and have served in war and other active-duty military situations. The following syndromes or concepts are useful ways to identify suicidal ideations.[65] The syndrome names are my own. They may appear like other documented symptoms, but that similarity would be coincidental.

## Acute Superman Syndrome

This condition is driven by a deep sense of the complete inability to be enough as a person, at least in the sufferer's own eyes. For whatever reason, the sufferer refuses to give himself a pass and instead mandates he work to achieve superhuman goals. It is often described as "driven," but it is better explained as "pushed." Climb the highest mountain, run the longest distance, lift the greatest weight, go the longest without sleep, and achieve more and more repeatedly. This condition is a relentless pursuer and acts as a placebo rather than a cure. While the activity itself can be admirable, it can sometimes mask what it is hiding very near the surface: depression and suicidal ideations. Those who suffer from this syndrome can do well for years and even excel in life if they are moving or being pushed by this invisible force. But at some point, when something necessary for the continuation of movement breaks down, that which was doing the pushing crashes down upon the sufferer, potentially causing catastrophic consequences.

This is a condition that often comes naturally because it so closely mirrors the typical military regimen. Those who serve have learned that training more, learning more, challenging themselves more, sacrificing more, hurting more, carrying a heavier pack, and taking more responsibility is part of military life. Practice and training are both positive stressors. Things start to go south when these activities are no longer required. When they have no future purpose. For many, the superman syndrome imposes imagined goals to fill the hole. A fear of future failure is one of the many symptoms driving the superman syndrome. You may have heard this adage before, "You better hope your past doesn't catch up with you." Most of the time it is used as a warning of impending judgment. The problem for sufferers of this syndrome occurs when this saying goes from *if* their past catches up with them to *when* it does catch up with them.

## Sudden Distance Syndrome

A sudden change in a veteran, assuming it isn't for the better, is a serious sign of concern. Sudden Distance Syndrome is often a signal of psychological distress, such as depression and hopelessness, which may have been triggered by many possible means. This syndrome typically involves the closing off or detachment of a warfighter from those previously allowed in and is often the result of shame or guilt, either contrived or real, felt by the sufferer. This condition often causes the sufferer to show a lack of empathy to events that would result in emotional and visceral reactions in people unaffected by this condition. They often seem somewhere else and cannot be present in the moment. When we see this symptom, the natural way most people react is to give the sufferer what they want, either consciously or subconsciously confessing, "Well, if you don't want me, then I don't need you." As an example, their response could be compared to the car accident victim in the following story.

Two friends decide to drive in separate cars following one another to a predetermined destination. The traffic is going along well as they drive on a long trip across state lines. The two are hours into the drive along this stretch of desert with hours still to drive before a rest stop. Then suddenly the leading car veers to the right, hitting the desert gravel where it overturns and rolls several times before coming to a stop upside down. The following driver screeches to a stop, exits the car, and runs to the crash scene. When he arrives, the driver is conscious but in shock. Confused by the shock, when the rescuing driver attempts to help, the hurt driver unconsciously makes a motion indicating he is all right and doesn't need the other driver's help. Taking the wounded driver at his word, the rescuing friend leaves the scene, gets into his car, and motors on.

At first reading, many would think they would never leave someone in such a grave condition. But this is what happens every day to our warfighters when they are in shock and showing signs of Sudden Distance Syndrome (SDS).

Let me be clear:

- SDS is a wreck.
- SDS means the warfighter is in shock and unaware of the gravity of the situation.
- SDS brings a reaction that often communicates to others there is no need for help.
- SDS can only be helped if a friend refuses the rejection, refuses to leave, and renders whatever first aid is needed until more help arrives.

# Chronic (Unbearable) Pain Syndrome

On multiple unfortunate occasions, I have been present and aware when those I loved and cared for were forced to live with unbearable pain. Their only choice was to live on addictive pain medication (prescription meds, illegal drugs, and/or alcohol) for the rest of their lives, all while waiting for some promised medical breakthrough or considering putting an end to the pain themselves. Chronic pain sounds simple enough until you experience it. For those with fishing experience, one victim described it this way, "It feels like a worm might feel when it is skewered onto a fishhook and then lowered into the water. First, there is the pain of the sharp metal hook penetrating your entire body. Then there is a sense of drowning. The worm may gasp for air much like you gasp for relief, but it does not come. Finally, the fish bites, not ending your pain, but only reminding you the pain can and will get worse with no end in sight."

The Department of Neurology at Columbia University calls it a "slow torture." They further state, "Unlike acute pain, this condition doesn't go away after your initial injury or illness has healed. It's marked by pain that lasts longer than six months and is often accompanied by anger and depression, anxiety, loss of sexual desire, and disability."[66] Understandably, many sufferers fall victim to drug and alcohol abuse. For some, these circumstances have led them to consider assisted suicide or voluntary euthanasia. As strange as this may seem, this option is available in several US states, as well as many European nations and Canada and Colombia.[67] I cannot possibly know how gut-wrenching such a decision must be to those who cannot imagine living one more day. And while I cannot accept euthanasia for human beings, neither can

I bring myself to condemn those who make that choice. From a moral perspective, I am adamant that euthanasia or assisted suicide should be reserved for suffering animals not precious human beings. The answer is not to fight to help the sufferer end their life; it is to fight to give them a reason to live despite the pain.

It is true. Unbearable physical pain can lead the sufferer to want it to all end so badly that they dream of death. This is particularly true with the warfighter because they have been trained to accept the tenant that the duty they have sworn to uphold comes with the possibility of a loss of life, including their own. The "option" of suicide when dealing with pain has been part of war for thousands of years. Whether it is the Roman soldier falling on his sword or the warrior of today killing himself, this is no new problem. The fact remains that many of those who have been conditioned to kill the enemy also lose the fear of their own death. I have seen the video testimonial of a soldier who walked into his tent in the Middle East, picked up his M4, rocked it back, and while uttering the words, "Well, I will just let God decide," shot himself in the chest. The good news in this case is that, miraculously, he survived. Since his recovery, he has made a commitment to help others who are suffering like he once did to find a reason to live.

Do not miss this point: the ability to fight for his life and to help stop others from taking their own lives resided in this soldier long before he shot himself in the chest. I believe this to be true in all who are wrestling with suicidal thoughts. The very fact that these ideations exist in their soul makes the sufferer capable of helping others.

## Denial Syndrome

Several years ago, I was asked to evaluate a friend who was showing deep emotional distress. After being with him for some time, it became clear to me that he had some serious mental health issues. I recommended that he be placed in a hospital for observation and that those around him draw close to help him as he walked through this difficult time.

Mental health issues are unbelievably painful to those who are experiencing them. They are also frightening to those who are close to the person suffering. To watch a person who has never shown anything but a sound mind and wide-ranging emotions degenerate into a bath of irrationality and disconnected feelings is not much different than watching a cancer sufferer decline physically. Sometimes the depth of the mental issue is such that it allows no rational consideration by the suffering.

For months my friend made some adjustments in his life and then declared himself healthy and whole. He posted videos online showing the world that he was sound of mind, merely an act to be sure. At one point he asked me to come to his home and see how much he better had gotten. I remember it being a rainy day as I approached his house. I was wanting to greet my healthy friend, telling myself he was restored and whole once again. I parked my car and walked to his door, but before I knocked, I felt a knot in my stomach. Then I told myself to accept whatever he truthfully was and not to be tricked. He greeted me with open arms and then took me on a tour of his house. That is when concerning signs began to show up. I'm sure he didn't intend me to, but I noticed ramblings, and instead of sitting and just talking to me, he would play music and show me his office, explaining all the trinkets he had collected over the years, and the conversation was disjointed and confusing. Lastly, there was a smell of alcohol on his breath, which he tried to hide with several pieces of gum. When I asked a probing question regarding what he was doing to get so much better, he simply changed the subject and changed location. After I was there for over an hour, he mentioned another meeting and walked me to his door. As I departed it was evident that he was as bad as he was before. Maybe worse.

As I walked to my car to depart, I knew that intervention was necessary to stave off a disaster. The problem was that anyone who came to him, even his family and friends, were summarily cut off if they didn't accept his self-assessment and narrative. He had essentially begun to live as if he were okay and denied that there was anything wrong. I cannot tell you how dangerous this situation is, especially if the person is a type A, or a very controlling individual.[68] Even though those around them can see clearly that there's a problem, they're afraid to confront the individual because of the potential backlash. In my friend's case, this went on for over a year, and then one day, the news came that he had taken his own life.

Veterans are often extremely motivated individuals. They have developed the ability to stand alone in the most difficult times and fight to finish the mission. Once separated from the regimented arena of military service this strength can often turn into a vulnerability. Sayings like, "I don't need anyone," "I can do this myself," and "Just leave me alone," are signs of a struggle, and those who are present to hear them need to make note of this as a sign of concern. Also, those observing this syndrome must make a conscious decision *not* to be controlled by the sufferer. Regardless of rage, silence, manic acts, and intimidation, those who are close must trust their gut and follow their instincts, which may include difficult prolonged confrontations. While it may be easier to leave the sufferer be, it is not in their best interest. This is when the warfighter needs others to literally enter the fight to save a life.

## Survivors Guilt Syndrome

This syndrome is one on my list that is among the most studied and written about. Wikipedia states the following, "Survivor guilts is a mental condition that occurs when a person believes they have done something wrong by surviving a traumatic or tragic event when others did not, often feeling self-guilt."[69]

This definition offers a conscious understanding of the survivor's guilt but doesn't begin to define the internal struggle found in those suffering from it. Many individuals suffer from this syndrome, and it is certainly not limited to the veteran or warfighter. *Medical News Today* published the following list of those who can suffer from survivor's guilt.[70]

- War veterans
- First responders
- Holocaust survivors
- 9/11 survivors
- Cancer survivors
- Transplant recipients
- Crash survivors
- Natural disaster survivors
- Witnesses to a traumatic event

- Family members of those who have developed a fatal hereditary condition
- Those who lose a family member to suicide
- Parents who outlive their child

While this list certainly identifies most of those who are possible victims of survivor's guilt, I believe there is a reason the first on the list are war veterans and warfighters. To me, they are hands down the most vulnerable.

# Extortion One Seven

At 2:38 a.m. on August 6, 2011, a US Army Chinook helicopter, call sign Extortion 17, entered the western opening of Afghanistan's restive Tangi Valley, flying alone. "One minute—one minute," transmitted Bryan Nichols, the pilot in command of the helicopter. Flying 250 feet above the valley floor at just under 70 miles per hour, Dave Carter, the pilot to the right of Nichols, guided the helicopter toward a carefully chosen landing zone just over a mile away. In the rear of the aircraft, the Chinook's passengers stood and prepared to storm out into moonless night once the wheels touched the ground. Extortion 17, however, would never reach that landing zone.[71]

This high-risk mission over the Tangi Valley, Wardak Province, Afghanistan, resulted in the deaths of thirty American special operators, some of whom I knew personally. I also happened to be friends with some of the men who were closely related to those who died in this operation, including one who called me from the region who could have been on the operation or QRF (Quick Reaction Force) but was not due to the company rotation. Many of my friends lost brothers that day and, without exception, demonstrated signs of survivor's guilt for not being there. By June 30, my concern grew most for the individual who was nearest those who died. I determined to monitor him over the next days, weeks, and months because I knew this situation and circumstances placed him among the most vulnerable to survivor guilt syndrome. Because this SEAL had a great support group, he navigated his guilt well and continues to this day to be a strong and competent warfighter and leader. But too many others were not so lucky.

This condition is not exclusively limited to proximity as some may think. Survivor's guilt may occur in those far from the tragic event. Missing a mission due to order of rotation or because the sufferer was in another region altogether for medical reasons does not lesson the traumatic effects of survivor's guilt. Thoughts of *I should have been there! Why did I get to live?* and *If I had only...!* raise thoughts of guilt. They play over and over in the consciousness of those suffering from survivor's guilt. It is a bombardment on the soul not unlike a mortar attack on a physical position. The difference is this emotional bombardment is constant and seemingly never-ending, an added trial prosecuted in the conscience of the individual.

In our experience, these five signs and syndromes are among the most dangerous. But there are more. With this information, we hope that both those who suffer from these conditions and those who wish to help them will take with them the message that none of these symptoms should result in nor require a death sentence. The knowledge and awareness of such conditions can make one an advocate for life as the sufferers of these conditions process through finding order and relief from them. The goal is not to remove the memory but to process it in such a way as to change the traumatic experience into a source of strength instead of a source of torture.

# Eyes Wide Open

With the high number of suicides happening daily, there is a strong chance that in our daily interactions, we will pass someone who is contemplating suicide. For most of us, our lives are already filled enough with our own difficulties and complexities to even notice when others are struggling. To notice would require ignoring our own problems that are right before our faces, but I can tell you this from experience, no matter how hard things are for you, you are able and competent to save someone else's life. By taking the focus off yourself, you may very well find the answers to your own problems. This will require a change in heart and in the way one views society. I am not saying it will be easy. In this era of suffering from the COVID-19 pandemic, we have become adept at not looking others in the eyes. We have learned to fear intimacy with others, especially those we do not know. I know there is fear, and I am all too familiar with the requirements of COVID-19 that mandate social distancing, but I have an answer. Since the eyes are the only part of us that we are encouraged not to cover, then look people in the eye. Just do it from six feet away. And when you have a sense about them just ask, "Are you okay?" The rest will come naturally.

# PART III

# RELIEF AND RECOVERY

The bravest thing I ever did was continuing my life
when I wanted to die.

–Juliette Lewis

## Power, Pattern, and Purpose

Each of us has patterns of behavior that drive our lives. They are by-products of our repetitive interactions with the environment, others, and, to some degree, codes found in our DNA. These habits can enrich our lives but can also have the opposite effect. When trauma takes place, it sets in motion a series of events that, if left unrecognizable to the soul, can be catastrophic. In its normal processing of various procedures and tasks, whether making repairs to one thing or another or showing emotions, the soul retrieves information from its memory banks. It also places new positive or negative experiences into its memory bank for future use. When a person has successfully turned a trauma (a shockingly negative experience) into a stored memory, he or she begins the process that

89

can lead to healing. Healing from the initial traumatic shock may range from, at minimum, creating a settled memory to creating a useful tool for improving one's life and, better yet, helping others with their struggles. The first step means shifting the vision from a continuously confusing and at times convicting mental activity to a settled memory.

Unsettling trauma establishes new patterns. And these patterns are almost always negative. Three main types of traumas are acute, chronic, or complex.[72]

- Acute trauma resulting from a single incident.
- Chronic trauma is repeated and prolonged, such as domestic violence or abuse.
- Complex trauma is exposure to varied and multiple traumatic events, often of an invasive, interpersonal nature.

For the warfighter, the experiences of combat—the sights, the smells, the images impacted on their minds—will undoubtedly invade "normal" life. The warfighter may become paranoid and hyper-aware. Sights and smells will cause an adverse reaction, one which the sufferer is unable to control. In response to a question on *Quora*, a question-and-answer website, regarding the smell of war, Jon Davis, USMC, wrote:

> I was deployed to Iraq's Al Anbar province. This is a particularly arid desert region which is important to understand the next point. When stepping off the plane you are instantly embraced by the heat and the smell. Immediately after the heat, depending on the time of year you are there, you get a smell that I have only been able to describe as the smell of "thousands of years of death and woe." It was somehow very different from that of training in the Arizona deserts of Yuma or even in Kuwait...Add to this the constant smell of yourself after not getting to regularly shower, bathe, or really function on any degree of civilized cleanliness and you have a

smell that I can only describe as pure and unadul-
terated man funk.[73]

Other smells include decaying bodies of both animals and humans. Also, the breakdown of infrastructure results in free-flowing sewage, body odor, and more. These smells produce an imprint on the mind, and even when in an environment where they do not exist, the slightest reminder of the smell will produce a stress-related reaction.

Over time, the straws of stress no longer lie neatly on the camel's back. They become so entangled and unmanageable that they infect our patterns, and quite frankly, everything in life is affected. The stress invades relationships, often resulting in their termination. Anger, rage can occur even in those whose disposition before the event was completely the opposite. Suffice it to say, this becomes unbearable both to the sufferer and those who know them. Because trauma produces these kinds of patterns, those traumas must be confronted for the sufferer to become stable. Thoughts frequently shift into actions, and repeated actions turn into behaviors. Therefore, it is so important to allow those troubled warriors in our lives to have permission to say *anything* to us to stifle the thought-to-action process. It could mean the difference between life and death.

Recently, I was counseling with a dear friend. After our session, she mentioned to me that I reminded her of her father, a veteran and a member of a special forces group. She went on to say that he was "really messed up." It didn't stick out to me at the time, but when I started to write this book, I realized something. All veterans need to have people looking in on them for signs of problems. And I am not talking of the kind of "feel sorry for you" help. I am talking about real help from someone who cares and will do whatever it takes to get at the truth. This is the kind of friend who looks for signs, like alcohol or drug abuse, outbursts of anger or rage, sleeping problems, and depression. You may not realize it, but these are all soul issues. The symptoms may have parked themselves in the victim's mind, but make no mistake about it, they are very active in their soul and can only be healed in the soul.

# 7

# PSYCHOLOGICAL FIRST AID

Out of suffering have emerged the strongest souls;
the most massive characters are seared with scars.

—Kahlil Gibran

Psychological first aid, or PFA, is a term used to describe simple tactics available for helping those suffering with stress, trauma, and thought of suicide. Considering the rising number of cases of PTSD and subsequent suicides, we feel everyone should have a basic understanding and ability to administer PFA when necessary. PFA allows us to mitigate normal life stressors from becoming chronic and leading to issues such as depression, PTSD, suicidal ideas, and suicide attempts. It means recognizing who may need help, how to support them, and how to refer them for professional help should the need present itself. PFA is the purposeful response to an event or series of circumstances that can cause an individual to spiral toward life-altering actions. It can be argued that there is a greater need for PFA than physical first aid in people's lives.

Speaking from personal experience, if I were to compare my need for physical first aid with my need for psychological first aid, the pendulum would swing hard on the psychological end. And, by most accounts, I am considered a rather "normal" person. We live in a time when there needs to be a cultural shift away from divisive strife that has engulfed societies and a movement toward actions that lead to honest discourse. This is not to suggest that we give up on our convictions and moral code. It is possible to still care about another human being with whom you have several deeply opposing positions on a myriad of issues. As a counselor, I engage people who often believe things that I not only do not adhere to but also have a deep distaste for. To help them, I must put aside my feelings to be able to see beyond the façade to help guide them to healing. In doing this, I'm able to give them a path toward the reconsideration of their ideals or beliefs.

I was once called to help with the cleanup at the scene where a person had died by suicide. When I arrived at the gruesome scene, I was met by a young man who was understandably in crisis emotionally. He was a good friend of the victim and was dealing with deep guilt because, although he had spent many hours with the victim, he didn't see the signs of his friend's distress. He wasn't crying or overly emotional as he recounted the horrifying experience, which alerted me to the need for psychological first aid. His trauma was being held at bay.

My first action was to communicate care. Care for what he had experienced. In the physical sense this is like pressing on the bleed to slow the flow of blood. Knowing someone was there to help allowed a place to let down his guard and release the anguish. All I did was show him that the deceased was not more important than he was. He imposed guilt on himself because of feelings of responsibility for the death. He needed a listener, someone who cared and was willing to help reframe his thoughts. While almost everyone around him was understandably focused on the victim and his family, he was the first person on the scene and had attempted to clean up the mess. During our time talking over the coming weeks, it became clear that this tragic event wasn't the only one he had endured. He had grown used to pain and, like most of us, had built a façade to keep others from seeing it.

# Issues

My wife and I love to watch football. We prepare for a game by making nachos and my famous guacamole. Amber is always cool and calm during the games, only making comments from time to time. As for me, well, I become another person altogether. Let's just say I am the exact opposite of her. I run the gamut of emotions from euphoria to the head-in-my-hands depression while Amber just tries to ignore me. As we watched the 2020 Superbowl between San Francisco and Kansas City, I was my typical self. Ranting, cheering, shouting, and walking back and forth across the living room floor. Soon, out of nowhere, Amber stood, grabbed my face and said, "Dude, you have issues." I shrugged her comment off and continued until the game was over.

The following day I was scheduled to conduct a presentation to the board of directors of a large company. Knowing the sophistication of everyone in attendance, I needed to be polished and knowledgeable of my subject. The subject I was presenting on was psychological first aid in business, such as identifying issues in corporate leaders who, by their job description, are required to be always in control. As I stood to speak, I remembered my wife's words from the previous day, *Dude, you have issues*. And so, I began my talk by quoting my wife, which brought laughter from my audience. I then turned my experience back on them by saying, "Ladies and gentlemen, this is a condition all of us in this room share. We all have issues, and when it comes to the corporate world, we spend a great amount of productive time learning to hide those issues because they are considered 'unprofessional.'"

We create facades that hide our true condition, our pain, and our destructive habits, each of which are guaranteed to negatively affect our productivity. While I am not advocating wearing our feelings on our sleeve in inappropriate situations, especially in leadership roles, there are times when our facades cannot hide conditions under extreme stress. If someone were to come into the workplace with a gaping wound, most coworkers would first attempt to stabilize the wounded while calling for an ambulance. It would be unthinkable to do anything else. But what if we apply this same mindset to psychological conditions. Every day when we enter our workplace, there it is a possibility that one or more of those workers will be dealing with serious emotional and psychological wounds. And if these conditions go untreated, the results could be catastrophic.

From time to time, wounds from the past will resurface. Death or impending death in the family, marital strife, and more can cause all of us to bleed emotionally. Financial pressures often open fissures in the soul revealing emotional wounds that have been held at bay long before the current crisis. Addictions that have been silenced for years can resurface, adding even more emotional stress. These are not anomalies; they are normal human responses to stress in all its forms. But for some reason, we have bought into this idea that it is "none of my business." And so those whom we see each day suffer in silence, dying a little more each day until they either self-destruct or just give up.

## Stigma

In many respects, corporations function along the same lines of structure, organization, operation, and goals as does the military, with some obvious extreme exceptions of course. Both memberships come with their own level of stress and stigma. If sharing emotionally troubled feelings can be problematic in the corporate world, they can be the "death knell" to a military career. For those in the military, stigma, particularly those involving psychological challenges, draw high levels of concern for the one suffering and those around him.

As an analogy, consider football, and most ball sports for that matter. The goal is to get the ball across the line and score points. The offensive line works to prevent the defense from tackling the quarterback. The main offense frontline defenders, very large individuals, work together to prevent any opposing team players from breaking through and sacking their quarterback. For those few seconds prior to hiking the ball to the quarterback, those linemen hold steady in their position, intensely prepared and ready for the oncoming wave of the other, very large individuals, all looking to crush the quarterback. In that instance, when the ball is hiked, all hell breaks loose, every player does his part to keep the quarterback safe long enough for him to handoff or pass the ball. Should one defender fail to block his opponent, the quarterback is sacked, and that one player is blamed for the loss of the play.

Now replace that team with a squad of soldiers, protecting an FOB (forward operating base) or outpost, when a group of insurgents suddenly attack. Soldiers suffering with psychological issues, real or perceived, are granted little exception by the team when lives are at stake, and every member must be at the top of their game. This fear of mental stigma carries across the board of military occupations, not just frontline functions. For this reason, men and women suffering from stress, depression, or other psychologically related issues avoid seeking mental help. The fear of being labeled inadequate, not-up-to-par, or unsat (not satisfactory) in any military unit presents a huge burden and stress on its own, never mind the actual stressors.

## Personal Responsibility

It should be our business to help the hurting when we can. In a world at odds with almost everything, caring about others' psychological conditions should be of concern for us all. The suicide rates today, in many ways, reflect society's growing ambivalence and lack of compassion for others. This condition does not necessarily reflect a lack of caring but rather a lack of knowing how to care for others. Multiple resources exist with an abundance of information on helping others. At the turn of the century in 2000, the U.S. Congress established the National Child Traumatic Stress Network to raise the standard of care and increase available service in the field of child trauma. From this network a guide book titled *Psychological First Aid: Field Operations Guide* emerged identifying many helpful actions for children.[74] The US Department of Veteran Affairs has also adopted this guide into its PTSD support for veterans website.[75] The guide is designed for mental health and other disaster response workers, it can be a valuable resource for better equipping anyone desiring to care for others. Two strengths highlighted in the guide are information-gathering techniques and culturally appropriate interventions. This stresses a need to learn how to appropriately speak with, and more importantly listen to, those suffering in a way they culturally understand. Listening is vital.

## Military Culture

About culture, the military creates a culture, out of necessity, that differs greatly from that found in civilian society. Lynn Hall defines it as "The

Warrior Society," a culture unique to the military.[76] She shares insights from Mary Wertsch, who states, "The great paradox of the military is that its members, the self-appointed front-line guardians of our cherished American democratic values, do not live in democracy themselves."[77] This diversity in cultural prospective should give us pause when peering into the life of a warfighter. Their perspectives on authority, the law, direct orders, conduct, and sacrifice follow a much more stringent and consequential path than one found in a society driven by loose guidelines and opinion.

"Is this okay?" A recent advertisement begins with some scenes of burning material in front of some buildings and then moves along to other chaotic scenes. All the while a commentator is asking in a concerned tone, "Is this okay?" One viewer commented, "What the hell does that mean?" What does "okay" mean? The word *okay* implies an adequate or acceptable level of approval (e.g., "the finished job was good enough"). Not excellent but not bad either. While the advertiser attempted to make an emotional plea to its audience, this viewer's logical perspective made it difficult for her to connect the ad with its intended purpose. From a military perspective, *okay* implies a "below standard," one that is a practically unacceptable standard level of quality. Peak performance is normal. To accomplish this expectation, training military recruits begins with instilling discipline and order. "Why" questions are particularly unacceptable. Marching in step may not seem important to most, but in military training, it is the foundation of what follows. Discipline, order, and strict adherence to commands is vital. In the field, split-second decision and commands are literally life changing. Taking the time to answer "why" questions is unacceptable. This mindset also filters its way through the family unit over time.

Authority, rank, command, all represent power and might, clear direction as well as care and security within the military. The Declaration of Independence stipulates that all men (and women) are created equal. That may be true at creation, but once in the military, rank and position brandish rule over subordinates without question. The 2000 Universal Pictures movie *U-571* depicts two great examples of authority in realistic form.[78] The movie is about the World War II recovery of a Nazi Enigma encryption machine. However, it also contains two scenes relative to this subject and the military culture to keep in mind when interacting with military members. One or more of the stressor straws may be entangled by this concept. As a subplot of this movie, the well-liked Lieutenant Taylor, played by Matthew McConaughey, is denied command of his own boat (sub). Although qualified, he worked more at integrating with the sailors and being liked by them than holding command over them. Lt. Commander Dahlgren, played by Bill Paxton, and to whom Taylor reports, challenges Taylor with a question. He requires Taylor to make a difficult decision about sending one of the men on a mission that would likely take the young sailor's life. Taylor hesitates to answer. Dahlgren then interrupts before Taylor answers and explains to him, "I'm not questioning your bravery. The question is: What about their lives? You and Mr. Emmett are good friends. You went to the academy together. Would you be willing to sacrifice his life? Or what about some of the younger enlisted men? I know a lot of those guys look up to you like a big brother. You willing to lay their lives on the line?"[79] In a later scene, Lt. Taylor is now in charge of the captured German sub, now severely damaged, and he is forced to make a decision. When asked by the other submariners what they should do, a confused Taylor exclaims, "I don't know." Chief Klough, now alone with Taylor, explains, "This is the Navy, where a commanding officer's a mighty and terrible thing. Don't you dare say what you said to the boys back there again, 'I don't know.'"[80] Certainly, military leadership holds multiple philosophies on *how* to command, but the point here is *to* command. The military requires absolute command, structure, and order from their disciplined subordinates. Any fractures in this system can be devastating not just to the structure but to the individual as well.

# Making Decisions

A friend once told me the following: What people do not understand, they reject. This maxim may not apply equally in the military world, but in cultures where democratic options are more readily available, it rings true. While the military requires blind faith and obedience to orders, current societal norm seems to garner understanding and agreement by speaking out loudly, quickly, and often. Under these distracting conditions, making decisions or taking action on any subject leaves individuals with little time to conduct fact-based research or think things through. All that remains are seemingly quick, "this feels right," opinion-based responses. Making decisions for small matters or major life choices is an integral part of living. It is a necessity to understand.

Modern technology and new ways to communicate with each other has brought with it many great benefits. Video chats across the world, virtual group meetings, text messaging, and other apps have brought people closer together. Unfortunately, this tech is a two-edged sword. Earlier, Socrates' description of the soul explained the theory of multiple parts or voices in your consciousness—that other opinion in your mind. Now, with modern technology, thousands of other opinions can be delivered daily. They each have a say, and they all demand their listeners to take their side or opinion on almost any subject. Making decisions between two options is difficult enough, deciding between multiple options/opinions can be devastating. Remember high school tests? Questions requiring a choice between "A" and "B" or "True" and "False" at least give you a fifty percent chance of getting it right. Questions with thousands of opinions to choose from can be maddening.

# EMT and PFA

Emergency Medical Technicians, or EMTs, are trained to provide the first level response to people suffering medical emergencies. Some technicians also have at least a minimal ability to recognize and support victims suffering and in need of psychological help. A good example of first responder or EMT training taught to young US Marines can be recited in a simple directive: "Stop the bleeding. Start the breathing. Treat for shock." Even the order of each command is specific to its level of importance. The training goes on to explain how to conduct each step, but it's the simple phrase that initiates the follow-on techniques to be applied in each situation. This method is proven, and it works.

Should you find yourself in a situation where you stand between someone's life or death, please keep these following simple steps in mind. As you read the remaining pages, you will find more depth as to how and why these steps can help you save a life or at the very least postpone death, thereby giving time for more help to arrive.

1. Check for potential physical dangers. If possible, without causing injury to yourself, the individual, or others, separate the individual from the tools or situation with which they may harm themselves. If the situation is dangerous, call 911.

2. Make a connection. In a case of suicidal thinking, a responder should not dive into offering solutions without first assessing the situation. Why does this person want to commit suicide? What or who is in the way of a good life? Listen attentively and allow the individual to vocalize fully before injecting your own views, analogies, or suggestions. Only by listening can you hope to find a connection point. And never ever say, "I know how you feel." You don't. You *can't*. Everyone's experience is different. Even if you had the same loss or trauma, yours is different in many ways, and how you respond and feel about the event will be as unique to you as theirs is to them. Furthermore, it can be demeaning. You may have had a similar trauma and the same feeling of loss, but you are now in a more stable place. A person contemplating suicide is still in extreme emotional pain. He or she may have only had a short time to process and reintegrate into a more stable position.

3. Point toward a way forward. Find a common point of reference other than what is causing the pain—anything to divert the conversation to a happier time, event, hope, dream, etc. Somewhere in this person's soul resides more pleasant thoughts and memories. Focus on them. Help the hurting individual reconnect and find a way forward in the short term. There are so many options for a good life. Perhaps the roads or paths this person has taken have become unfulfilling, and suicide has risen to the top in his or her list of options. The sufferer has found that none of the others work for them. Ask this person about the roads he or she has have or have not tried. Perhaps

100

suggest a few. Sometimes just thinking about possibilities is enough to keep a person searching for a better life rather than ending it. Not every path is a winner. In fact, most people travel many wrong paths and course correct along the way, even if it means reversing course for a distance. With that in mind, know that for a suicidal person, even the wrong road is better than no road in the sense that any road will buy time to eventually finding the right road. On this point, further in this book, you will find some helpful hints about asking the hurting person to write down their traumas. Include in this having them write about their hopes and dreams.

4. Seek professional aid. I commend those who pursue psychology, counseling, therapy, and other professions for helping distressed persons. For all others, be they friends, family, or new acquaintances desiring to help those suffering with suicidal thoughts, these brief instructions are meant to be used in an emergency in order to buy enough time for the sufferer to get professional help. Time and professional counselors will take care of the rest.

# 8

# SPEAKING A NEW LANGUAGE

Great minds discuss ideas,
average minds discuss events,
small minds discuss people.[81]

—Various attributions

Having a conversation with trauma victims can be challenging, particularly those with trauma suffered in war. Losing someone close to you can be debilitating. It can also generate a hurricane of feelings that are difficult to articulate. It's an extremely frustrating feeling to realize you may never be able to talk out your experience because those around you no longer speak the same language. Enlisted personnel begin their separation process from civilian society at boot camp. Boot camp focuses on instilling discipline, the ability to follow orders without question. In general, asking "why" will only get a recruit punished not educated. There is good reason and purpose for this difficult training. First, it gives everyone the same understanding of their role in the group, or as close as possible. It also enhances team participation. Officer's training carries a much different purpose. It is expected that someone prepared to complete a four-year undergraduate degree already holds a healthy discipline level. Their training focuses more on military leadership skills.

In both cases, transitioning from civilian free-will thinking to military mission-focused thought begins here. Afterward, their specialized skill training continues to fine tune their focus on "mission first" and allows them to remain purpose driven. Then training moves on to practice, lots of practice, endless practice, followed by hands-on conflict with opposing forces when necessary. Unfortunately, the U.S. involvement in the middle east provides more than enough work for every military skillset. Within a few years, it is difficult to recognize the civilian you once were.

When returning to civilian life, you find yourself, again, in a foreign country. You recognize your family and friends. They welcome you with open arms, and yet there is a sense of distance. The joy, laughter, and hugs have lost some of the warmth and closeness that was once there. On the outside, everything is as it was before, but on the inside, there is something different. You are no longer that young man or woman who left home to be part of the armed forces. Transforming from a civilian life to one in the military required training, practice, and lots of effort. It stands to reason that returning, reengaging, and becoming part of your civilian family and community requires as much time and effort as entering the military.

## You Will Never Understand

Often conversations with veterans begin with the words, "You will never understand." The fact of the matter is that no one will ever know nor understand your thoughts to the degree you may want them to. Claiming that no one will understand is a lie intended to keep the speaker trapped in their current situation. It may come across as a statement of bravado ("My traumatic experience is so bad; how could you understand?"). It may just be an effort to reject all who ask.

To this last point, many people ask veterans questions about their military experiences, not for the veterans' sakes but for their own purposes. Perhaps they want fame by association or just to use veterans' stories as gossip fodder. It's a type of taking that makes the veteran feel even more alienated. Much like the early burrows of New York City, where immigrants from different countries gathered because of their common language and familiarity, veterans gather for the same reasons. The goal is not to remain separated but integrated.

As to stating that others will not understand, it is a statement of speculation. First, being able to speculate on what another person can know or understanding in the future is not possible. While speculation may turn out to be correct in the future, at this moment, it is just a guess. Second, when sharing trauma, even with others involved in the same event, each person will have their own individual interplay with the memory of the event. Some will reengage life with only a small scar, an uncomfortable memory. For others, that same event will cause a "full stop," an inability to escape its consequential replay. The first is not better nor stronger than the second, only different. The building blocks established in their soul were formed differently. Meaning, every person develops at a different pace, under different circumstances, and with a different understanding of how things should or could be. The challenge of integration boils down to being able to translate languages and traverse feelings. Learning to speak a different language is required on the part of both parties.

Feelings, on the other hand, are like landmines. Some engage tears of joy or laughter. However, stepping on a sensitive feeling can cause an explosion. Always remember, when you hear the spring click, *do not jump*. Instead, prepare to defuse the situation with statements such as, "You're right, I will never know what you've been through, but..." Now begins the opportunity to engage each other, the one seeking solace and the other stretching out a new hand of friendship, sharing stories both good and bad, getting to know each other.

## Topic and Purpose of a Conversation

Whether you receive a call seeking help from a friend or family member or notice the signs of extreme depression in them, know their life is upside down and that they are at their limit of knowing what to do next. How should you engage them? Once engaged, where would you take the conversation? What questions would you ask? What stories would you share? The quote at the top of this section, attributed to Socrates, Eleanor Roosevelt, and others, offers some insight into having a conversation. Of the three subjects—ideas, events, or people—ideas are the most helpful when having a conversation with someone distressed to the point of suicide, but many times a good event will work as a starter. The weather is a good starter with almost anyone, but not so much with a depressed or traumatized person, so you'll have to be more creative. Questions about an idea they have or had before often result in better engagement, making it easy for follow up questions and comments. The main point here is attempting engagement and creating an opportunity for them to open up and share their thoughts, some good, some not so much.

## Listening

Starting the conversation should then take you to your primary role, listening. The worst thing to do is to make the conversation about yourself. Your hopes, dreams, and reason for living may seem helpful in leading others to join in with sharing their own, but leading with this may only enhance how seemingly unattainable their own goals, hopes, and dreams have become. At some point they tried and failed, not just once, but many times. In their mind they tried, they failed, over and over, and now they're losers. They have concluded their life is not worth living. It's important to make sure you listen to what they're saying. Ask questions about them. Avoid making conclusions during this process.

Many years ago, when I was a young volunteer teacher and director of the children's department at our local church, an elderly lady came up to me and asked if she could share a story. The services had ended, and the parents finally were coming around to pick up their children. I was exhausted, up late the day before preparing for classes. Sundays began early because we met at a school gymnasium and had to move all our equipment in and out for the services. Two services later, when I was hungry, tired, and ready to leave, this nice old lady begins her story.

She started by telling me how she felt about her recently deceased husband. As she continued, I started to feel like she must have hated this man. My mind was jumping from one Scripture verse to another. Platitudes and stories of grace and forgiveness poured into my mind. The more she spoke, the more I wanted to—nay, needed to—fix this woman. How could she be so hateful toward her deceased husband? Through every event in her story, I kept hearing this inaudible thought, *Don't say anything yet, just listen*, so I reluctantly held my tongue. Not an easy task for me at the time. About thirty to forty minutes later, she stopped. Then she started crying. I thought, *Oh my God, I've broken this woman.* Maybe I should have said something earlier. Then surprisingly, she thanked me. She said to me, "Thank you, thank you for listening to my story. No one, not my children, not my friends, no one has allowed me to finish telling my story. They all just wanted to fix me, tell me why I shouldn't think this way or that way. I loved my husband. He wasn't perfect, but I loved him, and I miss him. I just needed to tell my story. I needed to get it out of my head. I feel so much better now that I have. Thank you." Like this woman, warfighters many times just need to tell their story. They need to put it out in the open and see if they're okay in the eyes of others.

Imagine that each person you will be conversing with is like a freighter of containers that are full of books that are full of stories. And they are looking to dock with someone in the hope of unloading their stories to anyone with an attentive ear. Each book in every freighter is a different event, no duplicates. With such an overload of information, how can you help?

In this example, consider yourself the tugboat. Your job as a tugboat, small yet powerful is only to guide the freighter to the dock. In some cases, the tugboat crew does double duty and is also able to help unload the cargo.

The best approach is to take the example of a tugboat, small yet powerful. This means listen long enough to determine which books/stories/stressors you can manage to unload from the freighter yourself in the time available. Then nudge the person slowly and carefully to get them moving again in a good direction or to a port, capable of unloading more of their burdens. Most often a listening ear will make a huge difference. Other times, you'll recognize that they will need professional help.

Always keep in mind, as a first responder, PFA, or QRF, your focus is the survival of the patient—at that moment. Their long-term survival is a different challenge. Ask yourself: *Why do I want to help? Why this person? What is my interest in interacting with them? How much, time, money, and effort can I afford to bring to the table?* You are making an investment in someone else's life. You are not responsible for paying for their life. You have limited resources and your own life to invest in. Know your limitations; some wounds require surgery, not just a Band-Aid or a few stitches.

## Veteran's Language

Many veterans' stories are difficult to share. They can contain an unrelatable blend of horror and humor that only veterans with a common point of reference can appreciate. When sharing these stories, it is very easy for the veteran to discern when the listener has formed an opinion of dislike and disgust with the story. It's as if someone is speaking in their ear, *They don't understand. They don't like what you are saying.* For the listener, the veteran's humor becomes horror and vice versa.

Take, for example, a helicopter pilot who spots a group of people—men, women, and children—gathering in the street. Enemy combatants or curious civilians? The situation is unknown. The pilot lowers his craft and hovers closely overhead causing the crowd to disperse while also causing some children to topple over due to the powerful downdraft from the aircraft. To a fellow veteran, it is a funny story. To a civilian, unaccustomed to battlefield conditions, it shows horrible treatment of innocent civilians. Your response will dictate a sense of comradery or adversity to the veteran. In turn, he will continue sharing or shut down all conversation, for he has entered hostile territory. Don't misunderstand, the conversation may continue, but the focus will have shifted to milder subject matter. In other cases, it can become blatantly hostile. The listener's focus at first is to build as much cross-cultural (military-civilian) communication comradery as possible. You do not have to agree; just understand the other's perspective.

Married couples are good examples and the most vulnerable relationships since they result from the greatest personal investment. The veteran will go in thinking he is in safe company, but the spouse who is unaccustomed to such environments may not understand the humor or the horror. This brings up another point. Those who serve in the military often become divided in the family aspect. They have their wife and children as one family and their military brothers and sisters as another family.

# My Family, My Unit

For those who serve along with their families, life isn't what most would consider normal. Most families get to choose where they live along with a community and schools they like and the atmosphere which fits their social desires. The military family doesn't have any of these choices. They set up "home" where they receive orders. The community and schools are what they are, and each military family must make do regardless.

The military family must accept that service deployments and work ups, which require months of preparation for the deployment, are part of the world they enlisted in. This can and often does mean months of separation with little meaningful contact. I have often been on counseling sessions with military spouses who struggle with the effects of this separation. It is common for bitterness to develop in the spouse left home to be both father and mother. When the military member comes home, the separation doesn't end on the tarmac with welcoming hugs. Soon the bitterness surfaces as the couple tries to share home duties and the lack of connectiveness is revealed.

There are several movies which catch this lack of connectiveness. But one scene does it better than most. In *The Hurt Locker*, a bomb tech comes home to his wife and child. After being on a dangerous deployment in Iraq for many months, he arrives home. After a few days home, he begins to do things completely unfamiliar with his regimen. One scene shows him accompanying his wife and child to the grocery store. After an awkward walk down the aisles, his wife asks him to go to the cereal aisle and choose something. He walks to the aisle and looks over the many choices. Bewildered and confused, he shrugs his shoulders and just picks one then returns to his wife.[82] This scene underscores the vast distance between his family world and his unit world.

The unit is, in many cases, more of a family to the service member than spouse and children. In the unit everything is shared. Each member in the unit is tasked with specific responsibilities which serve the collective good. They face physical challenges together, fight together, suffer together, and more.

The difficulties military families experience become untenable when the time of enlistment ends. Moving from an active-duty professional warfighter to a veteran means leaving the unit or second family for good. This loss of comradery can be a festering sore in the family unit. The adjustment sometimes is overwhelming and can lead to divorce and separation from social norms. Once a warrior is alone and often distraught, suicide becomes a serious temptation. I have been asked many times how to mitigate this issue since those who serve cannot avoid the duplicity. My response is always education. From boot camp to the end of enlistment, there must be purposeful interaction and direct discussions about the family unit. Each serviceperson must be aware at all times of the importance of the natural family, and when there is an issue which arises, the family at home must be given priority.

# Responding

Understand the difference between speaking, sharing, making a point, preaching, and teaching. It makes a difference in how the listener interprets the story, the point, the information, and your concern for their well-being and your intent behind conversing at all. In this situation, your purpose should be focused on untangling or unburdening some of the stress the veteran is holding. Traumatic events, like those experienced by veterans, ink the conscience like a mental tattoo. Listening to those stories can be as repulsive as watching a gory scene in a movie. Always be prepared for the possibility of uncovering such a story when conversing with a veteran. Keep your verbal responses, physical demeanor, and facial expressions in check. Your duty here is to allow the veteran to share their story and to collect information, not make judgment calls on the humor, horror, or morality of the story. Afterwards, the evidence will let you know what is needed and how to respond.

# 9

# THE POWER OF A LISTENER

*Listening is a magnetic and strange thing, a creative*
*force. The friends who listen to us are the ones we*
*move toward. When we are listened to, it creates us,*
*makes us unfold and expand.*

—Karl A. Menninger

Being married for over four decades, I have learned the hard way the
difference between hearing and listening. My wife is adept at knowing
which of the two I am employing when we communicate. Truth is, I
am more of a natural hearer than a listener. I'm usually hyperaware of
everything that is going on in my surroundings and can easily look like
I am listening when, in fact, I am only hearing. Knowing the difference
between the two is vital to a successful life in relationships and life in
general. This is true even when engaging children. I vividly remember
an experience I had with my granddaughter, Marlea. She was only about
four years old, and we were sitting on the steps of our Civil War-era
home. She was chattering away like usual, and I thought I was listening
when she suddenly got up, stood directly in front of me, and grabbed me
by the cheeks. With a stern face, she then said emphatically to me, "Papa,
you aren't listening to me!" I was shocked! A four-year-old child knew

the difference between hearing and listening. Realizing she was right, I took her on my lap, apologized, kissed her on the cheek, and started listening.

Obviously, we were created with ears so we can hear, and hearing has its purpose even when not engaging an actual person. But when we engage a human being, several dynamics are in play. Listening involves shutting off those things going on outside of the conversation. Most people put up the front they want you to see at first, which often hides who they really are. I'm not saying this is wrong; vulnerability is often dangerous when trust isn't first established. Having said that, trust is only established in the listening mode. When someone knows you are listening, they will lower their guard, and you may potentially engage them on a deeper level. This is especially true when dealing with those who may be suffering from suicidal thoughts. They don't wear their feelings on their sleeve, but when speaking to a listener, the entire atmosphere changes. And listeners are the people who change the world, one person at a time. I would bet that among those who have considered suicide but didn't go through with it, the decision not to take their own life was in some way due to an engagement with a person with the qualities of a listener.

## Qualities of a Listener

Literally, anyone can become a listener. It is a matter of choice and discipline. And I can tell you from experience that the more you learn the qualities of a listener the richer your life will become. When you engage another person and tap into their soul through listening, your perception of yourself, others close to you, and the world changes for the better. There are several reasons for this. In listening, you are engaging another person with your quality time. Quality time is the willingness to give others your full attention. In fact, if individuals find that they can't give others their full attention, I encourage them to do the other person the favor of postponing the talk until the listener can give the speaker quality time.

Now there is an exception to this idea: there are some who are undeserving of your quality time. And you will have to make that choice between whom you can be with and those who will not benefit from it. There are some who have an agenda-based purpose and only want to use you or persuade you to take the same position. I call these people toxic, and you owe it to those who truly need you to cut these toxic people off. But if you wake up every day with the determination to be a listener, you will find those who are worthy of your quality time.

# Methods of Communication

People communicate through word, gesture, and spirit. The human being is made to communicate, and I have heard it said that communication is the basis of life. When there is no communication, there is no life. This is true in corporations, families and marriages, and all relationships. The level of communication determines the level of life. Companies that are successful are so because they understand this principle and make it a priority to pass along information on all three levels of word, gesture, and spirit. As people, we need communication, and we will do almost anything to obtain it.

## Word

During the Vietnam War, many brave Americans were captured and placed in POW camps, the infamous Hanoi Hilton being one of them. Men languished in rat-infested cells for years. Their captors intended to keep them in isolation to underscore the torture. While the Americans couldn't do anything about their physical isolation, through innovation and risk, they found a way to communicate. In Vietnam, the "Tap Code" was used by isolated POWs to let each other in on questions interrogators were asking so that everyone's answers could remain consistent and so they knew which of the other prisoners were not doing well. Because it was not overly complicated, new POWs were able to pick up on it quickly. This communication allowed them to maintain a critical connection with each other during a time when isolation was meant to torture them further.[83]

## Gesture

I have always been fascinated by the ability of listeners to read body language. I know there is a science to this idea, but personally, I learned to read body language just by watching people. Body language is a form of communication, and if you tune into it, you will be able to see what isn't easily spoken. If you can identify a person's body language, you can ask questions that you wouldn't otherwise think to ask. This may seem like probing, and it may be, but since you have already been allowed in due to your show of quality time, there is almost always an open door for deeper and more revealing conversations.

Most people understand the general idea of body language, but there is also an actual subset defined as suicidal body language. In a 2014 Penn State article, Adam Greene wrote:

> The biggest emotion that relates to suicide is depression. According to the Mayo Clinic, "Depression is a mood disorder that causes a persistent feeling of sadness and loss of interest." There are multiple obvious signs of depression, such as crying and fidgeting; however, there are many other signs that are not as easily spotted. One sign to look out for is a person's body posture. Studies show that a depressed person will tend to slump their bodies [sic] and they will not "stand tall" while walking. They will look like the Hunchback of Notre Dame, so it won't be hard to miss. Besides slumping their bodies, they will also keep their feet very close together. They do this to take up as little space as possible.[84]

Slumped and withdrawn, closed postures are strong indicators of depression, and depression is a strong precursor to suicide.

Narrowing one's presence, whether relating to the space to stand or the number people with whom one interacts, often leads to isolation. Depressed individuals tend to withdraw from social groups, friends, and even from their families. They begin to isolate themselves from others for several reasons, including guilt, shame, and a desire to avoid confrontation. Even holding conversations becomes difficult. Prolonged isolation and lack of communication can cause mental and physical problems. In a *Science Alert* article, Sarita Robinson explains, "For example, solitary confinement can have negative psychological effects on prisoners—including significant increases in anxiety and panic attacks, increased levels of paranoia, and being less able to think clearly."[85] As another example she says, "Natascha Kempusch—an Austrian woman who was kidnapped at the age of ten and held captive in a cellar for eight years—noted in her biography that the lack of light and human contact mentally weakened her. She also reported that endless hours and days spent completely isolated made her susceptible to her captor's orders and manipulations."[86] Natascha's vulnerability to her captor was increased due to her lack of communication with others. Subsequently, even though his actions were abusive, on a subconscious level, the abuse was a better stimulus than none.

Of course, body language is not an exact science, but it can be a good guide when deciding to ask a person about their state of mind. Other signs of depression include facial micro-expressions such as droopy eyelids, lack of focus, mouth curved in a frowning position, and furrowed (semi-angry) eyebrows.[87] There is a saying that the eyes are the mirror of the soul. I would add the eye is also the access point to the spirit. I have yet to meet a combat vet who didn't have a unique way of communicating their spirit. To describe it best, I would use the words "locked down." But this look isn't due to what most people would think. They are warriors, and a warrior always locks down to anyone who is not in the circle of trust. It is because of this that learning to see what is behind the eyes is vital to helping a soldier who is suffering within. It isn't mind reading or some sort of psychic activity; rather, it is the willingness to look beyond the obvious and sometimes intimidating gaze into the soul that is screaming to be heard regardless of whether the warfighter wants to admit it. This exchange can also be another method of discernment.

## Spirit

We communicate through spirit. Yes, you read that correctly. As described above, the spirit can be another word for the soul. It can also be referred to as an aura, something seen but yet not physically visible. Most of us go throughout life not interested in this part of others, probably due to the difficulty in tuning in to another's spirit. Regardless, all humans present a message through their spirit. Our spirit signals the true nature of our constitution. When a person has a pure spirit, no matter what package they come in, those around them will feel that the person is pleasant to be around. Newborn babies are the best examples. On the other hand, wounded people emanate a wounded spirit. Those with suicidal thoughts in particular present an atmosphere of hurtful wounds without the need for words nor gestures. It is not uncommon for those around a wounded individual to pick up on that feeling, but too often, others do not take the extra step to find out why the individual may feel that way.

Empathy, the ability to understand and share the feelings of another, like the soul and spirit, is an unmeasurable, intangible quality that people depend on for survival. Without this spiritual connection, psychopathy, antisocial behavior, and a general callousness can develop within the person. Empathetic people show a gentle or loving spirit toward others.

The reverse is also true in people with a lack of empathy or a bad spirit. Examples of bad spirits can be found in cult leaders like Charles Manson, David Koresh, Marshall Applewhite, and Jim Jones. Their vile spirits and lack of empathy toward others enabled them take advantage of those with wandering and weaker spirits. This mixture allowed these leaders to convince their followers to commit heinous acts consistent with their own bad spirit. While researchers have identified the specific location in the brain generating empathy, it's only a first step toward identifying the intangible mechanism involved in empathy, the functioning spirit aspect. Furthermore, empathy is not stagnated (a go/no-go process); it is trainable. It can be developed.[88] Unless there exists some form of traumatic brain injury affecting the empathetic part of the brain, even the least empathetic, emotionally distant, or just seemingly bad natured folks have in them a potential for developing a kinder, gentler spirt.

# Neutral Approach

During the 2020 presidential election, our nation found itself in seemingly constant debates over what the future should look like. At times, it appeared society was locked and headed toward either a revolution or a civil war. The communication among Americans accelerated to a fever pitch with political and social unrest at historical highs. Neutrality in opinions had left the building, and fighting for one's social standard, both physically and verbally, became a daily *Jerry Springer Show* type broadcast. Considering such a toxic atmosphere, one might ask, "Is it possible to put aside my own strong feelings about life, step inside the life of a hurting veteran, and bring a message of hope?"

The answer is a resounding yes! To be a great listener, personal biases must be shelved. A listener isn't there to judge the veteran's words, comparing everything the person says to their own perspectives of life. Often hurting people knowingly or unknowingly push the listener's buttons, just to see how the listener reacts. Quite possibly, some of the veteran's comments will stand against most of what you value. However, if you continue to listen, you will be afforded an opportunity to impart words of value into their life.

# PART IV

# APPLICATION

Up to this point, we've tried to capture the essence of suicidal thought. Stress and trauma weigh heavily on its targets. While the term "victim" has been used numerous times in the previous chapters, this does not by any stretch of the term imply weakness, cowardice, or fearfulness. In fact, almost all the men and women we have worked with are extremely strong, courageous, and fearless. These traits are mighty weapons against tangible enemies, but they fail against intangible enemies, those that attack one's soul. When trauma is viewed as an enemy attacking the soul, the sufferer is no longer a victim but rather a target. As explained in earlier chapters, suicidal thoughts result from a relentless onslaught of bad stressors, some self-induced, but most caused by external factors and events.

The elements, definitions, and constructs of the warfighter's soul, for us, are intended to help the reader recognize the combatants and terrain in which this personal war is taking place. As with physical war, intangible war takes on different shapes, different terrains, different combatants, different frictions (for you who understand Clausewitz), different chaos (for the rest). As military strategists must assess each conflict individually, we, too, must approach each person suffering with stress and depression individually. There are no fixed formulas, only a few persistent examples. And many of those found in the ever-growing psychologist handbook, the DSM (Diagnostic and Statistical Manual of Mental Disorders), are fraught with exceptions. Exceptions play a role as much as weather and other variables in combat. Similarly, as you will read later, in a court of law, even well-established precedence is constantly challenged because of the exceptions and differences to previous establishing cases.

The challenge here is to frame the issue. Isolate, the issue from all the external fluff, the extemporaneous drama that carries no weight for the immediate problem. If all the memories and stories of a single person were written, you would be facing a freighter full of boxes, each full of stories, and all wanting to be heard. Whether you're facing a traumatized person face-to-face or the one in the mirror, start by taking on only one issue. Your task is to untangle and remove one single straw before moving on to the next. Please keep this in mind as you continue reading.

Framing is the process of isolating the issue from its participants. When confronting an enemy, in general, the issue involves the goals being sought and the methods used to attain those goals. For example, a married couple starts out married because of an admiration and respect for each other, an attraction for each other, and shared goals. They get divorced because one or more of those things have changed in a drastic manner. Identifying what changed, beyond the simplified "you changed" excuse, allows the couple to isolate the change as an independent item and separate that item from their relationship. This framing process of isolating the issue from the person equally allows us to identify a distressed, depressed, and potentially stigmatized victim from the main, still present, capable, and functioning person trapped inside.

# 10

# BUILDING MEMORIALS

They say forgiveness is giving up hope on having
had a better past. I'm ready. I want to let it all go.
I'm just not sure how to do it.

Aggie Blum Thompson

In 2017, our team and I (Greg) flew to Israel to, among other things, broadcast the opening of the new US Embassy in Jerusalem. It also happened to be the seventieth anniversary of the birth of Israel and the feast of Pentecost. Our schedule was very full as we traversed the Holy Land.

One day, after we finished filming early near the Jordan River, I found myself sitting alone in a high place overlooking the majestic scene. It was a hot, dry day, but there was a breeze blowing, which made it tolerable. This atmosphere and the fact that I was alone for an extended time allowed for much-appreciated catharsis. I remember feeling as though I was close to either sleeping or dreaming. Then, my love for history consumed my consciousness, and I began to visualize the historical significance of what I was seeing. Thousands of years ago a sea of people called the Israelites consisting of twelve tribes of people crossed the Jordan River below me into the promised land of Canaan. When the Israelites crossed over the Jordan and stood for the first time in the promised land, we are told a transrational voice came from heaven with a command. They were to stop and send a representative from each of the twelve tribes and construct a memorial built of twelve stones. As I visualized this act, I wondered out loud, "What was so important about building a memorial?" It had to be important because the last thing these oppressed people would have wanted to do after spending forty years in a desert eating manna day and night would be to stop at the edge of their destination and search for stones.

I can only liken it to when I was a child and the day finally arrived for us to depart to Disneyland. My brothers, sisters, and I boarded our old Pontiac and began the journey to the "Greatest Place on Earth." For months, my siblings and I spoke of our Disney vacation trip, dreaming of the rides, the food, and the fun. And the day arrived like Christmas morning, and we knew that when we could see the Matterhorn, which stood forty-five meters tall, we were close to our dream. After spending what seemed like forever parking, we ran to the gates to purchase our tickets. With tickets in hand, we excitedly got into line to go through the turnstile and entered the park. That is when our mother and father would make us stop and sit in front of the Welcome to Disneyland sign to take a picture. And if that wasn't frustrating enough, after the family picture was taken, we had to sit facing our father while he laid down the law. What to do if we got lost. Where we were to meet for lunch and dinner. What would happen to us if we didn't watch out for one another. And more. Then, once Dad was finished and certain we were clear on everything, he would release us into the fantasy world of Walt Disney.

The Israelites had wandered in the desert for forty years longing for the promised land. Then, when they finally enter their promise, God stops them. It kind of seems to me like God was messing with them. But then it occurred to me to focus on the meaning of a memorial. When most of us think about a memorial we think of it as a place designated for mourning the loss of someone. But a memorial is not just a place to say goodbye to a loved one; it also symbolizes the beginning of another new dimension.

I believe, as many do, one who has died does not cease to exist. Their soul simply passes into an eternal existence. So, what does this all mean? God had the Israelites build a memorial so that when they went on to occupy Canaan, they would have said goodbye to all that the desert represented. Historically, the desert represented what happens when one rebels against the Creator. They took forty years to go a very short distance so their souls could be cleansed of the slave-like mentality. Sometimes the quickest way home is not the best way. In response to a similar question about the forty-year trip to the promised land, Rabbi Corey Helfand wrote:

> In his poem "The Road Not Taken," Robert Frost wrote, "Two roads diverged in a wood, and I—I took the one less traveled by, and that has made all the difference." I think that there is something to be said for taking the easy route because it makes us feel safe. At the same time, I also think that there is something profound in taking [the] road less traveled, even if longer, windier, and more danger-ous along the way. Sometimes, the harder we work for something, the more we appreciate what we've accomplished once we arrive at our destination.[89]

For these Israelites, the memorial would be a sign of new begin-nings signifying the moment they shed the old rebellious, idol-worshiping selves, allowing them to embrace a new self. This physical act would become, for generations, the equation for putting off the control of self and putting on a new person.

## Trauma and Memorials

Most of us see breakthroughs in terms of discovery. For instance, the dis-covery of the cure for cancer would be a massive breakthrough. Anyone who has had cancer or knows anyone with it, hopes that pharmaceuti-cal companies and scientists will discover some unknown compound or mixture of discoveries not yet known that will eradicate the scourge. I recently read of a story of a fourteen-year-old girl named JS, who lived with her mother in London. JS was diagnosed with a rare form of cancer, and by August 2016, she had been told her illness was terminal and active treatment would come to an end. She began researching cryonic preservation online—a controversial and costly process that involves the freezing of a dead body in the hope that resuscitation and a cure may one day be possible, and JS decided she wanted to be frozen after her death.[90] This is just one of many such stories, and it seems apparent that we are predisposed as humans to see the future and its discoveries as the best place to put our hope. While I agree with this in general, I wonder how many answers to life's issues have we missed because we are so determined to make history instead of learning from history.

When dealing with post-traumatic stress, or for that matter any traumatic event or memory, I have found nothing more effective than holding memorial building events. The World Health Organization reports that 264 million people worldwide are affected by depression.[91] This problem is not getting any better as it seems the more the issue is focused upon, the worse it gets. As a person who struggles with depression, I know how it manifests itself and what pain it can bring both to the depressed and to those who love them. I am okay with the medicines and the counseling that helps so many. "Building memorials" is a technique that allows for a detachment from the mind-matter that darkens the soul. Building memorials consist of three acts. The first is the admission to oneself of what is hidden and may reside in closed off parts of the soul. *What happened to me?*

This is the question many of us refuse to ask ourselves. Why? Because we avoid pain and will do almost anything to not feel it again. The problem is the pain, unless we face it, will create more and more pain. It is like a virus that feeds off weak cells until there aren't enough healthy ones left to keep us in good health. This is what is at the heart of a suicidal person. The lack of facing what happened to me sets in motion the denigration of all happiness. When the time comes when we are taken over by the virus, a suicidal person is so sick that death seems almost good. For the warfighter, the pain of what happened to them is exacerbated by the haunting questions of *What have I done?* or *What should I have done?* These negatives pile upon each other over time, and it is these compounding stress contributors that lead to the unusually high number of suicides among the warfighter community.

It is interesting to me that in the five books of Moses, the war was almost constant, much like it is now. It means that thousands of men fought regularly in bloody and close quarter combat. A study of this time must reveal much regarding the treatment of the psychological dynamics related to the warfighter.

The second part of building memorials is to write out what is in the soul. One of my mentors, Dr. Edwin Cole, taught me and thousands of other men an important principle. He said, "If it isn't written, it doesn't exist." This may not hold true in physics, but in the intangible world of the soul, it is true for building and maintaining human character. This is the reason journaling is so cathartic as a practice. The practice of writing things down has the tangible effect of taking thoughts out of our soul and moving them to the paper. What may be unspoken can be written, and when it is, something happens that can only be explained as the emptying of the soul.

Think about it for a minute. What if you could take all the pain that was inflicted upon you, that you inflicted on others, and finally that you inflicted on yourself and empty in on a tear-drenched paper? To build a memorial you must be willing to engage in this act of looking back into the desert of your life and boldly recognizing what you were. This act takes real courage. If we act willingly, the thoughts tormenting us, those we have been running from possibly our whole life, will begin to evaporate. You may ask, "Is it that easy?" The answer is no! There is nothing easy about confession to self. We have no one to look at but ourselves, and the act of writing is our confession to ourselves, taking responsibility for the one life we must live.

The most difficult parts of the soul to deal with are those traumas that were forced upon us. Because we were a victim of another's acts or events outside of our control, we feel as though we are helpless to deal with them. Our own mind can lie to us. It will say that we just must live with it. The pain is part of our fate. Nothing could be further from the truth. What happens to us doesn't define us. How we deal with those events defines us. Consider the horrors experienced by the Jews during the Holocaust. They did not choose this for themselves.

In a *New York Times* article, William B. Helmreich spoke about his book, *Against All Odds*, saying, "No book talks about the survivors regarding anything but their pathologies...There are no social histories. Until now, most sources drew from limited samples. Yet only 18 percent of the survivors ever saw a psychologist. The survivors had lives before and after the war. Why did I write this book? I felt it would be a travesty if survivors were only remembered as the skeletons they looked like when they emerged from the camps. Hitler made them look that way. Why give Hitler a victory by leaving this impression?"[92]

But those who survived had a legacy deeply entrenched into them regarding how to leave the horror behind. Following their ancestors' example at the Jordan River, they set up memorials. The proof is found in the success of these survivors who became doctors, thriving business-men, legal experts, professors, and entrepreneurs who raised a people who would build the new nation of Israel. These wounded people turned their nightmare into memory, and as a result, they couldn't be stopped. They denied Hitler his dream to enslave and destroy them, pressing forward to become one of the most prosperous people per capita on earth. This despite still being an often-hated people. That is what happens when you stop allowing what happened to you define you. A few years ago, our good friend Gary L., having survived the Holocaust, went skydiving for his ninetieth birthday. He jumped out of the plane screaming, "[Truck] you, Hitler. Look at me now!" [First word changed for your sake.] A fine example of triumph over adversity and trauma.

Aron Ralston's example of hellish conflict is one of person versus nature. In a 2019 story, a man named Ralston set out for a hike in a dangerous area. While hiking Ralston slipped and an eight-hundred-pound boulder fell onto his arm. He was trapped for many hours when he decided that to survive, he must take radical action by cutting off his own arm. The harrowing experience took 127 hours. Today, Ralston, while missing an arm, enjoys a life of sports, helping other disabled hik-ers, and much more.

You or someone you know may have been in hell much longer than

127 hours. It may also be a very real possibility that writing your memorial, looking back, and acknowledging what has caused you so much pain, will hurt as much as cutting off your arm. For you to find the courage to cut may seem too far, too impossible, but I assure you it is not. The loss of an arm is acceptable. The loss of your life and soul is unacceptable. It has been said that a price cannot be placed upon human life. The value of a human life cannot be assessed. The worth of a human life cannot be quantified. This is written in the universe and into the heart of all human beings. To take one's own life is to deny all these eternal truisms and to deny oneself and the world the uniqueness of a gifted and special human. Take the next step, build your memorial—write it down. Then…

# Burn It

Soon after learning of the process of building memorials, I was invited to speak at an event attended by leaders who had great success in business, the arts, music, and politics. After a full day of speaking, I asked all the men if they wanted to join me at the fire pit. It was a cool evening and what I consider a perfect environment for the memorial process. I must admit, presuming that due to the great success each man had attained, I felt that few of them would have any issues to deal with. As each man found his place on a rock or a chair, I began to tell the story of building memorials. As I spoke a calm came over the group, and it was clear that introspection was taking place. Some men were looking intently into the fire, others looking into the moonlit night, and others looking down at the ground. After finishing my talk, I paused for a few minutes and then passed out pencils and paper before instructing each man to go for a walk and take as much time as was needed to put on paper whatever he was inspired to pen. Over the next thirty minutes, men would arrive back at the fire holding their written, unprocessed trauma. As I watched them, I observed something very interesting: how the men held their paper. Some had their list rolled up tightly, others folded into a tight square covered in the palm of their hand. Some had their list folded in half and held it over their heart. These actions betrayed the emotion of shame, pain, anger, and even fear. For these men, this was their moment, and the determination to destroy what they had lived with for so many years was etched on their faces.

As each man sat down that night, the third part came into play, which is to destroy the power of the trauma thereby creating a closed memory, one that can cause meaning and purpose rather than constant torment. One of my main concerns with the way the psychological community treats trauma is they are adept at the process of identifying it but often cannot process it into something positive. While the identification process is vital, it isn't a complete treatment until the trauma's power is destroyed. And while the destruction process is symbolic, it is more effective than any drug prescribed to numb the pain.

After ten minutes of silence, with each man sitting quietly at the fire, I said, "Men, what you have in your hands are not just words. They are your enemy, and while each of you has been successful up to this point, if you don't destroy that enemy's hold on you, it will ultimately win and become a destructive force within you, taking from you all you love and cherish. You have all taken a courageous step, but for this to be complete, one final action is required. I want each of you to place your trauma on the fire and watch it turn to ash. This step completes the building of a personal memorial, allowing those building it to identify with the self, which will go forward with renewed purpose and freedom.

# 11

# CHANGING THE PATTERN

When you change your thinking,
you change your beliefs.
When you change your beliefs,
you change your expectations.
When you change your expectations,
you change your attitude.
When you change your attitude,
you change your behavior.
When you change your behavior,
you change your performance.
When you change your performance,
you change your life.[93]

—John Maxwell

Traumatic patterns or habits are difficult to break, but difficult is not a new thing to the warfighter. Like any habit, we can become addicted to it. Even when destructive, we must have it. Whether subconscious or conscious, there is no upside to traumatic habits. And the answer is certainly not a drug, especially when that drug only masks the pain. I have watched too many of my good friends come home from combat and within a very short time be prescribed an opiate-based drug. And while I know there is a place for the use of these drugs, they should not be doled out just to put off dealing with the real issues. Our warfighters give their all, and when they come home, every hospital should be available to them, and if they need an army of therapists, then we should give them that army, free. There is only one outcome to ignoring them, and that is death or at least some portion of it. I think the world is still in need of the courage, honor, and strength emanating from our warfighters.

## Pattern-Busting Accountability

It is often the case that those suffering from suicidal thoughts do so alone. They don't speak of the suffocating turmoil and total loss of hope. There are several reasons for this, with the greatest being that warfighters end up sidelined, made irrelevant, forced into an institution, or something even worse—ignored. Other reasons differ greatly, but the point is accountability to the right person or people is vital to eradicating suffering. Alone, stress is magnified. To hide what is going on inside is to live two lives: the hurting one inside, and on the outside, the one everyone else is allowed to see. The "I'm ok, I can handle it" life is a lie. It takes creativity to live two parallel lives. Unfortunately, that creativity is eternally wasted when the true condition of the soul wins out. Living two lives is inherently unnatural. One life will always be a lie while the other will be emaciated due to the symbiotic relationship with the lie.

"The man who is left alone to define his life while experiencing a time of trauma and difficulty will always define his future skewed." I spoke these words to thousands of men during an event in the Philippines in the early months of 2016. Little did I know that I would be challenged by my own words due to traumatic events that began unfolding shortly after my arrival home.

It all started with the untimely death of my friend and mentor of over thirty years. He was fifty-nine years old, and together we had traveled the world. During these trips, we spoke almost incessantly about our dreams of changing the world. There was never a sign of anything but success, and more and more of our dreams became a reality. I loved working with him in war zones, disaster areas, and places in the world that were in total disarray. We went from the pinnacles of government lobbying for the people to the death and stench-ridden squalor of Cambodia. But if I was doing it with him and our teams, I was in my element.

Then one night I received a call. Yes, that call. My friend had suffered a stroke. None of us who loved him believed in anything but a total recovery. Anything else just couldn't be possible; we had our plans, and this wasn't one of them. Over the next year, he suffered several more strokes and ultimately lost his life to brain cancer. During that time, the part that hurt most was the look in his eyes knowing that our dreams would not be achieved. After his funeral, I was struck with the loss of vision because my vision wasn't even mine. It was ours! For months after his passing, I fought to determine a new path. Little did I know that my loss was just getting started.

In January 2018, I received another call from a friend who was close to my family. He called me early in the morning before the sun rose. He began the conversation by asking me how I was. I answered with the typical doing fine response. In a shaky voice he asked me to sit down. I pressed him with a kind of nervous humor thinking he was messing with me. I sat, then he told me that our first-born son Adam had died. Losing a child, no matter what the circumstances, brings a shock no one is ever prepared for. To my four children and Adam's many friends, the funeral only marked the beginning of our grief. I remember those days as hazy and numb. In my career, I had helped many families work through this same type of catastrophe, but I never expected it to feel like it did.

In my attempts to rise from these two tragedies, I began traveling again. This time it was with a team of people including my dear friend's wife, who now headed his organization. The team traveled to Cambodia to help the poor and destitute and to take children from the jungles across the border into Thailand. They were treated at the Presbyterian hospital in Bangkok for every type of ailment from needing new prosthetic eyes to having shattered bones. Our trip there took us into the filthiest place I have ever been to. On one day, we received intelligence that a group of children was living in these terrible conditions. The squalid place, as you might image, was so fly infested we could hardly see. And worse, it reeked of rotting human body parts, most likely discarded by the lackluster medical care facilities they have there.

After spending some time there and arranging for support for the children, we departed. After several weeks, we returned home. Almost immediately after our return, I began to feel pain in my elbow, which over a couple of weeks grew into a baseball-sized cyst. When I went to the doctor to have it looked at, I was immediately taken into surgery to have it removed, and I was placed under the watchful eye of a doctor from the Centers for Disease Control. Then several weeks later, I was once again rushed into surgery for doctors to place some sort of antibiotic directly in the wound. I spent over two months in a sling. Looking back, this lack of mobility and the frustration of it all exacerbated a growing depression.

Several months passed, and we were asked to travel to the middle east. It is my practice when traveling either to or from a foreign country to immediately orient to the time zone upon landing. This often requires me to stay up for many hours at a time. As I arrived home from this trip, I decided to take my iPad and sit on my deck until bedtime. Unfortunately, this time I was unable to fight the fatigue and fell asleep in my chair. About two in the morning, I was stirred and awoke in a daze. I stood up and attempted to get to the old civil war era door when I stumbled and fell six feet onto the concrete leading from our front step. I passed out and awoke sometime later in a pool of blood, with deep cuts and unable to move my arm—the same arm that became infected in Cambodia. Since my wife was asleep, I decided to drive myself to the hospital, which, looking back, wasn't the best decision. X-rays revealed I had broken my arm in thirteen places, requiring two surgeries, a plate, and thirteen screws.

After all this, I found myself, for the first time in my life, closed off to the world. Inside, I was depressed because I was having such a hard time dealing with the death of our son. I felt guilty and spent long hours going over and over what I must have done wrong. Since he died of a drug overdose, leaving behind four sons of his own, I *had* to be the reason for the way he turned out. I had even convinced myself that all these terrible things that happened to me were some forms of judgment. For months I was depressed, and this guy, who always had all the answers, was left with none. The unyielding emptiness was killing every productive thought, leaving me with only one outlet, walking.

Every morning I would wake, have my coffee, and head out to walk the dirt roads near my home. But even through the music playing on my iPod, the haunting voices were driving me further and further into a deep, dark hole. I remember one summer day walking as the sun rose. I stopped walking, suddenly looked to the sky, and cried out, "I cannot take this anymore!" That same day, without knowing what I had said on my walk, my wife reached out to our friend, a former SWAT officer and detective, Aaron Davis. She told him what was going on and asked him to find me. Not only did Aaron find me, but he immediately got into the mental hole I had dug for myself and told me his story.

You see, Aaron knew what I was dealing with. Aaron was a police officer in Middle Tennessee at the time, but he also had a job clearing construction sites of debris. One fateful day just before leaving in his police cruiser, he received a call from one of his workers at a construction site telling him he needed a trainer hitch. Aaron, thinking he could drop it off while on patrol, put the hitch in the passenger seat and departed. Soon after his departure, he received a call that two suspects were seen committing a crime. He hit his lights and headed to the scene. The added speed and the quick turns caused the hitch to go under the passenger seat, which would soon become the weapon that changed his life.

Officer Davis soon found the suspects and arrested them. Once seated in the back of his police car, one of the young men found the hitch and, with his feet, was able to get it into his hands and began beating Aaron over the head. Bloodied and beaten, Officer Davis was still able to wrestle the two down again and restrain them. By the time other officers arrived, Aaron was unconscious and covered in his blood.

Due to traumatic brain injury, Aaron was forcibly retired without any benefits. His career was over. Aaron, however, relying on his faith, was able to forgive the two men and move on with life. His contributions to others are unquantifiable. He has helped more people both personally and corporately than anyone I know, including myself.

# No Man Is an Island to Himself

As I think of this quote, I am reminded of the movie in which Tom Hanks washes up on an island and spends the next four years completely alone. In *Cast Away*,[94] Hanks plays Chuck Noland, a successful and gifted man, who works as an executive for FedEx. However, he is marooned on an uninhabited island after his plane veers off course in a storm and crashes in the South Pacific. Chuck is the only survivor.

Having survived the crash and the turbulent ocean waters, he washes up on the island with only the FedEx plane wreckage and delivery packages to keep him company. As the years pass, the time alone began to take its toll. During one scene in the movie, he opens a package to find a volleyball ball. He paints a face on the ball and names it, what else, Wilson. Extremely lonely Chuck begins to speak to Wilson as if it were human. He is driven to near madness and even plans to kill himself until he finally decides it is better to risk his life getting off the island and back home than to die alone on it. It is always risky trusting others with our personal lives especially when we are already in a vulnerable place emotionally, but like Chuck in this story, the reward is worth the risk.

# The High Cost of Parallel Living

Subconsciously, when we are traumatized, there is a tendency for the sufferer to develop two separate lives, as I pointed out previously. One of the lives seeks to project that all is good and that everything is under control while the other suffers with the stress of its reality. The thoughts of one part of the mind are always in conflict with the other. Duplicity is something that is sure to cause both the sufferer and those close to him to cycle from one emotion to another. This hamster wheel life is not a life at all. This parallel living will cost you all forward motion in life. Because the hard drive of the mind is so full of conflict, there remains no room for creative thinking and forward motion. Therefore, it is vital to process this condition and eliminate the duplicity. Once trauma is turned into a stored memory, that memory becomes the catalyst for a stronger and more resilient human being. Trauma may have created the circumstances, but it is the sufferer who decides what those circumstances become.

# A Familiar Story

A soldier with PTSD fell into a hole and couldn't get out. When an SNCO walked by, the soldier called out for help, but the SNCO yelled back, "Suck it up, son. Dig deep and drive on," then threw him a shovel. The soldier did as he was told and dug that hole deeper.

A senior officer went by, and the soldier called out for help again. The officer told him "Use the tools your SNCO has given you," then threw him a bucket. The soldier used the tools, and he dug the hole deeper still and filled the bucket.

A psychiatrist walked by. The soldier called, "Help! I can't get out!" so the psychiatrist gave him some drugs and said, "Take this. It will relieve the pain and you will forget about the hole." The soldier said, "Thanks" and followed his advice, but when the pills ran out, he was still in the hole.

A well-known psychologist rode by and heard the soldier's cries for help. He stopped and asked, "How did you get there? Were you born there? Did your parents put you there? Tell me about yourself; it will alleviate your sense of lone-liness." So, the soldier talked with him for an hour, then the psychologist had to leave, but he said he'd be back next week. The soldier thanked him, but he was still in the hole.

Another soldier, just like him, happened to be passing by. The soldier with PTSD cried out, "Hey, help me. I'm stuck in this hole!" and right away the other soldier jumped down in there with him. The soldier with PTSD started to panic and said, "What are you doing? Now we're both stuck down here!" But the other soldier just smiled and replied, "It's okay, calm down, brother. I've been here before. I know how to get out."[95]

Never be too proud to shout for help. Unless you are living on an uninhabited island, I am sure there is someone near you who can and will be that hand of help. I am also sure that your soul will reach out when you are near them. Discernment, an inhabitant of the soul, often referred to as "my gut," tells us things. It works very closely with the conscience and creates clarity when we are in the presence of good people and bad people. Discernment is a part of the soul that can be developed much like a muscle. This ability is always active, even when trauma has taken place. Discernment simply means to judge well.

There are two steps to getting help when we are dealing with suicidal thoughts. The first is to acknowledge to yourself you cannot stay in this frame of mind. We must be truthful with ourselves and willing to humble ourselves to ask for help. The second step is to find the right help. Good, honest people are easy to find, but you must search for them through many who are not so interested in helping.

Our society is full of people who cannot seem to do a good thing if their own lives depended on it. They are toxic, partisan people with little or no core. Trust your discernment, your gut, to help find the good people, those with a listening ear and caring heart. They may be family members, close friends, and even one of your "hard-charging" teammates. It is important to find the right person to allow into your life. And possibly, as you read these few sentences, you already have the right person in mind. Whoever it is, they will not be perfect or always say the right things, and that's okay. All you need is to have someone who will genuinely listen and help you climb out of your hole.

# Gold in the Dust

Gold is hidden in the dusty heart filled with unsettled trauma. Purposeful, life-giving gold, but the decision to continue forward is left up to you. Opening up to a friend is like pulling open the curtains in a dark room. It allows the sun to shine in, maybe only for a moment, revealing a new hope and the endless possibilities life holds.

# CHANGING THE PATTERN

I remember years ago when my wife, Amber, and I were just dating. Her parents owned a large house with horses in the pasture. Since the house was on a corner, the bus stop was located adjacent to the pasture. Each morning the kids would arrive and wait for the bus to come and take them to school. One sunny day, there was some commotion at the bus stop, and a fight broke out between two boys. The yelling and screaming were so loud that most of the neighbors were standing on their doorsteps wondering what was going on. After a few minutes, the bus arrived, and all the commotion stopped.

That evening, Amber and I were sitting on the couch watching football when there was a knock on the door. It was one of the fighting boys along with his mother. We were then told that, while fighting, the boy had lost a family heirloom, a gold coin worth a great deal of money. She asked permission to search the dusty horse arena in the hope they would find it. After several hours, there was once again a knock. We were told that they searched every square inch of the ground and were now convinced that another kid must have seen the coin and taken it.

Several years passed, and I never let go of the thought that the gold coin was still in that pasture. One cloudy day after a night of rain, I remembered the gold coin incident. With an awakened interest to find it, I walked out into the pasture to the spot where I thought the coin might be. Logically, that spot would be near the corner where the bus stop was. I searched for over an hour and then decided to give up. Right about then, the sun broke through the clouds, and about twenty feet to my left, I saw something sparkle. As I walked toward the sparkle, the sun disappeared once again, but I continued my search while walking bent over. Suddenly I saw it. The night rain turned the dusty condition into hard dirt, and as I reached down, I picked up the long-lost gold coin.

When the warfighter finds a person who is worth trusting, along with the qualities of patience and understanding and the ability to call out what is inconsistent with healing and hope, he has found that lost gold coin hidden in the dust. The patterns trauma leaves are areas that we must exposed so we can eliminate them and put new, healthy patterns in their place. I have met hundreds of warriors who were suicidal, but instead of doing it, they found someone to trust and asked for help. In almost every case, the once hurting person I knew ended up doing something amazing. "Bram" is such a person.

# Bram

When I first met Bram, a name he was given in the SEAL teams, he was living in a trailer on the base, which is not a good sign. In his case, this was due to an unfortunate circumstance he didn't see coming. He arrived home after a six-month deployment. Departing the plane at the airfield that day, Bram was expecting the same thing all the other returning warriors did, the embrace of loved ones and the joy of making it home safely. Walking toward the crowd searching through all the faces, Bram started to feel a chill, one that would become his reality to deal with, like it or not. His wife was gone, leaving him with an empty home and empty bank accounts. I cannot imagine what it would feel like to have this kind of rejection. I understand the anger, the depression, the haunting thoughts of betrayal that would visit him in his dreams and waking moments. It is so cruel, and since it is not all that uncommon, it can sometimes turn into thoughts of self-harm, like alcoholic binges, unchecked risks, and more. This was a low place for Bram and set the stage for our encounter.

Shortly thereafter, I was honored to become one of the many friends who stood with Bram while he dealt with what life handed him. I cannot overstate how important it is to be there for those who are dealing with such circumstances. Often, knowing the strength of such individuals, it is assumed that they will navigate it like they do everything in their professional lives. This is a bad assumption.

Not only did he make it past his traumas, but he has gone on to many successful ventures, philanthropic endeavors, and personal successes. He is now the owner of a business that hires mostly veterans, and his company has grown to over 130 employees and is known as a safe place where rejected and traumatized people feel welcome. Because Bram had been adopted as a child, he and his new wife, Robin, adopted a troubled child, giving him the same chance Bram once had with his own adoption.

They are well known for their willingness to give and, in some instances, literally until it hurts. In 2017 when Bram and Robin heard that a stranger in Colorado would die of a genetic disease if she didn't receive an organ donation, Bram didn't hesitate to offer a portion of his liver. Melinda, a mother of three, was diagnosed with polycystic kidney disease, which caused ever-increasing organ failure. Bram traveled to Colorado and underwent the testing to see if he was a match to be an organ donor for Melinda. After clearing all the medical and screening hurdles, the pair underwent successful surgeries, and Bram was able to donate 30 percent of his liver to Melinda. During his surgery, I had the pleasure to be with him. I will never forget the week following the surgery and seeing this bright, beautiful woman, along with her husband and children, celebrate their newfound future.

The best news is that Bram's story is only one of the many I know of. Because Bram found a friend in his own time of need, one who was willing to help him navigate his crisis, Bram has become that same type of friend to others. Through his life, business, and Life of Valor conferences that call men to a unique manhood, Bram has helped hundreds of men find a brighter future.[96] And you can do the same.

# 12

# TAKING LIFE BACK

Our chief want in life is somebody
who will make us do what we can.

—Ralph Waldo Emerson

"The final straw" when referring to breaking a camel's back points to the one that caused the broken back. This term is more commonly used to identify the final cause of failure of anything that was working right before that last change or added weight, as explained earlier in this book. As problem solvers, we tend to look for this type of failure. What happened or what changed right before it failed? When we find the breaking point, we can remedy the failure, and we move on. This approach works well when repairing things or processes. People, however, are fluid. People change from moment to moment. Perhaps not much, but even the slightest change can make a fix become ineffective even if it worked before. When considering a person's development through life, each event, each person they encounter, and every bit of knowledge they acquire affects, to some degree, their life course. Of these events and people, their effect will vary between beneficial on one end and destructive on the other.

While the camel's fate consists of delivering straw from the field to the farmer's storehouse, a person's equivalent of straw consists of

138

memories and hopes, their disappointments, traumas, dreams, goals, and desires. And each of these comes in different levels of intensity. Furthermore, each person is unique in his or her ability to carry the weight of each item. The same event can be a passing bit of bad news to one person and devastating to the person standing right next to him. From childhood to old age, each event that happens in one's life leaves some type of imprint. Each of us endures both positive and negative events. How we respond to each situation and stimulation makes us who we are.

Reading this book, I'm sure many of your own experiences or events have come to mind. This chapter exclusively deals with the impact of negative events. From birth, when parental influence impacts the core of a child's growth, good and bad events will leave lifelong marks. Beyond parents, mentors can help shape a young person into a well-functioning adult. As we read below, even bad childhood influences can be overcome and corrected. This chapter includes methods for taking control back from negative influences.

# Breathless

A child's birth alone leaves most fathers breathless, overcome with instant awareness of the need to protect their children, to mold their children, and to teach their children the dynamics of responsibility and authority. Contrasting these attributes as provided by a good father to those offered by the gang leader, one can easily see the opposite nature of each. The father gives of himself for the child's growth while the gang leader takes from the child. A father's influence on his child is undeniable. Therefore, we fathers *must* learn to take the raising of our children as the most serious responsibility in life. Being absent either physically or emotionally can have consequences for generations. Fortunately, the intervention of good father figures, exceptional mothers, family members, and outsiders can change or nudge the individual's life course.

# Mentorship

The importance of mentors cannot be overstated. With over seventeen million children living in fatherless homes,[97] mentors are more needed than ever. Every mentor to whom I have I've ever submitted has a story that moved them toward mentorship. These individuals lived and overcame some of the same issues they help others overcome. This story is what makes them so powerful in molding those who lack a father figure. Mentors are military leaders, coaches, teachers, business leaders, and more. What sets them apart is their innate yearning to help others by speaking truth, helping those they work with face their fears, create challenges for their pupils to overcome, and instill courage. They allow failure to teach. The mentor brings out the best in those who have a father hurt. For those who have a void due to a father's absence, there is no more powerful phrase than, "I am proud of you." This little phrase alone can erase a generation of pain, changing the direction of a life forever.

## Father Hurt

When things go wrong early in life, trauma can find and exploit these weaknesses. A Navy chaplain friend once told me that 80 percent of those who enter Basic Underwater Demolition training, or BUDS training, either have a poor father figure or no father figure. While I cannot vouch for the whether this statistic is accurate, my many years of working with these unique individuals underscores it. This type of negative influence is often referred to as "father hurt." The traumatic effect of harmful or missing fathers in a child's life is evident. Fathers abandon their families for many reasons. The more common reasons include insecurity, domestic abuse, and substance abuse issues. A lessor shared reason, hereditary predisposition, identifies patterns of behavior passed from parent to child. Simply put, this happens due to the father passing down the same pain he received as a child. Regardless of how or when this negative behavior started, it can be passed down from generation to generation. A child's response to their father's negative influence will, in many ways, determine either a negative or positive future. While there is always the possibility of course correction, the longer that child follows a negative path, the more difficult it is to correct. Following is one example of such a breakdown.

# The Counterfeit Family

Due to the great dysfunction in the family structure today, a void is created when family breaks down. A void subconsciously invites just about anything to fill it. And when it comes to the family structure, this can be catastrophic. There are many examples, but the most common one is found in gang life.

When thinking of gangs, one might imagine a mob of inner-city kids wreaking havoc, dealing drugs, and living lawlessly. In many cases, this could be accurate. Alternatively, a gang may more accurately represent a counterfeit family structure. In these subcultures, there is a designated leader who, through intimidation, simulates strength that is really narcissistic authority. This becomes the means he uses to mold those under him into what will serve him best. This "leader" disguises his dysfunction by demanding loyalty to the gang and absolute obedience from those who join. In many cases, the "father hurt" issue creates gaps in the child's ability to continue maneuvering through life's unexpected challenges. For example, how parents relate to each other sets a foundation for how the child's relationships with others will develop.

The proliferation of gangs is easily traced to their ability to generate an enormous amount of profit with little skill and a sense of family and belonging, thereby filling gaps directly attributable to some type of father hurt suffered by the gang member. The gang offers security, protection, and guidance. Provided the member does his or her part, the gang unit supplies his or her needs. It establishes governance and purpose. The gang leader sets up rules of conduct and responsibility. The leader establishes moral conditions for their subjects to live by. As bad as these moral codes may seem to outsiders, they frequently contain forms of benevolence toward their members, their families, and even for outsiders in their ecosystem. Regardless, most moral codes within gangs run askew of our more common understanding of morals and legal standards. The larger part of society works at maintaining a properly set moral compass even while struggling to survive.

Consider the number of times a gang lieutenant has taken control of the gang by murdering the leader. One example is the notorious "Teflon Don," John Gotti (1940–2002). Gotti grew up in poverty. His father John Gotti, Sr., was a day laborer struggling to provide for his family. He did not abandon them, but due to the situation, the children were left without guidance, short of provision, and lacking in security for the future. In this environment, it is understandable how John, Jr., and his brothers turned to the obvious option available to them. By no means does this excuse Mr. Gotti for his choices, but the patterns described above can be seen in this example. After earning his membership in the gang (Gambino crime syndicate), John Gotti rose in its ranks and began to explore opportunities beyond the established gang codes of operation. Before Gotti, dealing drugs fell under the "unacceptable" list of gang rules. Gotti had much grander aspirations and pursued dealing drugs on his own. It was under this situation that Gotti deescalated further and determined to take control of the gang. He then arranged and ordered the murder of his boss Paul Castellano.[98]

Gotti's story represents an all-too-common continued negative evolution of an individual resulting from a combination of negative events and the subsequent choices the person makes. As exemplified here, a moral imbalance between survival (extreme self-interest) and benevolence (care for others), creates a foundation that allows illegal activities, such as dealing drugs, operating protection schemes, and even murder without remorse, to flourish.

In a healthy family structure, a good father takes on three responsibilities. They are to guide, guard, and govern the family unit. While this may not appear as very democratic, a good father will balance each family member's desires with the whole family's needs and resources to best accommodate and provide for the whole family unit. When these three dynamics are not in force, the family suffers, and the children are left vulnerable to a world of predators, predators who prey on those craving acceptance, guidance, structure, and security. A father guides through his words and his example. From the moment a child takes his or her first breath, a father's influence begins to shape the child. A newborn knows and understands little. His or her existence is based on a choice between good or bad. Contentment develops into joyous desire. Conversely, lack might grow into fear then greed, then extreme selfishness.

# Sexual Abuse

While poor parenthood can be detrimental to a child over the course of his or her life, sexual abuse in most cases is instantly damaging. Children learn early on to trust their parents. Their life depends on the parents' provision. However, few traumas destroy trust more than sexual abuse. Children more than anyone are the most vulnerable due to their inability to fight off predators and their lack of understanding. This issue has changed virtually all modern society, and it continues to get worse by the minute.

Predators evolve from all walks of life. Sexual desires ride on a scale between disgust and lust. A healthy understanding of sex contains a balance between a medical/physical knowledge of the subject and that of the pleasure-pain principals. As with any desirable interests involving the human senses, satisfaction on its own demands more. Furthermore, sexual satisfaction tends to encompass all five senses, thereby intensifying its future desire. The growth of sexual desire arrives naturally in humans as a part of natural procreation. Most children are taught to develop moral concepts designed as control mechanisms for these desires. However, when left untrained, individuals are prone to develop unhealthy sexual appetites. Furthermore, influenced by outside forces such as pornography, "sex sells" commercialism, and the general public's ungated views and attitudes on sex, building moral concepts in children becomes a near impossibility. By allowing uncontrolled sexual actions and addictions into their home, parents influence all who live in that home, including their children. Under these conditions, these same children are vulnerable to acquiring the same habits and in danger of becoming future sexual predators.

Predators with financial resources and worldwide contacts have created a multibillion-dollar child sex trafficking industry. Sexual lust stifles parental patterns of guiding, guarding, and governing. It mutes discernment and ignites a fantasy-filled altered life, allowing a distorted view of sex to contort what once was pure. The US Department of Health and Human Services reports that one in three girls and one in seven boys will be sexually assaulted by the time they reach age eighteen. Moreover, about 30 percent of abused and neglected children will later abuse their own children, thereby continuing the cycle of pain and violence.[99] This indicates a strong chance that a percentage of those who enter military service very likely may either be a victim of sexual abuse or at least exist with the symptoms of it. This condition exacerbates all the other issues the warfighter faces.

# What Can I Do?

Since we have looked at the issues of "father hurt" and sexual abuse, which I consider two of the largest issues in society today, one must ask the hard question: *So, what do I do about it?*

To take our lives back we need to address the issue of control. The real question is this: Who or what has control of our lives? Are we being driven, or are we driving? Is our life a pattern of habitual drives, or is our life one of positive discipline?

If your life is controlled or driven by poor habits, then you are undoubtedly suffering, and there is a strong chance that you've decided that there is no way out. I can categorically say this is not the truth. No matter what the reason, restoration is possible, and health can be restored both mentally and physically.

Our experiences in life give power to new patterns of living, which may be helpful or destructive to our life's purpose. As humans, we are all born with DNA that drives our physical self and determines how we view and deal with what unfolds in life. Let's take the psychological response to danger as an example. Some individuals are born to run toward danger and offer themselves to mitigate or stop the threat. Others, though, are not born with the same response. They freeze up when danger is close, and finding shelter or a way out is the first thing on their mind. The experiences both individuals have in these situations will give power further, leading to their fight or flight response. Simply put, the fighter becomes bolder to enter danger, and the person of flight becomes more cautious, depending on their life experiences. Each experience has a profound effect on the patterns of our life and purpose. We are the sum of our experiences that make us who we are, for good or bad.

In instances where power is given to a negative pattern, this pattern will drive decisions and determine how individual purpose is revealed or denied. Tim's life is an excellent example of this.

Tim was a young, homeless man who had lost all hope in life. Severely abused for most of his childhood, he turned to drugs, crime, and superficial existence. Like many who share similar stories, his life had spiraled downward, and he was closing in on a cliff. Tim's bad decisions and actions had become suffocating and untenable. With the police looking for him and nowhere to turn, he determined to end his life. He invaded several homes while the occupants were away, not to steal money or food but to find a weapon to end his life. After invading several homes, he found a gun in a drawer with the ammunition sitting next to it. This twenty-eight-year-old soul was tired and wanted his pain to end. He traveled to an unpopulated area of the city with the stolen gun and settled behind a large metal building housing an airfield. Clearing the weeds away, he laid out his filthy, tattered sleeping bag; Tim decided to sleep one more night, determined to end it all when he awoke. When the sun arose the following fateful day, Tim had nothing else on his mind but suicide. He unpacked the gun, made sure it was loaded, and put the barrel in his mouth.

Just then, Clark, a manager of the airfield, just happened to come around the corner. Clark was a seasoned warfighter who had retired several years earlier. While the sight of a man with a gun in his mouth would shake up most people, Clark reacted with calm derived from his years of training and experience. He asked the young man if he wanted to talk. Still sitting on the ground with the barrel of the gun still in his mouth, Tim slowly relaxed, lowered the gun, and allowed Clark to sit next to him. Several minutes passed before Clark broke the silence and began talking and letting Tim know that he wasn't in any trouble. Then the conversation went to introductions as Clark watched the gun in Tim's lap, ready to disarm him if necessary. After an hour or so, Clark asked if he could have the weapon to make sure it was safe. Tim handed it over with a sigh of relief, and Clark just placed the gun in his belt. About this time, several other employees came around the corner looking for Clark. The men were introduced to Tim, and everyone departed like buddies to the lunchroom. Through mentorship and Clark's encouragement,

Tim settled his legal issues and accepted a job working at the airfield. He became one of the company's best employees and, to this day, lives a vibrant and purposeful life with his wife of five years and a son.

Tim shouldn't be here.

He didn't matter to anyone.

He wouldn't be missed.

Animals would likely scatter his remains.

Tim's experiences gave power to destructive patterns that almost took his life. But chance favored him when Clark came around the corner that fateful day. Life and death hung in the balance, and this time life won.

Destructive patterns have a voice, and in Tim's case, the voice led him down further and further into darkness, hopelessness, and despair. In the absence of another voice, no other possibility existed except suicide. In Tim's mind, at least then, the voices would stop with his death. But when Clark came into the picture, a new voice was introduced. And, notably, the power behind the words of despair and hopelessness were no match for the power of the positive words coming from Clark that day behind the metal building and in the weeks, months, and years to come. The script was flipped!

Since I began writing *The Warfighter's Soul*, I have heard dozens of stories about what happened when the gun didn't go off, when a person intervened at just the right moment to thwart a plan to make all the pain go away. In almost every case, there was a Clark involved, a stranger who happened on the moment and who became the power that led to a purpose that was yearning to be discovered.

# Renunciation

There is a way we can deal with strong bondages that can break forever the hold they have on our lives. When done with authority, you can forever reverse the agony caused by the traumatic experience. You are free to reject and, more than that, to renounce any bondages of habit or trauma you carry. These are straws you carry that have no destination and no purpose other than to burden you with needless weight. It's a week pack when only a day pack is needed. To renounce is to take a stand and say formally or publicly that you no longer own, support, believe in, or have a connection with this burden or this trauma. It no longer defines you.

This definition of *renounce* is one of the strongest I have ever heard relating to the method of gaining freedom from the hold of trauma. The most important part of this definition to recognize is the word *say*. When we renounce a trauma and its hold over our thoughts, will, and emotions, it is not just done with passive mumblings. We carry out a renunciation after a deep and thorough look at the issue we seek to renounce. What proceeds this powerful act is the verbal admission that the problem exists and the understanding of how it came into being. We also must admit to ourselves the depth to which the issue has imbedded itself into our life. To renounce isn't about cutting off the top of the weed; it's about cutting it out by the roots.

In the South, from time to time, there are tornadoes and wind gusts that either break trees in half or cause them to be uprooted. Recently we had a wind gust called a *derecho* come through our ranch. This is straight-line windstorm that, in our case, was seventy miles per hour. What struck me most about this derecho was the damage it caused on the two or three-hundred-year-old trees. Some were completely uprooted. These trees were hundreds of feet tall and up to five feet wide, but when I looked at the roots, I was surprised at their shallow depth.

I use this as a metaphor of the shallowness of what torments us. When we have been controlled by a destructive force for many years, we cannot imagine anything strong enough to take it down. But I see the act of renunciation as having the same force as a derecho storm. When we renounce, through our words, we unleash enough power to completely uproot our tormentor. And no matter how high and wide our enemy is, it cannot withstand renunciation.

The second part of the description of renunciation is "you no longer own." When we are bound to an event or bondage, we become slaves to it. In the truest sense of the word, we do whatever it tells us to do regardless of how denigrating it is. We become its property and will be treated any way our owner says. To renounce our slave owner is to declare through the authoritative means of renunciation that we will no longer be owned. That we will no longer allow ourselves to be either defined or controlled, and we are claiming the right of all humans, which is to define our own lives and ideals for ourselves. It no longer owns you, and you will no longer own it. To renounce is to regain freedom and restore wholeness to our identity. This means those who have been freed now have renewed control over their destiny.

Lastly, the act of renunciation is to declare that you no longer support or believe in the control of the negative event over your life. What we support and believe defines us as individuals. This is true in every aspect of our lives and will, to a great extent, determine the quality of our lives. When we have been bound to an event or traumatic circumstance, our beliefs are held captive. We believe through the lens of the painful experience and, as such, create for ourselves a life that is a far cry from what we could be or become. When we renounce the power a traumatic event has over us, we become free to define our beliefs once again, which will completely change our constitution. Therefore, in freedom, we no longer seek to end life. The power of shame, guilt, and enslavement to past negative events is released, and as free people, we can build a new outlook on life. We can run into the future and make it grand. Unburdened of needless straw, you are free to build a new life. Modify the skills you have for good purposes. Concentrate, dream, set goals, and plan toward those good things you admire. Fill your time with learning new beneficial skills. Continue to gain knowledge and understanding. Help others.

For us to take back life, we need to recognize that the power of renunciation is not only able to stop the pain of what had been done to us but can stop what is happening through us. For instance, all sexual perversion is the result of one allowing fantasies to develop in one's mind. What begins with a perverse thought can grow into a perverse act, which can result in the unthinkable. I became aware of this issue years ago when I worked with a campaign designed to stop child trafficking. As the executive director of the not-for-profit organization for over three years, I became aware of the most heinous crimes done to children as young as babies. Children who were rescued from their traffickers often describe torture that would cause most people to become physically ill. Seeing the faces of these abusers can and should elicit rage. But the truth is that these people, for the most part, began their lives like all others. The trouble comes when they allow fantasy to develop. And because they didn't renounce this imagination, it pressed them from the thoughts of abuse to the actual act of abuse.

The same rule applies to those who murder, physically abuse others, steal, and prey on the weak. There is no destructive behavior that cannot be broken through the power of renunciation. We must realize that any active deviances that exist in our daily lives, whether new or the result of destructive action, must be taken to renunciation and dealt with as we would deal with any enemy or monster.

Most young men and women join the military for all the right reasons. Love of country, love of freedom, following in family footsteps, and a desire to help those who cannot help themselves. But to help others, those who serve must not only train physically to be effective but also train themselves emotionally to be of a mindset free of monsters. It is only then that a life can be offered to others to bring freedom.

Start your new journey untouched by the past with this declaration of renunciation:

> *I declare that you, _____, are evil and, you are the enemy of my soul. I acknowledge that your rule over my life has been illegal and unjustified. And while I have been your slave, this moment, this day, this second, I renounce your hold on me and command you to lose your hold over my mind, my emotions, my thoughts, and my life. I hereby declare that I am free, never to be a slave again.*

# PART V

# THE CAUSE

What would cause a seemingly rational person to commit suicide? I propose the answer is a judgment, a bad judgment.

Throughout this section, I will attempt to show that a person under enough stress or pain can be pushed to the point of deciding to end his or her life. To explain this proposition, I shall use various metaphors and analogies to other life-changing events or traumas, such as a high school graduation or murder trial, in an attempt to show how these events compare to extremely traumatizing ones. I want you to become familiar with how "dramatic leaps" can leave gaps in a person's perspective on life. It is these gaps and subsequent judgment calls to fill them that leave the traumatized individual in a disparate position of having to find the disconnect between a once healthy optimistic view and now a fatalistic pessimistic view of one's life.

I will also compare our national system of jurisprudence—the nation's system for maintaining order, discouraging disorder, and delivering consequences for disorder—with an individual's personal system of justice operating within their soul. This is not a review of psychology's role in the legal system nor a contrast of that role. Psychological jurisprudence considers the role of psychology in the court system, particularly during the trial process and the presentation of evidence. Rather, I posit that our system of jurisprudence is simply a type and a shadow of that which naturally occurs in the mind of every human as they develop from birth. And this personal justice system continues developing and changing until death.

Furthermore, from their exploratory years of youth to their more cynical and wiser years, each individual human's developmental process proceeds through endless acts of discovery. When something new enters the room, their mental space and soul processes the new information to make it fit with all preexisting information, experiences, and conclusionary beliefs. Each experience, good or bad, self-induced or inflicted by others, is processed through the simple child-like procedures in the beginning. Learning the rules of playground games or the new social rules in high school can be challenging. Imagine the high school graduate now entering college or their first job. Both scenarios are equally challenging because the rules change. It is not so much how they changed but just the fact that they are different. New rules, new procedures enter, and some old, well-established and understood rules will no longer be needed. A lot of change occurs in terms of responsibility between high school and a job or college level studies. Most students adapt, but some do not. Many of the rules and procedures grow into complexity, yet most people are able to adjust. At the same moment of change, individuals are able to reestablish once static thought "filtration systems" with the traumatic changes into new, modified states of existence. But what if a person can't make the proper filter adjustment?

Think of these filters as a type of Japanese pachinko board. This board stands vertically with nails driven into it at different locations. The player then drops a small steel ball to make the ball fall through the nails, bouncing on some nails, to make the ball land in one of several small cups at the base. Doing so successfully rewards the player. Consider the board as the young mind. The nails are knowledge and understanding, simply lessons learned. Some pins may represent things to be avoided, like don't touch a hot stove. Others are very helpful for keeping things in order. The owner of the board (mind) constructs the placement of pins (filters) as they please according to his or her overall understanding and experiences. These carefully placed filters help the person guide newly dropped balls, new experiences, into the proper cups or memory categories. With each new experience, the player might make some adjustment to the pins, or filters, or perspectives on how the world works to keep functioning properly. Any change to the current system means the owner must adjust their current working filtration system. Minor changes are manageable, but larger changes or a multitude of changes in rapid succession make the system difficult to reorganize into a once-again working system. Ever wonder why humans have a propensity to reject change? To quote humorist Will Rogers, "People change...but not much." With each new discovery, every new parental rule, every event, the human mind (pachinko board) adds more filters and directives to keep their every growing philosophical view of life in proper perspective.

The mind accomplishes this by processing new events through its "judicial system," beginning with the basic questions, "Is this good or bad?" and "Is this right or wrong?" In simple terms, a trial court passes similar judgments, but with more official sounding terms, such as *guilty* or *liable*, which mean "he did the crime" or "she's responsible for the accident." But what happens when the court docket (scheduled trials) overwhelms the judge or a large, complex, and egregious case is brought to trial? One where the owner of the pachinko board is accused and brought to trial. The owner/judge is now on trial, and a guilty verdict may include the possibility of a death sentence. The victim, the judge, and the accuser are the same person. What kind of trial court is this? Who are the parties involved? What was the crime? As one's mind begins to spin endlessly from one issue to the next and then to the first again, as this whirlwind of issues builds, even the most insignificant stressor can become a devastating and convicting trial.

In 1885, W. Wynn Wescott, MB, deputy coroner for Central Middlesex, England wrote a comprehensive study of suicide.[100] In it, he stated, "In every age of the world, and in the history of almost every country, we find instances more or less numerous of men and women who, preferring the dim uncertainty of the future to the painful realities of the present, have sought relief from all their troubles by suddenly terminating their own existence."[101] Many assumptions regarding mental illness were not well defined at the time; however, the list of causes included in his book identify many stress factors that still affect people today. Some of his more prominent factors include debt, misery, disappointed love, loss of children, loss of employment or position, and bodily diseases and pain.[102] These may sound a little foreign to modern vernacular, but their meaning does not differ much. They each represent some event or trauma in life that creates a new stress, a new trial to be adjudicated. And, depending on the individual's ability to handle each stress, the outcome of each trial may be favorable, or the result could be devastating. As you will read in the following pages, events, and circumstances, many beyond our control, can deliver life-changing blows to our life as we know it.

# 13

# ELEMENTS AND THE BATTLEGROUND

Sun Tzu says, "Ground on which we can only be saved from destruction by fighting without delay, is desperate ground...On desperate ground, fight." For, as Chia Lin remarks: "if you fight with all your might, there is a chance of life; where as death is certain if you cling to your corner."[103]

—Sun Tzu and Chia Lin

Consider these three battlegrounds. The first is society, the large group consisting of people an individual may or may not know. The second involves the individual's group of acquaintances, whether it be family, friends, or fellow employees. These are people with whom the person maintains some type of direct relationship. The third battleground occurs within the individual's mind. This chapter attempts to define the mind and soul of the individual. If asked, "How do you explain the human mind, the soul, the spirit, the conscience, and common sense?" how would you respond? All are common terms and easy to explain. The more challenging question asks, "How do they differ?" Explaining the differences can be difficult, especially when many definitions overlap, and some are ambiguous. For example, common sense is common to everyone. But ask anyone for a list of rules included under the title of "Common Sense," and their responses might be vague at best. These common-sense rules, even in their unclear state, are vital in a person's conduct, behavior, and mental balance.

In 2020, Peggy Sanders wrote a short article about rules and common sense. In it, she states, "The most common is the Golden Rule: Do unto others as you would have them do to you. Or he who has the gold, makes the rules. How someone applies the rule demonstrates their character."[104] These two rules seem to argue against one another in order of priority. Should caring for others be more important than acquiring wealth or vice versa? Her last comment answers the question. It depends on who you want to be. Your application of these and other rules results in your character. A person's character rests as much on the rules they follow as on the degree to which they apply them.

The application of rules works much like the volume control on a sound amplifier or the temperature control during a church meeting. Adjustments are necessary, but the direction chosen and how we apply it can be challenging. It is a veritable living organism unto itself. Both, US law and the Holy Bible recognize that "the word is alive," and every situation, no matter how similar, is different. Common sense is difficult to come by, even in the most simple situations such as telling the truth. We may always want the truth, and at the same time, we may not want harmful truths. Take shopping for shoes, for example. Some shoes are ugly, and you may decide not to buy them. However, when a coworker, wearing those same "ugly" shoes asks, "How do you like my shoes?" how would you respond? You can say, "They are ugly," which might be truth to you, but you know your coworker loves those shoes. So what would you affirm—what you think is true or what your coworker thinks is true?

Now for a more extreme example. Imagine yourself a former high school graduate returning home, to a former state of normal, from this situation:

About halfway back, we took a break. On our way down, we had passed a lot of "dead," both ours and theirs…Someone told me that bodies that had died by concussion would swell up to unbelievable proportions. These three must have suffered that fate. One looked like he was ready to float down the streets of New York in the Macy's Thanksgiving Day Parade. This bloating was not limited to the stomach, but every arm, leg, and finger as well…with the exception of his nose, which was hidden in between large swollen cheeks. His bulbous mouth had lips so black it was hard to realize that it was, in fact, a mouth. A purple tongue forced its way out toward the sky.[105]

The writer goes on to describe this scene as unbelievably horrid and the following actions as even more horrible. How would you, as a twenty-year-old, explain this to your friends in a way they might understand? This writer was unable to speak of this action in any form until some sixty years later. As you might imagine, readjusting to "normal life" after having experienced such encounters can be difficult. One's earlier thoughts of truth and common sense now lay far from common.

As painful as that story may sound, it reveals how the "ugly" side of life and death can change one's world perspective dramatically. Bad things happen; many are unavoidable. Every judgment one makes, even as simple as deciding the temperature setting for the church sanctuary during the Sunday service, is relative and dependent on a combination of past and present experiences. We have no intention of dictating the "correct settings" for any situation nor what is "normal" for warriors as they return from war. We do hope to make you aware of some of the soul-based mechanisms that can be adjusted. To that end, we begin with some general definitions of the terms introduced previously and offer a description of how they interact.

**The Human Mind** – "The element of a person that enables them to be aware of the world and their experiences, to think, and to feel; the faculty of consciousness and thought."[106]

**The Soul** – "The soul has been referred to as the spiritual or immaterial part of a human being."[107] That which is alive and yet intangible. In the academic world of metaphysical consciousness study, the term *consciousness* has been used to separately identify the difference between a person's physical body and its mechanisms from that which is the untouchable person, the theories of dualism.[108] Principally, the inability to quantify and measure the soul provides the most fodder for creating a variety of theories on structure and operations of the soul. Arguably, every approach, whether psychology, philosophy, medical, or neuroscience, runs into a seemingly impenetrable wall when attempting to access facts and truth as it relates to consciousness or the soul. Research in cognition, behavior, and neurology all struggle with identifying this connection between body and soul.[109] More recent academic efforts have extended an arm toward the study of spiritualism. Not as a definitively identifiable type or religion, but rather as the possibility of a yet-to-be scientifically identified entity. Additionally, the theory of awareness (the world outside of self) and self-awareness (knowing oneself) only begins to address the idea of consciousness. The soul and the initiation of a person's life require a higher level of hypothesis, research, and theoretical conclusions along with a layer of belief and faith as our attempts to discover the soul continue.

**The Spirit** – "The non-physical part of a person which is the seat of emotions and character, the soul. The non-physical part of a person is regarded as their true self and as capable of surviving physical death or separation. The non-physical part of a person manifested as an apparition after their death; a ghost."[110] Theoretical as shown below, one's spirit may be identified as an inseparable subset of the soul.

**The Conscience** – "A person's moral sense of right and wrong, viewed as acting as a guide to one's [behavior.]"[111] Historically, this twelfth- or thirteenth-century word evolved as describing a "faculty of knowing what is right." It implies an existing knowledge within oneself making the person capable of knowing and distinguishing between right and wrong.[112] That may be its intended meaning, but a definitive meaning is more elusive. To refer to one's conscience is to refer to one's ideals of right and wrong, one's moral sense. Unfortunately, moral sense has a flavor of individuality as broad and immeasurable as common sense. Attempting to find an exact match between any two people might be described as futile. Nonetheless, for the sake of a peaceful society, we must all try, search for those points on which we agree, and know there will be many on which we do not.

**Common Sense** – "Good sense and sound judgment in practical matters."[113] While searching for a clear understanding of this term, I picked up a small book entitled *Common Sense* by Thomas Paine. Surely, the answers or lists of common-sense rules could be found in such a book. There are answers, but not any bullet point or numbered lists as one might expect. Paine addresses the state of human nature and the need to balance the desire to enjoy personal and social freedoms with a need for the government to provide security. He basically sets the stage for allowing people to enjoy their personal freedoms and the need for a structure to keep individual freedoms from interfering with or damaging the freedoms of others. In his opening chapter he writes: "Society is produced by our wants, and government by our wickedness; the former promotes our happiness *positively*, by uniting our affections, the latter *negatively*, by restraining our vices. The one encourages intercourse [communication], the other creates distinctions. The first is a patron, the last is a punisher."[114]

In conclusion, he creates no list, only the container necessary to keep individuals from hurting each other while enjoying personal freedoms. Paine's representation of common sense is a far cry from modern definitions applied to this term. Modern definitions seem to imply a fixed standard known by everyone. Everyone may indeed believe his or her definition of common sense is common. However, articulating a list of common-sense rules is a bit more challenging. Putting them into priority—even more so. Venture to say, everyone's list does look the same from a distance but not so much up close. In the end, any attempt to establish a list of common-sense rules would be met with endless argument.

**Belief** – "Something one accepts as true or real; a firmly held opinion."[115]

**Faith** – "Complete trust or confidence in someone or something." From the Latin *fides*.[116] An elevated conviction to one's beliefs. Also, the root word in the US Marine Corps motto, *Semper Fidelis*, meaning "Always Faithful."

A functioning mind draws from the body's physical resources through sight, sound, touch, taste, and smell. The person uses these five senses to collect countless bits of information surrounding the body and feeds this information into the mind where the data is processed, and "something" happens. Physicians, medical researchers, neurologists, and the like work diligently to identify and articulate the physical properties and activities that take place when this "something" happens. Psychologists study, collect data, and make statistical conclusions as to why humans behave and respond the way they do. But why humans think what they think is a much more elusive question.

Simply looking at the definitions above, we can begin to picture the building blocks of our thoughts, assumptions, conclusions, feelings, actions we take, and words we speak. Take a look at the following illustration, read it carefully, and make note of the story it might build for you concerning how the things you think, say, and do are affected by and filtered through the images, voices, smells, ideas, and other inputs you have accepted into your soul.

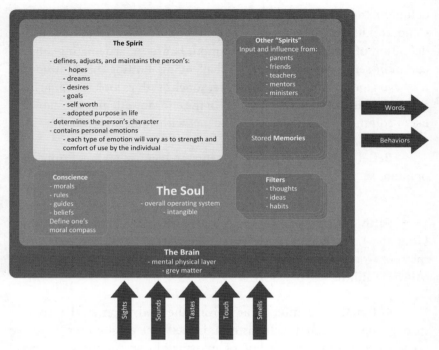

Figure 1: The Soul

From childbirth, and perhaps sooner through DNA transfer or some other mechanism, information and processes begin to feed into a person's soul or operating system, if you'll pardon the computer analogy. Each component of the soul—whether spirit (as in purpose and character), the repeating influence from others, or stored memories, to name a few—all operate together and are driven through a collection of filters toward continued growth and mental stability. These filters may include reasoning skills, empathetic emotions, and a series of like/dislike qualifiers and scales of importance. From a physical perspective, the soul receives input through the brain's connection to the body's five senses. Without more, this would result in a huge storage array of information, but thanks to the soul, humans are far more than data storage banks, as we are about to find out.

# 14

# MORALS, THE LAW, UCMJ, AND ROES

The years '89 and '90 were years of elation and hope.
A powerful and much-loathed regime not only
collapsed unexpectedly but did so with surprisingly
little violence. Amid its ruin, a new international order
seemed to be taking place, built on a respect for peace,
democracy, and human rights. So transformative did
the moment appear that many advanced thinkers
predicted nothing less than the coming end of warfare.[117]

—David A. Bell

Elation and hope, what a happy time that must have been. The war was over, and people could go back to their normal life as farmers, shopkeepers, and business executives. No more conflict. Here, David Bell's words described 1790 French Revolutionary forces collapsing the "Old Regime" of the French aristocracy. The kingdoms of royals were finished. There would be a government by the people. Again, no more conflict. These same comments and predictions may have been felt by many, as those some two hundred years later, when at the end of the 1990–1991 Gulf War, the people of Kuwait and Iraq saw the hope of normalcy return. In a flash, the US military, led by General "Stormin' Norman" Schwarzkopf, and coalition forces quickly disposed of Saddam Hussein's Iraqi regime within months of the regime's invasion of Kuwait.[118] Hope restored, no more conflict. However, only ten years later in 2001, a massive terrorist attack on September 11 would engulf the United States in a war on terror that continued into 2021. No more conflict?

Most people desire order and peace. They want constancy in their lives. Not the same thing over and over but a place where they can feel some sort of person control, whether in peaceful contemplation or on a risky adventure. A freedom to explore and expand their own mind. More specifically, their soul. If only that were possible without the endless difficulties and challenges we are forced to face daily. How might we mitigate them? Perhaps a set of rules to help keep some of the potential problems out of the way.

Attaining peace, democracy, and human rights is a sampling of "just causes" sought after, although difficult to achieve, in most communities of people. Guidelines, rules, laws, ethics, and the like are delicately balanced to achieve and maintain the best state of existence possible. *Delicately balanced* being the operative term. The game Jenga comes to mind. It begins with a tall stack of rectangular wooden pieces. The play involves removing a lower piece and restacking it at the top. Eventually, a player will move a piece that causes the entire stack to fall. If we agree on an earlier statement that the word is alive, then it may be true that the law should live accordingly. Changes in the law transpire at a pace constant with social change. The person's soul, as described previously, is then challenged with applying the laws as recorded in their memory and those requiring change. For example, in the Bible, Cain killed Abel, but did he commit murder, first-degree murder, manslaughter, or involuntary manslaughter? It appears that this was not a case of self-defense, which might relieve Cain of the charge, but the text offers little evidence other than the fact that Abel is dead and that it was Cain who took his brother's life. How are we to judge?

When making judgments, two of the most challenging moments

in a warfighter's career include the moment before pulling the trigger and then right after. The question "Did I make the right choice?" can haunt someone permanently. Keeping the myriad of rules in order and not bouncing around in one's head could mean the difference between a memory secured away as experience or one remaining an open wound unable to scar. Parents teach rules to their children to keep them safe. As adults, these same children pass them along to their children. Countries equally are founded on basic rules and general principals or constitutions. Both rules begin as general rules. Work hard and be good to one another, they say. However, complexities ensue requiring more clarification and clear direction. Circumstances change, and the rules must be adapted. They require more specific detail to account for the countless scenarios that might occur requiring additional guidance or resolution. On the national, first type battleground, the US Constitution depends on the US Code to offer additional detail and specificity toward its citizens' expected conduct. The military uses the Uniform Code of Military Justice (UCMJ) to maintain order and resolve incidents particular to the military. The Geneva Conventions worked toward creating international rules for war, establishing protections for the wounded and provisions for the Red Cross and chaplains on the battlefield in an effort to prevent the possibility of total and unlimited war.[119] On a finer level, battlefield Rules of Engagement (ROE) are established for particular and potentially changing circumstances that can vary from one incursion to another, which are not specifically covered in any of the overruling laws or constitution. Operational briefings dictate the mission goals, strategy, tactical employment, and ROEs. What members can and cannot do.

For some perspective, imagine the ensuing chaos from this rule; Marines, also known as "Teufel Hunden" or "Devil Dogs" to the German soldiers at the battle of Belleau Wood in WWI,[120] had a saying, "Kill them all and let God sort them out." Clearly, it was more a term of bravado than actual directive. This would be an impossible rule to apply in any battle engagement where an enemy's death might land a warfighter in military and/or civilian criminal court. Rules, even outlandish rules such as this, are processed through the same procedures in the soul—established at the time. So, for a young person, the rule may find its way into a prominent place on the mental board than it would on the mind of an older, more cynical person.

# Morals—Without Them All Is Lost

Having viewed so many rules and laws, let us consider personal morals. Contrary to popular belief a common set of morals, or "true north" on everyone's moral compass, is as uncommon as common sense. There are many morals, right and wrong, good and bad choices, but no definitive list. Furthermore, rules adopted by individuals as their own are as diverse as highlighted Scriptures in people's Bibles. Please don't misunderstand, our morals are the substance by which we each maintain personal order as we float through the chaos life throws at us. Without them, all is lost. We become a ship with no rudder in tumultuous seas.

With so many decisions to make and so many rules to follow, it is possible to understand how complex and convoluted order can become. Add to this the voices of authority demanding obedience to their view of justice, some honorable, others selfish, and some even diabolical. "Ours is not to question why, ours is to do or die"[121] may seem like the easiest solution, but there is the inevitable question that even children learn to ask early in life: "Why?" Sometimes the question is warranted, and other times it may endanger the one asking. In the context of military orders, asking why can be dangerous. Answers to such questions may provide fodder for making personal judgments. Personal judgments may result in actions out of sync with team efforts, thereby creating chaos, conflict, and possible danger for the other members. Choosing obedience to one's morals, ROEs, commander's orders, US law, or international laws when some conflict occurs between any two of them creates a trial environment in one's soul ripe for personal trauma or moral injury.

# 15

# CAUSATION

Commit a crime, and the earth is made of glass.
Commit a crime, and it seems as if a coat of snow fell
on the ground, such as reveals in the woods the track
of every partridge and fox and squirrel and mole.
—Ralph Waldo Emerson

For most practical and scientific matters, *Causation* identifies the facts, actions, and culprit(s) by which something happened. In legal terms, causation requires both "cause-in-fact and proximate cause."[122] This second element can be the most troublesome. It involves a determination of how directly connected the cause is from the affect. Was it foreseeable? Was it a freak accident? In a courtroom, well-trained lawyers and judges adjudicate all types of cases. The act of finding fault, placing blame, and then assigning an appropriate sentence becomes extremely difficult considering the variety of facts and perspectives they must consider. Unknowingly, when bad events happen or things go wrong, stress and trauma, whether we caused it or not, just walk into our life. These two bad actors create a type of legal case in one's mind. They bring their accusations and instigate a mental trial or prosecutorial process demanding a sentence of guilt and shame.

In a trial courtroom, all the facts and circumstances must be delicately balanced to reach a righteous result. Generally, trials fall into two types of cases: civil and criminal. Civil law is an area of justice concerned with wrongful acts or infringement of rights involving another person's property or rights. Criminal law concerns crimes against the state—laws created by the state necessary for maintaining a civil society in general. It can get confusing, especially when they overlap in a case. For example, consider a murder. Historically, murder falls in the realm of criminal law. In modern times, both criminal law and civil law can play a role in the same event.

In the particularly well-known O. J. Simpson murder case in the late 1990s, Mr. Simpson was accused of murdering his ex-wife, Nicole Brown Simpson, and her friend, Ron Goldman. Both print and televised news media covered this case for months while the trial dragged on. To the surprise of many and the horror of some, the jury found O. J. Simpson not guilty. The jury determined that the state's evidence fell short of meeting the "beyond a reasonable doubt" threshold required to convict for murder.

Keep in mind that no one in the jury nor the police detectives nor any of the millions of people watching the trial play out actually witnessed the murder. To reach a conviction for murder, the prosecutor must convince the jury that the defendant did commit the crime while the defendant must prove otherwise or at least show that the evidence against him leaves too much room for doubt. Neither *possible* nor *probable* should be enough to convict in a case of murder. While the term *possible* requires little more than opinion, *probable* means the evidence proves a likely or "common-sense" determination of guilt. However, probable cause would be enough to make an arrest. The prosecution must then convince the jury that their evidence is more than probable. In the Simpson case, the court trial found him not guilty; however, the subsequent civil case brought by the families found him liable for their wrongful deaths.[123] While the state failed to prove guilt beyond a reasonable doubt, the plaintiffs in the civil case only needed a 51% probability, a preponderance of the evidence, to find the defendant may not have killed the victims but that he was liable or responsible for their deaths.[124] As you can see here, the Simpson murder case involved two cases, one for murder and the other for civil liability—multiple trials with different results.

In criminal cases, and particularly in murder cases, where charges are brought against an individual, three trials take place. First, the jury trial conducted in the courtroom, over which a judge presides, determines the defendant's guilt and future residence. With the prosecution on one side and the defendant on the other, each presents a possible or probable explanation of the crime along with their evidence. The fourth member, the jury, determines whether the prosecution proved their theory to be beyond a reasonable doubt, a standard of proof required in murder cases. This type of trial may or may not be witnessed by anyone other than these participants and people closely connected to the defendant and victim. Generally, there is only one trial unless a mistrial is called, an appeal is requested claiming an error in the process, or some new evidence has been found that may reverse the result of the case. This theory of appellate law assures court accountability, allows society to correct mistakes, and offers a hope for the convicted.[125]

A second type of trial, a trial of public opinion, occurs to the extent that a case is publicized. It may consist of a small community or millions of participants, depending on the extent of the word-of-mouth or media coverage. This trial requires no rules of the procedure or a presiding judge to assure the process and evidence remain within the law. It does not require evidence at all, nor does it require a presumption of innocence. Each participant is allowed to use any threshold for accepting or rejecting evidence. This public jury determines guilty or not guilty based on popular opinion, not necessarily fact.

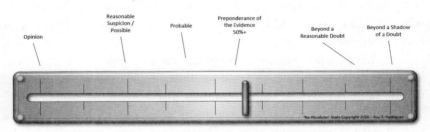

Figure 2: Proof Scale

The third trial, and quite possibly the harshest, "the personal trial," plays out within the defendant's conscience, his soul. Few if any others witness this trial. The outside world, those outside the defendant's mind, only witness a distracted person, one who seems confused at times, angry at times, or perhaps distant at times. Rarely, but on occasion, they may also seem happy and smiling. Generally, to people who know him, this individual seems different than the one who previously engaged with others freely. Many voices in this defendant's conscience argue the case, weigh the evidence, and declare their judgment, which is sometimes guilty, other times not guilty.

Unlike the first two trials, which have a termination point, personal trials tend to linger. Many, and I dare say most, linger in one's mind until the end of one's life. The arguments, the evidence, the memories, and the stories are spun and re-spun over and over in a series of retrials. Regardless of the verdict, the trial begins again the next day or when the next trigger revives it. To further complicate matters, in this private courtroom, bad events may add new charges. To numb the pain, the defendant may increase his or her alcohol consumption or begin using drugs. New voices appear at this mental trial with accusing cries of "alcoholic" and "loser." These new spiritual witnesses scream their accusations relentlessly, mercilessly, and loudly. In addition, old charges can be brought up again and all combined into the same retrial. They need not be related and may include all types and levels of offenses.

Should the accused be found guilty during this mental trial and the counts against him or her mount to a high enough degree, the internal judge may render a punishment of death. Sadly, and regrettably, upon carrying out this sentence, the defendant and all parties of this private trial die. The outside world, friends, and family only see the evidence of another suicide.

What or who caused the problem? How reliable is the evidence? When it comes to suicide, like murder, those left behind are left looking for the same answers. What caused their loved one to commit suicide? The best answers are usually little more than opinions and generalizations. Probabilities and even possibilities are even more difficult to determine for good reason. The principal and typically only witness to the suicide can no longer answer for him or herself. Even when they leave a note explaining the reason, it's characteristically only a partial reason. It could be the main reason for their decision, but it is highly unlikely that it would be the only reason. Try to imagine one single tragic event that might cause a person to go from happy-go-lucky to such a depth of depression or despair that he would resolve to end his life.

A CBS News presentation on the subject suggests that the idea of a single-event cause is a myth.[126] In a 2013 *Molecular Psychiatry* journal article, M. A. Oquendo, et al., note that an increase in suicidal behavior occurs when an individual with existing negative motivators, such as pessimism, aggression, hostility, and despair, is exposed to a major depressive episode of stress.[127] In other words, the straw that breaks the camel's back only works when the camel is already carrying too many straws. Even the strongest camels have their limitations. However, while the defendant is still living, his or her sentence of death is reviewable on appeal. Criminal defendants are afforded defense attorneys during a trial because the law knows the requirements for prosecution, defense, procedure, and all the exceptions in the rule of law demand a high level of expertise to process the case fairly. An appeal equally requires an attorney or a legal counselor to help the defendant, now appellant, through the process and to present an argument as to why the sentence should be reversed. Neither defendants nor appellants should attempt to appear at court without a good legal advocate. It is just not a good idea to do this alone. Neither is it a good idea to suffer in the personal, third type of trial court or appeals court alone. Therefore, all mental health care professionals, regardless of specialty, recommend that you speak to someone about your issues, troubles, burdens, straws, cases (pick your label) rather than dealing with them yourself.

# Rights and Privileges at Trial

Those unfortunate defendants who have endured a criminal trial involving first-degree murder may find several similarities between those events and the misery involved in PTSD. Accusations and demands for justice can be relentless and debilitating. The process of bringing charges in the judicial system involves a gathering of evidence, including questioning potential suspects. Reasonable suspicion, a low hurdle to cross in the "Proof Scale" provided earlier (see Figure 2), brings the suspect into the interrogation room. Here detectives primarily seek a confession from the suspect. Short of that, any incriminating evidence shall suffice in support of a grand jury indictment. Tactics authorities may use for securing such evidence include lying. It's a common theme in numerous detective and crime drama movies. While it may seem unjust to the defendant, the US Supreme Court supports this tactic.

Fortunately, defendants possess their rights in opposition to the states' rights. The Fifth Amendment right affords a defendant protection against self-incrimination and due process of law, for example.[128] The defendant has a right to say nothing at all. Moreover, the defendant has a right to protect himself from double jeopardy, meaning the government cannot try someone twice for the same crime regardless of the outcome.[129] The defendant also has a right to legal counsel, an attorney, under the US Constitution's Sixth Amendment.[130]

These are all helpful rights involving cases brought against the individual within the confines of federal and state legal systems. Unfortunately, these rights are practically useless in the courts of public opinion and personal conscience. Within a person's conscience, many voices speak for and against conviction. Recorded comments for anyone and everyone who may have spoken to the defendant, albeit tangentially, may screen accusations from the past. The sounds of naysayers shouting, "I told you that you would never amount to anything" can be heard in the individual's mind as if they were in the room. Comments from loved ones equally crying out, "I know you're innocent" or "It was justified" bring hope, but is it enough? On some good days it is. On others, not so much. One voice sounds out as the accused's defense attorney. If given the right tools, as described in later chapters, it is possible to build defenses, to offer exculpatory evidence, and to bring excusable justification or even a final judgment of not guilty. For this to occur, time is required, which we all have in limited amounts.

# Demystifying the Legal Moral Case against You: Stress and Trauma

A nurse asks a patient suffering from chronic pain, "On a scale of one to ten, with ten being the worst, what level of pain are you experiencing?" How should the patient answer this question? How should one measure pain? Intensity? Longevity? As sciatic back pain suffers know, the pain comes and goes. One moment it's bad, the next is good, and then it can be bad. Does the ability to endure pain count toward this measurement? Some people can endure pain better than others. For example, a military-trained patient having endured numerous traumas, head injuries, broken bones, cuts, bruising fights, may have a high pain tolerance. Stories are abundant of warriors continuing to fight or rescue fellow soldiers despite their own wounds.

On the other extreme, many people have a very low tolerance for pain. You may have witnessed that panicked and screaming victim reach a pain level of ten following a paper cut. Before judging either, consider the amount of pain endured by a woman during natural childbirth. Were that mother asked what pain level ten meant, she might answer, "Childbirth just before the baby's head emerged." Individuals having suffered traumatic dismemberment or third-degree burns may recognize this type and level of pain.

Stress works much the same as physical pain. Some stress is mild, such as deciding whether to work on some home repair or to watch a fun movie. Mild stress may last only a few seconds. A more difficult stressor might involve deciding to pay the rent or the car payment while not having enough money for both. At the higher extreme, consider someone having to tell his spouse that he is having an affair, or worse—finding out his spouse is having an affair. Then, there are the extreme traumas involving death.

As with pain, stress varies in degrees of intensity and longevity as "stress is a feeling of emotional or physical tension. It can come from any event or thought that makes you feel frustrated, angry, or nervous." According to an article from the National Library of Medicine, "Stress is your body's reaction to a challenge or demand." [131] But there are multiple types of stress and stress-causing events. Throughout the normal course of human development from birth until death, every person will traverse stressful events every step of the way.

Life is equally filled with eustress, or positive stress. Unlike distress, or negative stress, eustress includes physical and mental challenges that help us grow and become more resilient. In general, "Stress is simply the body's response to changes that create taxing demands."[132] Change is difficult for all, some more than others, but change is inevitable. From the most minute and inconsequential, such as moving through time from one second to the next or going one step forward as you walk along a path, to the more severe changes such as losing your employment or losing a family member to death, change is inevitable. While unavoidable, how you engage with and endure change will dictate your body's response to the change. Positive stress causes the body to focus its energy and can improve performance. It can also be exciting and motivating.[133] Distress brings enduring concern, decreases performance, and can contribute to mental and physical issues.[134]

Acute stress, or short-term stress, helps when facing danger or encountering exciting events.[135] Everyone encounters this type of stress regularly. Loud noises, shocking news, minor injuries, and countless other incidents cause the mind and body to react with an initial fight/flight/freeze response. This stress dissolves once the cause or solution to the incident is found.

On the other hand, chronic stress lasts much longer. Worrying about issues or situations for weeks or longer can develop into chronic stress. Financial worries and concerns over relationships can grow into chronic stress. Regardless of a person's economic demographic, rich as much as poor individuals can suffer from excessive worry over actual and potential money issues. Other examples include an unhappy marriage and work-related issues.[136] Work-related issues will many times revolve around a root fear, such as the lack of money. Disagreements, overwork, and disliking one's job can cause a fear of losing that job and subsequently a fear of losing one's income. This combination may easily become chronic, lead to anxiety or causing depression. Anxiety is stress based on bad possibilities. Anxiety is "a feeling of worry, nervousness, or unease, typically about an imminent event or something with an uncertain outcome."[137]

> Depression and anxiety disorders are different, but
> people with depression often experience symptoms
> like those of an anxiety disorder, such as nervous-
> ness, irritability, and problems sleeping and concen-
> trating. But each disorder has its own causes and its
> own emotional and behavioral symptoms.[138]

Future predictions concerning the loss of employment or business, fear of divorce or separation, and the possibility of one's death or that of a loved one may quickly build into overwhelming anxiety or depression. Eustress and acute stress are beneficial to growth and survival; however, distress, chronic stress, anxiety, and depression are destructive and burdensome. These are known as the straws that broke the camel's back: the past and future charges against a person for wrongs committed and personal failures that person carries. One particularly heavy and debilitating conditions suffered by many veterans is post-traumatic stress disorder (PTSD).

> [PTSD] can occur following a traumatic event. It is
> characterized by symptoms of re-experiencing the
> trauma (in the form of nightmares, flashbacks and
> distressing thoughts), avoiding reminders of the
> traumatic event, negative alterations in thoughts
> and mood, and symptoms of hyper-arousal (feeling
> on edge, being easily startled, feeling angry, having
> difficulties sleeping, and problems concentrating).[139]

Two key elements found in this description include "symptoms of re-experiencing the trauma" and "reminders," also commonly referred to as "triggers."

These two elements fall directly in line with our earlier discussion of personal trials. The symptoms here are indicators of individuals rehashing a traumatic event. Perhaps they are trying to find solace or relief. Ultimately they are looking for a final verdict—one that will declare they are either guilty or not guilty. For in doing so, they can move toward freedom or forgiveness. Either is better than the endless replay of the trauma. The second element, "triggers," identify the types of input, whether in the form of sound, image, smell, taste, or touch that causes a recall of the event that led to the trauma, thereby triggering a re-trial in the person's mind. If you witness someone suffering severe mood swings or any of the symptoms listed above, know they are in need of an advocate—someone to stand with them during their trial and encourage them toward a reintegrated life.

# Life Expectancy and the Inevitability of Death

As of January 2020, the oldest living person is a Japanese woman named Kane Tanaka. She had just turned one hundred seventeen.[140] The record for the longest living person in modern history is held by Jeanne Calmet (1875–1997) of France.[141] She lived to be one hundred twenty-two years and one hundred sixty-four days old. Jeanne appears to have remained active throughout her life, having taken up fencing at age eighty-five, acted in a movie at age one hundred fourteen, and becoming a recording artist at age one hundred twenty.[142] Many would say she lived a full life.

While her longevity may be inspiring, one hundred twenty-two years may be a bit more than most of us can hope to achieve. Medical data about life expectancy estimates the average age for US citizens to be seventy-nine years, as of this writing.[143] That is a thirty-two-year increase from the 1900 estimated average life expectancy of forty-seven years. Jeanne was twenty-five at the time of that estimate. Certainly, many things have changed since the beginning of the twentieth century. Better living conditions, medical advances, reduced risk, and other factors play a role in extending a person's life. A person's life choices equally play a role in increasing or decreasing the number of years they should expect to live.

Today, life insurance companies use calculators to predict a person's life expectancy. The equations used in these calculators, or more accurate estimators, consider several well-studied factors affecting how many years a person should expect to live. To do this, the calculator starts with the current life expectancy average and then deducts years for bad habits, like heavy alcohol consumption, or adds years for good habits, such as diet and exercise. There is little doubt, although some people may wish to live forever, that history has proven every person ever born will pass away at some point. It may be accurately stated that every human comes with a termination date. Referencing the life insurance company's model, this date fluctuates depending on how a person chooses to live his or her life. For example, according to the chart, the "Stress" factor seems small when compared to the others. It only deducts two years from one's life expectancy. However, stress is known to increase vulnerability to drug and alcohol addiction.[144] Together, these three factors reduce the individual's life expectancy by eighteen years, not just two. An individual under enough stress has a high risk of becoming a heavy drinker and drug abuser. In the article "Chronic Stress, Drug Use, and Vulnerability to Addiction," Rajita Sinha points out that a person's response to stress depends on the intensity, controllability, predictability, mastery, and adaptability of the stressor, as well as the person's "personality traits, availability of internal resources (including the physiological condition of the individual), [and] prior emotional state (including beliefs and expectancies)."[145] As a result, two individuals under similar conditions respond differently to the same traumatic events. One continues life as before while the other succumbs to addictive behavior.

This information on life expectancy serves two purposes in context to suicide: First, it reinforces the well-known and often ignored knowledge that death is inevitable. Second, it confirms that death is permanent. Neither appeals court, do-overs, nor re-spans (gamers) allow a dead person to return for another shot at life. All hopes, dreams, and desires are erased as well as one's fears, shame, and guilt. Principally, victims succumb to suicide because of the latter. All those negative events are wiped clean, but so are the positive ones. Overall, stress begins with a single problem and grows with each subsequent problem. Unless there is a lessening of the combined load, every person eventually reaches a breaking point. For some, an overload of bad stressors makes a verdict of guilt crescendo into a punishment of death. The resulting suicide terminates one's life expectancy prematurely and ends any available reprieve or merciful salvation in a court of appeal.

# Finding Hope: Appeal and Reprieve

The Mayo Clinic states, "Most often, suicidal thoughts are the result of feeling like you can't cope when you're faced with what seems to be an overwhelming life situation. If you don't have hope for the future, you may mistakenly think suicide is a solution."[146] Continuing with the self-trial analogy, deciding to end one's own life does not begin at any particular stage of the process. It takes many bad events before depression begins to set in. Depression and hopelessness then build into thoughts of suicide over time. This process slowly increases feelings of hopelessness, worthlessness, and helplessness.

Hope and self-worth are two major contributors that allow humans to continue reaching for the future. Death is inevitable, but that does not prevent us from reaching beyond the stars, a child dreams of great adventure and achievements. As they get older, children reshape their goals according to their abilities and changing desires. Adults equally continue this process, albeit in a more controlled fashion, in a sense of recognized limitations and perhaps fears of failure. Our value or self-worth begins to take a hit, and we lower our expectations. That value is also affected by others' judgements. Comments of "you can't, you won't, you'll never, and you're just not good enough" take their toll on a person's self-worth. Self-worth is a type of meter we use to measure our importance to the outside world.

Achievements push the scale of self-worth up. Defeats bring the scale down. This self-worth scale seems to make sense and appears to have a balanced way of keeping track of one's worthiness, personal value, and/or capability. However, this method of measurement has an underlying flaw. Achievements, victories, accomplishments, etc. are often weighted less than those badges of disappointment one might receive. It's not a one-for-one exchange. Ask any Marine, "What is the Marine Corps equation for measuring a Marine's successfulness?" and they will tell you, "One 'aw-shoot' (to put it nicely) wipes out ten 'atta-boys' every time." It's a comical retort, and perhaps it's a Marine thing, but the quote is quite telling of how much more weight we tend to give defeats in our lives than we do successes.

Everyone decides the level of importance each have, good or bad. People with low self-esteem put more weight on defeats than on successes. They think about those defeats more. Personality and social psychologists agree that people with high self-esteem focus more on their successes than defeats.[147]

Perhaps, we can view this another way. Whether sports, the arts, or academic activities, participants are awarded trophies, ribbons, certificates, and diplomas of accomplishment. They collect those awards and prominently display them for all to see. This "Wall of Fame" maybe as simple as a refrigerator door or a doctor's office wall. Then there are the collections of Olympic medals, Superbowl rings, Pulitzer Prizes, and Medals of Honor. On the other side of the room, the opposing wall, or "wall of shame," holds all the reminders of past failures. These reminders tend to scream loudly and constantly.

So how does a person with low self-esteem shift to high self-esteem under these circumstances? Even if a person's "Wall of Fame" is empty and the other wall screams of one's defeat like the crowd in a sports stadium at full roar, it is possible. Reaching out to old and new hopes and dreams in an instant can fill the one and silence the other. It only requires practice and tenacity. Keep chasing hope and your dreams as passionately as someone sentenced to death begging the appellate court judge for leniency and mercy.

## Conflict and Combat

"Life imitates art," claims Oscar Wilde in his essay "The Decay of Lying."[148] Wilde uses this phrase as a way of describing conflicting philosophical positions of romanticism and realism. One emphasizes the importance of feelings, emotion, and art, and the other approaches life in a more analytically reasoned manner loaded with facts and figures. These two philosophies continue to both conflict with each other and, at the same time, complement each other. Reversing Wilde's phrase into "Art imitates life," we find the more common use of the phrase.

People read stories and watch movies and dramas principally

because of the conflicts involved. The people facing struggles draw our attention because of our curiosity to discover how the story turns out. The hero versus the villain is a common theme in adventure movies as well as love stories. Some of our attraction to this comes from our desire to see how others handle familiar situations. Crime dramas, love stories, adventure stories, and movies all have an attraction to some type of struggle, a bit of unknown or mystery, and an association or similarity with the reader or viewer. From birth, humans arrive with a struggle or conflict of some type, and this does not end until death.

In literature, movies, and life, conflict appears in many different forms and generally sits between two opposing participants. For those readers familiar with the various types of narrative conflicts, you will see similarities and some differences in the following list. The more common designators of "Man" and "Person" are replaced with "Self." This was done to help the reader better personalize the conflict types.[149] Additionally, one of four common categories—physical, classical, psychological, and supernatural—are added to each type for more clarity.[150]

1. Physical – Self vs. Another Person

2. Physical – Self vs. Nature

3. Physical – Self vs. Machine or Technology

4. Classical – Self vs. Destiny

5. Classical – Self vs. Society

6. Psychological – Self vs. Self

7. Supernatural – Self vs. God

8. Supernatural – Self vs. the Unknown

While more commonly used for artistic direction, we also find a "Life imitates art" value when considering how each also contains a common point of reference to real-life struggles humans face. Please forgive my belaboring on conflict types. The reason for this is to help you as you try to identify the issue at hand. As an example, difficulties between you and your boss at work easily fall under the "Person vs. Person" conflict. After a major accident or destructive storm, you may have heard a victim crying out, "God, why did you let this happen?" What happens when the car doesn't start or the phone doesn't work or the power goes out? The thought of conflict on its own can be disturbing, and thinking about the more serious prospects of physical combat only creates a more distressing situation.

Mankind, throughout history, has struggled to find ways to live peacefully with one another; however, this struggle generates its own controversies. Controversy in search of a solution can flow into intrapersonal conflict as well. Moral dilemmas are of this psychological type. But how do we resolve conflict? Our earlier discussion on rules, laws, morals, and the like identifies humanity's efforts at reducing conflict. They result from humans' attempt to better define and regulate our social contract, the theory of working together. On this theory, Celeste Friend explains, "*The Social Contract* begins with the most oft-quoted line from Rousseau: 'Man was born free, and he is everywhere in chains'…Humans are essentially free, and were free in the State of Nature, but the 'progress' of civilization has substituted *subservience to others* [emphasis mine] for that freedom, through dependence, economic and social inequalities, and the extent to which we judge ourselves through comparisons with others."[151]

As soon as another person enters the room you are in, you no longer rule alone. A contract is created allowing both people to remain, unless Cain again kills Abel. Social contracts and attempts to work together have yet to eliminate conflict, but they have come a long way in helping to limit the combative extremes thereby keeping societies at relative peace. Relative at least to the more extreme methods of conflict resolution. In Cain's example, he all too quickly chose to use one of the most extreme of combative solutions—murder. In one final act, Cain removed his conflict, or so he thought. The sad and unfortunate result of many intrapersonal conflicts is that the sufferers choose the same solution—to murder the perceived troublemaker. Of course, from a biological perspective, the outcome will differ. Unlike Cain, who lived on, intrapersonal conflict involves opposing forces within the same person, so killing one kills them both.

Why is conflict important in understanding suicide? Pretty much any action, conversation, and thought can turn into a battleground, and in this struggle for dominance, practically any type of resolution can follow. Take, for example, this conversation between two fishermen. A fisherman catches a huge fish and tells his friend about it. The friend then replies with his own story, "Well, let me tell you about the one I caught." A simple comparison, you might think, but the basis for conflict is there. Whose fish is bigger? Whose story is more important? While this type of conflict is a far cry from the struggles found in marriages, at the workplace, or in war, it is combative nonetheless. This simple conversation starts as a story of one person's fishing experience, but as soon as the friend offers the bigger fish story, the conversation becomes a contest. A contest to answer the question of which fish is bigger, while it may sound silly here, is still a contest. And a contest is just a milder form of conflict. Who is better, stronger, faster, smarter? Who's a better leader? Who has a better plan? Is it right or wrong? Is it good or bad? Whose fault is it? See the point?

This fishing conversation could just as easily take a different turn. Rather than challenge the storyteller with a bigger fish story, the friend could have congratulated the fisherman on the successful catch. The direction of the conversation rests with the listener's response. Is the fishing storyteller sharing a fun experience or bragging? Is the respondent sharing a similar story or challenging with his own bigger fish story? The point of this fish tale is that even the simplest conversation can be escalated into a combative conversation and just as easily be defused with a kind word of congratulations. However, don't misunderstand: not all conflict is so easily dismissed.

All this writing about conflict, combat, and war may sound a bit militaristic; it should—intentionally. War and conflict are both defined by their similar elements: goals, desires, and methods for achieving them, achieving them through might if necessary. Military might, method, and thought can be found in almost any conflict between humans. Almost any contest, challenge, game, and even conversation can contain essential

CAUSATION

elements for conflict: two or more parties, a difference, and a goal.[152] And then there is the interest of third parties who have no investment in the conflict and who do not look for a reward after the conflict. They just like to fight, which brings us to the subject of goals, the reason we fight.

## Military Thought

Carl Von Clausewitz offered some perspectives on strategy and the interplay between war, politics, and society.[153] For our readers not familiar with Clausewitz, his book *On War* is arguably the most used text for the study of military thought and strategy and the theory of war. Within his writings, Clausewitz proposed that war is always an instrument of policy,[154] implying that the person or persons in charge (e.g., politicians, the makers of policy) determine whether to initiate a war. Politicians equally determine the goal(s) of war. This includes defensive (protecting what one has) or offensive (taking from others) goals. Once the goal is established, the military in turn focuses on strategy and execution of war. (Keep in mind, a mini war between two people contains the same elements of goals and methods for achieving those goals.) Strategy dictates the best course of action for achieving the goals.

Along with goals, the policymakers dictate limitations for the conduct of war. Limitations are necessary elements to avoid unnecessary problems, and they come in various forms. Globally recognized rules established by the Geneva Convention relating to human rights laws play a grand role in terms of international war. A basic rule of "don't argue in front of the kids" may be a simpler yet equally important family rule. A variety of other rules on the national scale include but are not limited to "Rules of Engagement," "Codes of Conduct," and "Rules of Ethics," to name a few. In addition, whether military or family, each member operates under their own individualized moral guide. Without such restrictions, armies quickly escalate their combat to an idealized level of "total war."

To understand total war, we need to look back no further than our own Civil War. Mere months following President Lincoln's issuing his "Emancipation Proclamation" in 1863, the year saw the emergence of large-scale and routine destruction in its application war.[155] Devastating conduct of armies included the destruction of property, theft, murder (not to be confused with the killing of enemy combatants), rape, and arson, to name a few. One eyewitness described Army General William T. Sherman as "[a man] eviler than Ivan the Terrible or Genghis Khan." Sherman himself claimed, "You cannot qualify war in harsher terms than I will. War is cruelty, and you cannot refine it."[156]

With no rules limiting war, all bets are off, and barbaric behavior is okay. Rules are necessary. In response to Sherman's acts, the Union Army issued "General Order No. 100," considered "the western world's first formal set of guidelines for the conduct of armies in the field."[157] Suppressing close range discretion held no control over the devastation brought on by World War I, trench warfare, and the development of more powerful artillery and chemical weapons. World War II appears to have reached the apex of total war with the development of destruction via the use of atomic weapons. World governments continue the effort of limiting war to this day for the same general purpose as instituted in General Order No. 100, preserving human rights and preventing the horrible extremes of conduct humans can exert if given enough freedom.

If, as Clausewitz noted, politicians, the leaders of nations, determine activation of war, then it transfers that leaders, in general, might make the same types of decisions, albeit at their level of influence. A husband (political leader H) and wife (political leader W) may be viewed as leaders of their realms of influence (nation A and nation B) within the family unit. This may sound a bit silly, but this analogy demonstrates the environment in which a war between spouses might erupt instigated by either leader. As you see, the number of combatants and the goals change, but the conduct remains the same at any scale. Consider the couple above planning an evening of eating out. There are two parties with similar goals, so far so good, until the questions begin followed by this typical script:

Spouse 1: "Where should we go?"

Spouse 2: "I don't know. Where do you want to go?"

Spouse 1: "I don't know. Where do you want to go?"

Spouse 2: (flustered) "If you don't know, then why did
you ask? Do I have to plan everything?"

And suddenly a conflict ensues. Every element is present: combatants—the two parties, the goal—dinner, and the conflict—diverse opinions of where to go.

# Personal Troubles

Let us consider for a moment self vs. self, conflict #6 in the previously mentioned list of conflicts, the one that happens to one person alone. Short of being able to battle this type of division physically, we generally turn to a more judicial process, the internal argument, the third type of trial. Intrapersonal combat and moral dilemmas occur within the mind of an individual. Unlike wars involving other people, where we find a variety of laws and rules officiating its conduct, intrapersonal war is open to the concept of true "total war." Within one's soul, due process, order and procedure, rules and guidelines can break down and drive an otherwise psychologically stable person into total collapse. To understand this idea of a moral dilemma, or moral injury, requires a closer look at the concept of the "moral" component. Definitions and theories of a single moral, morals, and morality are complex and endless, but the idea of a single moral rests on one person's decision to adopt one rule to define a way they wish to act and think for the purpose of how they wish to live.[158] Each person, knowingly or not, collects a set of rules which they apply to all future decisions they make. Where do morals come from, and why do we need them anyway?

The US Declaration of Independence reminds its citizens that, "We hold these truths to be self-evident, that all men are created equal, that they are endowed by their Creator with certain unalienable rights, that among these are Life, Liberty and the pursuit of Happiness."[159] This opening comment represents the initial "moral" of the nation when it was conceived. "Self-evident" implies we should all know and agree to this comment. "Created equal" reminds us that, on a human level, we are equal. And we all have the right to life, liberty, and the pursuit of happiness until, as mentioned earlier, someone else enters the room. Then the negotiating and contracts begin.

At birth, all babies begin life equally—that is to say, they are not aware of what it means to exist, much less to be different. They don't know they are he or she. They don't know they should have two arms and legs. All of these differences are taught to them. Even the concept of difference is taught to them. In babies we find the epitome of innocence; however, from their first breath, innocence begins to erode. Their once "blank slate" view of the world becomes filled with differences. This difference is good; that difference is bad. This process begins with rudimentary building blocks of explorative tasks: *What is that thing in front of my face? What is a face?* A baby's first entrance into the world, traveling from a warm, dark environment into a lighted, apparently endless place of things must be shocking to some or welcoming to others.

Their initial method of expressing to others what is good or bad is through their cries. If something good, the baby remains quiet, but if it's bad, the baby lets everyone within earshot know. Parental difficulties begin right away when trying to resolve the question, "Which cry belongs to which problem?" Is the baby, cold, hungry, soiled, startled, or something completely different? As they get older, another self-evident truth reveals itself: everything changes. Bad is good, and good is now bad or vice versa, depending on the "exceptions" or "disclaimers" added to their once fixed rules of behavior and operating through life. Moral rules of good and bad, right and wrong, begin at birth. Throughout infancy, their rules are initially shaped by the parents' response, but as they get older, their rules are shaped by their own observations, then by others' influence and by their own reasoning as that part of their soul develops. Their set of morals begins with some simple rules but soon develops into a complex system of self-imposed codes to live by.

Jean Piaget (1896–1980), a Swiss psychologist, studied and wrote some very insightful observations on the moral growth of children.[160] He suggested a moral begins as a simple rule. Rules are important learning blocks in the mind. Games are more than mere entertainment for children; games contain "an extremely complex system of rules, that is to say, a code of laws, a jurisprudence of its own."[161] Rules have no greater or lesser power; they are just rules. Rules become morals, an imperative rule when a sense of high consequence is added to it. This authoritative sense, whether added by their older, stronger peers, in the case of games and social groups, or by their parents, helps create an individual's moral code.[162] As the child matures, parental influence wanes while social influence grows.

At the core of adult social influence, we also find the rules of social governance. The US Constitution, for example, first established the main rules of the nation. Think of them as the main house rules. They were followed by federal law, which added the detail of how this house is to be run and includes the consequences for breaking the rules. Each state, as a member of the family, then created the rules, state law, regarding conduct and consequences for their own room in the house. As you see the pattern here, each city then sets up its own ordinances and regulations and so on.

As mentioned previously, the UCMJ is subordinate to the constitution as a federal law over the military branches. Most of the time, the law that has a higher level of authority or jurisdiction (place of authority) has control over a particular requirement or consequence. At the bottom of the scale are personal rules. One's morals only govern one. However, one's morals also drive and maintain one's belief system. When laws, rules, and rights collide or conflict with one's morals, it is the individual who must choose to accept, reject, or adapt to the new rule. Concerning an individual's conduct and belief system, external governing rules and orders generally have a lower level of importance. As long as they fall within personal moral guidelines, no problem exists. However, when the new rule rises to an imperative higher level and conflicts with an existing moral, the individual finds himself in danger of moral injury.

One glaring moral conflict all warfighters may face concerns the possibility of and, for many, the actual occurrence of having to kill another individual. In his seminal book, *On Killing*, Lt. Col. Dave Grossman explains that people in general, even combat soldiers, object to the idea of killing others. He writes, regarding a study following World War II by Army Brigadier General S. L. A. Marshal, "The results were consistently the same: only 15 to 20 percent of the American riflemen in combat during World War II would fire at the enemy."[163] This detail may seem like shocking news to many but is completely understandable on a human level. When confronted with moral dilemmas, an individual resolves the issue, when possible, on the side of the moral rule contained within his soul over the governing rule demanded of him. The US military solved this issue with improved training, says Grossman. To emphasize, he notes that when S. L. A. Marshall was sent to study the Korean war in similar fashion, he found killing rates had improved to 55 percent, and continued training method improvements brought the Vietnam war rates as high as 90 to 95 percent killing effectiveness.[164]

The military's psychological training, while effective for effectiveness' sake, took little account of its side effects. Only afterward did the "fallout war" taking place in the warfighter's soul reveal this cost. In addition to creating better killing machines, the military equally broke the trust given to them by the individual member—the trust of an assurance of moral integrity. Men and women enter the military under a sense of purpose and duty toward family, country, or, more generally, the "all men" stated in the Declaration of Independence. They trust their efforts will make a difference and that, in return, they, too, will benefit. Their country and its leaders will care for them by assuring a continued flourishing and peaceful place to live. It is regarding this care where the individual realizes he may have been deceived.

Erik Erikson, "a German-American developmental psychologist and psychoanalyst known for his theory on psychological development of human beings,"[165] tells us that children look to their parents for guidance, instruction, and care. In return, the children offer a level of trust and reliance on to the parents.[166] The children trust that the rules and guidance from their parents will remain consistent. Change to this constant requires training the child, even if the rule seems contradictory to currently held beliefs, to be able to make meaning or find purpose for the change. Erickson continues, "Parents must not only have certain ways of guiding by prohibition and permission; they must also be able to represent to the child a deep, an almost somatic conviction that there is a meaning to what they are doing."[167] In adult terms, the implication remains the same. Adults continue to need direction but more so direction with meaningful purpose. Good leaders, like good parents, can provide both.

And then there are those who cannot or do not lead well. When good leadership fails, those they lead are left with a sense of betrayal. While some betrayal is easily dismissed, severe betrayal may engender devastating ramifications. For example, regarding a homicide, as described earlier, the killing of another human being is not murder if commissioned by justified authority, such as being under justified military orders. But what happens when the warfighter finds the orders were unjustified, such as the result of poor leadership? This type of betrayal begins the internal third type of trial. To resolve the conflict, the suffering individual begins to debate which is right, their existing justified moral decision or the new opposing judgment. The longer the debate remains unsettled, the more likely an injury may occur. A moral injury results when the rules remain in conflict.

Often, we hear parents say of their sons and daughters after they return from war, "They're not the same. They don't say much. And their eyes...they seem dark, as if they aren't even looking at us." Severe intrapersonal conflicts can have this effect on its victim. The wrestling match between ideas, reasons, the presentation of evidence, and the retrial of events consume their mental processing cycles to a point that leaves little power for responding to those outside their mind. As for the darkening of the eyes, could it be that, during this period of introspection and involvement with their internal conflict, their sight is turned inward? Not biologically of course. Without serious external forces, the human eye will not roll back and look inward. On their own, no words are required; a person's eyes can speak volumes. One might gaze with wonder, another might stare with positive, curious emotions. However, a person glaring by showing this negative, angry emotion may be looking for trouble. And anger can be a detonator to war.

> Wars spring from unseen and generally insignificant
> causes, the first outbreak being often but an explosion
> of anger.
> —Thucydides

# 16

# SOUL AT RISK

> You have been weighed, you have been measured,
> and you have been found wanting.
>
> —Adhemar

This familiar quote is often attributed to the movie *A Knight's Tale*, featuring Heath Ledger and Rufus Sewell. Count Adhemar (Sewell) first uses the quote to gloat over William Thatcher/Sir Ulrich von Lichtenstein (Ledger) after defeating him in a jousting competition. The quote appears to have originated from the word *tekel* as interpreted by Daniel to King Belshazzar in the biblical story of Daniel.[168] The reference in both cases relates to a person's value or capabilities, not just their physical weight. Thatcher was deemed incapable of defeating his opponent in a jousting match whereas Belshazzar was judged unworthy of ruling his people by God. Both stories relate to one's physical and mental ability, value, or self-worth.

Measuring one's worth or value on one attribute, such as a physical skill or ability to lead, is a difficult task on its own. Taking a full assessment of someone's overall value or worth is extremely subjective and driven more by opinion than fact. There are so many skills, abilities, qualities, and other points of value to be found in a single person that making a valuation of current and potential future qualities is impossible. It is difficult enough for anyone to accurately assess their own self-worth, much less being able to evaluate someone else's. Furthermore, self-assessment can generate over-valuation or, conversely, the most severe under ratings. It is in these most severe appraisals of oneself where suicidal thoughts make their appearance, thereby placing the soul at risk.

Before we conclude, I would like to close this book with two final stories. First, an army medic, having endured multiple traumas, details his struggle with suicidal thoughts. And second, a military spouse who attempted suicide at a young age yet survived now enjoys a successful life as a grandmother. Both, for a time, had weighed and measured their lives badly. Fortunately, their scales were corrected, and they found new hope.

# Once an Army Medic

The following story reflects the experience of a US Army medic and the struggles that followed his release from the army. His life, unfortunately, like many, took a dark turn after being medically released from the army. He lost several friends in combat and at home. It's impossible to imagine the daily pain and turmoil he continues to endure. However, with the help of his family, friends, and fellow soldiers, he found a way. His story is one of survival, perseverance, and success. We are thankful he allowed us to share it. Please note the names have been changed for privacy reasons. Also, some minor editing was conducted for grammatical purposes and language.

## Email Reply

First, let me thank you for the opportunity to share a part of my story. The opportunity is eerily fitting as I wasn't comfortable sharing my story, talking about my [problems] publicly, etc....until a childhood friend passed. Four months before his death, I had nearly met the same fate, but I didn't tell many people. Few knew what was going on in my life, which, to be honest, increased the chances of me being there again. But after his passing, I reached out to three of our mutual friends. We had all grown up together, but I kind of lost contact with them over the years.

This might be a little weird, but it stuck with me. While I was talking to my lifelong friends and listening to them describe their pain and anguish about our loss, part of me was experiencing an "after life" moment. Like, these same exact conversations would have been taking place with these exact same people, but it wouldn't be his death they were discussing. It would be mine four months prior. They would have been wishing they had reached out to me more, kicking themselves…or all the other "what ifs" we deal with in situations like that.

I gained enough strength in those conversations to tell my friends, starting with those three, what was going on in my life. From there I started telling my story to those around me and then to complete strangers through comedy and social media. I'm nothing special; I am not a hero. I am a regular dude with a troubled past, who has created a better life for himself. And that's the message I want to share.

## My Story

I couldn't figure out how I got there—huddled in the corner of my apartment, curled into a ball, fighting for my life. This was not a noble fight, however; I was far from the mountains of Afghanistan, fighting addiction, depression, anxiety, and the demons of PTSD.

During that weekend in September of 2017, a disastrous attack against my life was being formulated, and I was going to be the perpetrator.

*Failure, failure, failure!* kept ringing through my head.

I had miserably failed at my marriage in the years following my deployment, allowing it to dwindle into a divorce by 2014. Within eight months of my divorce, my commander recommended me for the Medical Evaluation Board, a place where warriors' careers are stripped from their grasp. The suicidal threats, hospitalization, and untimely single-vehicle accident—all within forty-eight hours—were enough to alarm my command of the trouble I was in.

I'd like for you to imagine an Ancient Rome-like coliseum. The massive structure being held in place with hundreds of cement pillars, each one adding to the structural integrity of the building. If all the pillars are strong, then the coliseum can withstand even the most extreme weather conditions, never faltering. But as those support structures start to get taken out overtime, the once unwavering building starts to sway. Without the proper repair, the building will eventually crumble.

And a crumbling structure is what my life resembled in 2016 when I was no longer a staff sergeant, combat medic, United States Army. I was just "me," another disabled veteran without a purpose. A decade of blood and sweat went into building a career that would exude pride; the army was all I knew. It was the only thing I was good at, but my coliseum was empty, and the pillars were collapsing at an alarming rate. No matter how much booze I poured into the cracks, the cement wouldn't reconfigure itself.

I couldn't stop. By 2017, I had drowned myself night after night for the better part of four years as sleep eluded me. I didn't want to sleep. I was afraid of what I saw when I tried closing my eyes. These types of images haunted me since 2007 after I discovered a gruesome scene Easter morning. What was supposed to be a day filled with soldiers laughing and eating, trying to comfort themselves on their first big holiday away from home turned into a day of loss. Two more friends were dead, a murder/suicide, and I will never be able to ask him why he did it even though he haunts me to this day.

The events that transpired two years later in the hills of Afghanistan would leave me with more images that I still cannot shake. On that day, an ISAF position was overrun in our AO. By the next day, over a dozen of our allies would be dead and countless lives would be changed forever. We would unload bag after bag…after bag. And then came the partial bags with various body parts, their owners' whereabouts unknown. Among those lost were three of my closest teammates…Americans. The stamp of war left an angry mark within me that may never fade, a tattoo on my soul.

It seemed natural to increase my drinking every time life didn't go my way. The addicted mind was convinced that there wasn't a problem. I kept getting promoted and even got a bachelor's degree in psychology?! *Pssshhhh…I got this!* I would tell myself, but the drownings continued through my divorce and my medical retirement from the army. There were nights that I would sneak into my son's room and watch him sleep, crying as quietly as I could. What was it going to take for me to get my [act] together? A question his mother would scream at me in 2017 after another arrest, this time causing me to temporarily lose custody of my nine-year-old. The innocent, child-hood joy that sparkled in that boy's eyes left the day he witnessed his hero taken away in handcuffs.

I repeatedly declared that I would not be my father's son, yet here I was at thirty-one years old…a spitting image of the man that I hated so much.

Level after level, my coliseum crumbled until the structure was no longer recognizable. The judge thanked me for my service and genuinely wished for my health to return but wasn't going to be lenient. The plea deal was denied, another column collapsed.

The shame, the guilt, the demons that I continued to face became too much for me on that September morning when the enemy attacked. No longer able to feel any emotions but anger, the thought of a better life escaped me. The charis-matic, outgoing young man that everyone loved was long forgotten. All that remained was the empty shell of a man, asphyxiating himself with booze. I "relapsed."

Addiction had taken full control of my life for the next four days and would leave me nearly dead before a concerned friend intervened. Both auditory and visual hallucinations paired with the immense physical pain I experienced over the following days provided insight to how close death was. I was terrified.

For many years leading up to this incident, I held the notion that I would welcome death with open arms. That it was going to be my sweet relief from the turmoil inside my head, but as I sat there looking into death's eyes, I realized I wanted to live. I wanted to live for one reason and one reason only—my son.

Hours before I relapsed that September, I took a picture of my son. It would have been the last time my son saw his father alive; it would have been the last post I made on social media. Each year since, on the anniversary of that day, I am reminded of how close I came to leaving him without a father. Yet, as I scroll through the memories that social media brings to my attention, I'm dumbfounded at the things that have happened since. The fulfilling job, the meaningful friendships, buying a house…forging an unbreakable bond with my son, now a resident under my roof 50 percent of the time! Unimaginable memories the suicidal addict would have scoffed at.

Now dedicated to restoring the mangled coliseum, I must acknowledge that the road to recovery wasn't paved with giggles, rainbows, and unicorns. Whether the janitor of a local elementary school or a dedicated soldier, life will kick your teeth in at times. It's inevitable, but its acknowledgement is powerful. Logic could argue that if life occasionally kicks you in the teeth, then it would inescapably not be kicking you at times! Those are the "good times," but they will happen again. A powerful statement of hope that the suicidal addict I once was could never fathom.

As the marching orders in life continue to push me forward, I must respect the enemy. I know that an assault could be in the next valley, and some of my wounds are still healing. Some may

never fully heal and the most dreaded thought…
new wounds are coming. Nevertheless, I am
reminded of the words Dr. Ray Rodriguez had
implanted into my twenty-two-year-old brain a
month before I deployed to Afghanistan as a combat medic with the 1st Infantry Division. Dr. Ray
pulled me aside from the gathering taking place
at my parent's house and said something to the
effect of, "You're about to see some ugly things. No
matter how bad it gets, on the worst day, remember
that nothing lasts forever."

I'll borrow that concept and add the previous idea that there will be good times, and I have
concluded that if I wait out this storm, there will be
a smile again. Some storms have been withering to
my soul, and others have been very long in nature,
but if I'm still here at the end of the day, then I succeeded. And I'll have another attempt tomorrow.

We thank this fine man for being with us, alive and well. As a
father, it was difficult knowing what that troublesome and mischievous
little boy was about to endure. Growing up, he was very strong-willed,
and it's part of the reason he survived, both in combat and in his struggle
with the temptation to find relief in suicide.

More than will, desire, ambition, or attitude, one must believe he
can survive all adversity long enough for the next "good day." The potential of death is a constant comrade. It is inevitable for us all, which is even
more reason to fight for every day of life we can get. Bad days are death's
opportunity to entice us to succumb to its inevitability. Whether the grim
reaper is rewarded for achieving our early termination or he is being punished by being shackled to us or he just gets tired of our company, don't be
fooled into jumping off early. The next good day is on its way. Make both
short- and long-term goals for yourself. Believing and having faith are
critical in living a good life, especially during troubled times.

# The Man in the Next Bed

Having suffered the trauma during the writing of this book, one near victim of suicide graciously revealed her story. She had attempted to commit suicide by overdosing on prescription pills. Her mother found her unresponsive, and she was taken to the hospital. Doctors pumped her stomach and were able to prevent further harm. While she lay on the hospital bed recovering, she noticed the man in the next bed. He had been crushed in a work-related accident, and he was fighting for his life. Her revelation? *How selfish am I? I valued my life so little that I was willing to end it while this man, barely alive, lies fighting for every breath.* In this case, this woman's survival was the result of the alertness of her mother and the hands of her doctors. We now know her salvation resulted from a renewed value and hope for the future inspired by the man's fight for life.

Ask any health-conscious person about muscle fitness and diet, and a slew of exercise techniques and healthy eating dietary recommendations will ensue. Ask them about hormones, and the crowd noise begins to dwindle. Ask again about the neurobiological interplay between hormones and anxiety or stress overload, and the room may grow silent with a few exceptions. The bottom line is that the human being consists of a multitude of simple elements combined into subsystems, working together as systems, and finally a functioning machine driven by its programming. In its simplest form, the computer is designed to replicate a human. Robotics emulate the skeletal, muscle, tendon, and ligament sub-systems. All computers in one form or another represent some part or function of the human body. Imagine if only the human mind had a similar component as the computer monitor to display its every thought. Therein lies one of the functions humans simultaneously wish they could do and probably are glad they cannot. How often have you said to yourself, when trying to explain something to someone, *if only you could see what I am thinking.* Then there are those times when you think, *I'm glad you cannot see what I'm thinking.*

Please excuse my comparing humans to computers, but it allows me a simple method for revealing the complex structure in both components and functions found within every functioning human. The analogy of automotive repair or home renovation would also suffice in comparing the human soul with all its parts and functions working together to create an individual, independent, unique, and special person, unlike any other, regardless of similarities. In doing so, the hope is that when something breaks down, it may be easier to identify the source and apply emergency procedures. These procedures may extend the victim's life long enough to find a solution—a cure for the ailment driving the human-machine toward a total shutdown.

# 17

# A RENOVATED LIFE

"How much time shall I invest in dread and fear of
impending death?" None, I say. Fear not death, for
death awaits us all. A time will come when death itself
shall be swallowed up in victory and we shall rest in
immortality. For now, embrace every moment of life
with thanksgiving and praise as if it were your last.
Consider every breath you take as a joy and a pleasure.
In doing so, fear and even death's knock on your door
shall lose its sting.

—Ray Rodriguiz

There are subjects in life that make most of us very uncomfortable. One
of them is about our life's purpose. In my experience, our purpose is
a subject that haunts us because it brings everything into question as
we scrutinize our lives. A dear friend of mine, one whom I have great
respect for, asked me a question. It was blunt and heavy. He asked, "Greg,
what is your purpose?"

I don't think of myself as easily ruffled, but this one passed all my
defenses and hit me in the heart. I felt flabbergasted for a moment until
I blurted the words out. My response surprised me because I didn't give

myself much time to contemplate the answer. I responded with the following: "To live life in such a manner as to die a good death."

The next day he texted me with the following: "Well, Greg, you may be dying soon because, as far as I can see, you have achieved your purpose."

During the following two weeks, I was hit with a ricochet leaving a bullet in my arm and I snapped my Achilles tendon playing pickleball. Jokingly I told my friend I was rethinking my purpose. But in seriousness, my answer stands!

In my early twenties, I found myself hyper aware of the way I live my life as well as how others lived theirs. This anthropological study just became part of my psyche. I would stare at homeless men and women and wonder. I would study people with "everything" and wonder. As the years went by, I took note of the many people I had intimately known who lived and died without making any difference.

Attending funerals, I often cringed when the officiant struggles to make something out of nothing. Hearing mourners speak in platitudes can be like listening to fingernails running down a chalkboard. Those speaking often know they are lying just to make things acceptable for the moment. I have also enjoyed meeting and knowing many who lived well and died a good death. I have also had the pleasure of knowing people alive today who, if they stay the course, will die a good death.

What is a good death? A good death is the culmination of achievements that go far beyond personal wealth—marked with self-sacrifice. It is part of a worldview which seeks to help others and the determination to rise over any personal weakness to make the world better. It isn't a life that grabs fistfuls of things and holds them tightly. A good death is to live with an open hand. It's the willingness to give as much as you can in life. A good death is not a perfect death. Only *one* person died a perfect death. Because he died a perfect death, we can die a good death. All humans fail, all are imperfect, all must live with what we have and struggle to do our best. *Perfection is not the goal. Staying in the fight is the goal.*

I was born with little more than what was necessary to get by. The bar was consistently low for me as my examples mainly just *existed* until death. To realize a good death, I would have to accept the risks life brings to those who refuse just to exist. To this day, I look for mentors who will look deeply into my life, wise individuals who aren't given to silliness and politics, who are examples of courage to challenge me. This triune discipline guides me to the best path toward opportunities that may change my life and the lives of others. This practice leads to purposeful living, which invites hope into the mind and emotions. As this purpose rushes into the consciousness, it evicts everything which fights against possibility and opportunity.

Our failures don't have the right to define us, which means that no matter how much of a dirtbag we have been, we can flip the switch and spend the rest of our lives reaching toward a good death. It's not too late, my friend, to find a good death. The story is still being written about your existence here. Dead men cannot read or hear these words, and since you are reading or hearing them, you can unclench your hand, opening it up to a new existence. The barriers of this world are only real to those who accept them. For you, there is no barrier, and there is a way; it's time to find it.

Constructing a skyscraper or a ship capable of withstanding strong winds and inclement weather requires a firm foundation and a well-structured framework with solid anchors for holding it in place and the floors and walls attached. Humans equally require firm foundations and a well-structured framework with solid anchors to withstand the winds of change. As one matures from infancy to adulthood, an enormous construction project is taking place. Parents, whether biological, adoptive, or surrogate, begin preparing themselves long before the child arrives. They prepare the material needed for building the foundation on which this child will begin construction. Should the foundation lack strength, it will introduce a vulnerability. Visibly, everything may seem fine. During small winds, it may continue to support the construction; however, should wind with enough force hit the building from just the right direction, a crack in the foundation will appear. Left unattended, this crack may compromise the stability of the entire structure and eventually cause it to collapse on its own.

A human soul begins in similar fashion with the laying of one's foundation. We've read Piaget's writings on the child's development and understanding of rules—rules of the game (i.e., their morals). These represent foundational rules for the individual, the core if you will. All other rules and laws lay on these foundations. This foundation allows the child to continue building, to venture out. The structure is purpose, and on this structure, hopes and dreams are anchored. Anchors are beliefs and faith. They come in a variety of strengths. From opinions (weak beliefs) to hypothetical probabilities to theories emboldened by an ever-growing list of facts finally to unshakeable laws. History has shown that even the seemingly indestructible ship RMS Titanic could not withstand the ripping force of an immovable iceberg. Equally, even the most well-constructed person in terms of body, mind, and soul can encounter a force, an event, that will penetrate his structure, resulting in trauma.

To some, demolition, or suicide, is the only option. We hope that this book has shown there is another option. Renovation is the best solution. For buildings or ships, the cost of renovating may outweigh their worth. For people, this is never the case. Human life is far too valuable for a person to judge himself and condemn himself to death. Renovation proposes finding areas of weakness and strengthening or rebuilding the weak areas. As you have read in the preceding chapters, there are many areas of the human soul. Every young person goes into the military as an unfinished work, still "Under Construction." Some parts of the building are finished and others not. Perhaps the most critical point to recognize here concerns the order of construction. Everyone builds at his own pace and in his own order. Some have experienced multiple hardships growing up, others not. Some entered the military with a sense of adventure while others are escaping traumatic lives. Some have strong minds and reason well, others not so much.

The military has very broad guidelines for those whom they accept into their ranks. For one, they have a broad range of jobs and tasks they need to accomplish. For this they need numbers, large numbers, of warfighters. Recruits are processed and trained for their specific job and duty. Very little consideration is given to moral structure or investigating the strengths and weaknesses of their souls. While warfighters are equally trained and capable, they are not foundationally the same. Weaknesses in their ability to process drastic changes or extremely ugly events can shake their foundations, framework, and anchors, thereby uncovering previously unrecognized weaknesses. This might explain why, when two warfighters encounter the same scenario, one comes out okay and the other will end up traumatized. Identifying and renovating weaknesses prior to such overwhelming stressors can help diminish and, in some cases, prevent trauma. For those already suffering from trauma, renovation is necessary. It may be more difficult but doable, as you have read.

Thank you for reading. We hope you have found the information, experience, and stories helpful. We also hope we have demystified the mystery of suicide and encouraged potential victims to find their way back to life, much like the young son did for his army medic father and the man in the bed did for a young teenage girl named Cheryl.

# ACKNOWLEDGMENTS

**From Greg Wark**

The words in this book reveal how much I value life. I learned most of what I believe from a shared life with the greatest woman I have ever known, my wife of over forty-five years, Amber Lea Lane Wark. When we met, I was a lost, purposeless man living day to day, mainly on the California beaches. She is the best of us, for sure, and is responsible for anything I am today or will ever become.

**From Ray Rodriguez**

Many thanks to Cheryl Rodriguez, my spouse and writing mentor. Your persistence in writing your own books was a constant encouragement for me to keep writing. The echo of your words, "Just write, Ray; you can fix it and rearrange it later," allowed me to reach the end and want to keep on going.

I wish to acknowledge my father, Alfred Ponce Rodriguez, for having survived the Korean War and for raising his family with the kindest strength and discipline. He and my mother, Romana, provided for us a perspective from which to view the good qualities of other people and to respect those first and foremost. Also, to be aware and cautious of bad traits but not to judge people by the bad slices of their lives.

Lastly, I wish to thank everyone who has shared their stories of loss to suicide. The loss of their family or friend to suicide is always a difficult subject. There are far too many names and stories to list, but one particular veteran of the Vietnam war comes to mind—a man I never met yet came to know through his family. His suicide left a lasting negative impression on his wife and children. Searching for the good in this man, through their stories of his former and later self, helped identify many of the initiators of suicidal thought. Suicide seems to occur most often when the good (hope) is drowned out by bad memories.

# ENDNOTES

1    Arthur MacArthur, as quoted by Robert Massicotte, "The History and
     Message behind Flag Day in the US," *Daily News*, June 13, 2020, https://
     www.ironmountaindailynews.com/opinion/editorials/2020/06/the-
     history-and-message-behind-flag-day-in-us/.

2    Washington's Blog, "America Has Been at War 93% of the Time—222
     out of 239 Years—Since 1776," Global Research, February 20, 2015,
     https://www.globalresearch.ca/america-has-been-at-war-93-of-the-
     time-222-out-of-239-years-since-1776/5565946.

3    Christian Oord, "Believe It or Not: Since Its Birth the USA Has Only
     Had 17 Years of Peace," War History Online, March 19, 2019, https://
     www.warhistoryonline.com/instant-articles/usa-only-17-years-of-peace.
     html.

4    Janet Kemp and Robert Bossarte, *Suicide Data Report, 2012*, US
     Department of Veterans Affairs, https://www.va.gov/opa/docs/Suicide-
     Data-Report-2012-final.pdf.

5    Kemp and Bossarte, *Suicide Data Report, 2012*, 15.

6    "2020 National Veteran Suicide Prevention Annual Report," US
     Department of Veterans Affairs, https://www.mentalhealth.va.gov/docs/
     data-sheets/2020/2020-National-Veteran-Suicide-Prevention-Annual-
     Report-11-2020-508.pdf, 3.

7       Patricia Kime, "Active-Duty Military Suicides at Record Highs in
        2018," Military.com, January 30, 2019, https://www.military.com/
        daily-news/2019/01/30/active-duty-military-suicides-near-record-
        highs-2018.html.

8       Barbara Starr, "US Special Ops Suicides Tripled in 2018, As Military
        Confronts the Issue," CNN Cable News Network, February 2, 2019,
        https://www.cnn.com/2019/02/02/politics/socom-military-suicide-
        spike-2018/index.html.

9       "Increase In Armed Forces Suicides Over Last Five Years, MOD Figures
        Show," Forces Network, March 26, 2020, https://www.forces.net/news/
        increase-armed-forces-suicides-over-last-five-years-mod-figures-show.

10      Sun Tzu, *The Art of War*, trans. Thomas Cleary (Boston and London:
        Shambhala Publications, 2003), 81.

11      Henry Campbell Black, Joseph R. Nolan, and Michael J. Connolly,
        *Black's Law Dictionary: Definitions of the Terms and Phrases of American
        and English Jurisprudence, Ancient and Modern*, 6th Ed. (St. Paul, MN:
        West Publishing Co., 1990), 221.

12      Black, *Black's Law Dictionary*, 1500.

13      Seth Paridon, "The Highest and Purest Democracy: Rabbi Roland
        Gittelsohn's Iwo Jima Eulogy to His Fallen Comrades," The National
        WWII Museum, New Orleans, February 19, 2020, https://www.
        nationalww2museum.org/war/articles/highest-and-purest-democracy-
        rabbi-roland-gittelsohns-iwo-jima-eulogy-his-fallen.

14      *Pirates of the Caribbean: The Curse of the Black Pearl*, directed by Gore
        Verbinski (2003; Burbank, CA: Walt Disney Pictures, 2004), DVD, 143
        min.

# ENDNOTES

15    "The Origin of the VA Motto: Lincoln's Second Inaugural Address," Celebrating America's Freedoms, US Department of Veteran's Affairs, Washington, DC, retrieved June 26, 2021, https://www.va.gov/opa/publications/celebrate/vamotto.pdf.

16    Bernie Sanders, "While Serious People Can Have Legitimate Differences," Facebook, posted February 4, 2017, https://m.facebook.com/berniesanders/photos/a.324119347643076/1312284712159863/?type=3&locale2=de_DE.

17    Leo Shane III, "VA: Suicide Rate for Younger Veterans Increased by More Than 10 Percent," *Military Times*, September 26, 2018, https://www.militarytimes.com/news/pentagon-congress/2018/09/26/suicide-rate-spikes-among-younger-veterans/.

18    Timothy Zahn, *Star Wars: Thrawn* (New York: Del Rey, Random House, 2017), 416.

19    Bernard Hamilton, "'God Wills It': Signs of Divine Approval in the Crusade Movement," *Studies in Church History* 41 (2005): 88–98, https://doi.org/10.1017/s0424208400000140.

20    R. G. Grant, *Battle: A Visual Journey through 5,000 Years of Combat*, First American ed. (London: Dorling Kindersley, 2005), 110.

21    Grant, *Battle*, 297.

22    William Shakespeare, *King Henry V*, in *The Complete Works of William Shakespeare* (San Diego, CA: Canterbury Classics, 2014), 532–69, 554.

23    Gordon Leslie Squires, "Quantum Mechanics," *Encyclopædia Britannica*, https://www.britannica.com/science/quantum-mechanics-physics; Jan Hilgevoord and Jos Uffink, "The Uncertainty Principle," *Stanford Encyclopedia of Philosophy* (Stanford University, October 8, 2001), https://plato.stanford.edu/archives/win2016/entries/qt-uncertainty.

24    Robert Lanza, "Does the Soul Exist? Evidence Says 'Yes,'" *Psychology Today*, December 21, 2011, https://www.psychologytoday.com/us/blog/biocentrism/201112/does-the-soul-exist-evidence-says-yes.

25    Edward J. Furton, "Is a Soul Conscious after Death?" *Legatus*, accessed August 7, 2020, https://legatus.org/news/is-a-soul-conscious-after-death.

26    Daniel 3.

27    Hebrews 11:1 NKJV.

28    "Oath of Enlistment," Army Values, US Army, accessed on November 1, 2020, https://www.army.mil/values/oath.html.

29    "Oath of Commissioned Officers," Army Values, US Army, accessed on November 1, 2020, https://www.army.mil/values/officers.html.

30    Eric Brown, "Plato's Ethics and Politics in *The Republic*," *Stanford Encyclopedia of Philosophy*, April 1, 2003, https://plato.stanford.edu/archives/fall2017/entries/plato-ethics-politics/.

31    Brown, "Plato's Ethics."

32    Meghan Keneally, "The 11 Mass Deadly School Shootings That Happened since Columbine," ABC News, April 19, 2019, https://abcnews.go.com/US/11-mass-deadly-school-shootings-happened-columbine/story?id=62494128.

# ENDNOTES

33    Kate Briquelet, "Feds Are Asking Epstein Victims about Sex-Trafficking Crimes," *Daily Beast*, June 3, 2019, https://www.thedailybeast.com/feds-are-asking-jeffrey-epsteins-victims-about-sex-trafficking-crimes.

34    "Child Trafficking Statistics," Ark of Hope for Children, April 9, 2019, https://arkofhopeforchildren.org/child-trafficking/child-trafficking-statistics.

35    "Protect Your Brain from Stress," Harvard Health Publishing, February 15, 2021, https://www.health.harvard.edu/mind-and-mood/protect-your-brain-from-stress.

36    John B. Lyttle, *If I Should Die before I Wake: One Marine's Experience on Iwo Jima* (New York, NY: Vantage Press, 2007), 54.

37    "Protect Your Brain from Stress," Harvard Health Publishing.

38    "Protect Your Brain from Stress," Harvard Health Publishing.

39    Erik Vance, "Unlocking the Healing Power of You," *National Geographic*, June 3, 2020, https://www.nationalgeographic.com/magazine/2016/12/healing-science-belief-placebo/.

40    Vance, "Unlocking the Healing."

41    Lorraine Smith-MacDonald et al., "Spirituality and Mental Well-Being in Combat Veterans: A Systematic Review," *Oxford Academic*, November 1, 2017, https://academic.oup.com/milmed/article/182/11-12/e1920/4661639.

42    Dave Grossman, *On Killing* (Boston, MA: Little, Brown, 1996), 183.

43    Phillip Carter, "What America Owes Its Veterans: A Better System of
      Care and Support," *Foreign Affairs*, September/October 2017, https://
      www.foreignaffairs.com/articles/2017-08-15/what-america-owes-
      its-veterans?cid=otr-press_note-what_america_owes_its_veterans-
      090617&spJobID=1245356576&spMailingID=54905134&spReportI
      d=MTI0NTM1NjU3NgS2&spUserID=NTMwNTAwMTIxMzkS1&
      sp_mid=54905134&sp_rid=cGNhcnRlckBnbWFpbC5jb20S1.

44    Tom Brokaw, "Tom Brokaw Explains the Origins of 'The Greatest
      Generation,'" NBC News, June 4, 2014, https://www.nbcnews.
      com/video/tom-brokaw-explains-the-origins-of-the-greatest-
      generation-273640003752.

45    Brokaw, "Tom Brokaw Explains."

46    Edwin L. Dale Jr., "What Vietnam Did to the American Economy," *New
      York Times*, January 28, 1973, https://www.nytimes.com/1973/01/28/
      archives/what-vietnam-did-to-the-american-economy-worsening-
      payments-deficit.html.

47    History.com editors, "Woodstock," History, March 9, 2018, https://
      www.history.com/topics/1960s/woodstock.

48    Andrew Tilghman, "The Pentagon Keeps Data on Millennials. This Is
      What It Says," *Military Times*, July 9, 2016, https://www.militarytimes.
      com/news/your-military/2016/07/09/the-pentagon-keeps-data-on-
      millennials-this-is-what-it-says/.

49    Robert Longley, "Differences between Communism and Socialism,"
      ThoughtCo., updated February 2, 2021, https://www.thoughtco.com/
      difference-between-communism-and-socialism-195448.

# ENDNOTES

50    Lee Edwards, "Three Nations That Tried Socialism and Rejected It," The Heritage Foundation, October 16, 2019, https://www.heritage.org/progressivism/commentary/three-nations-tried-socialism-and-rejected-it.

51    Edwards, "Three Nations."

52    "Conscription in the United States," Wikipedia, last modified May 17, 2021, https://en.wikipedia.org/wiki/Conscription_in_the_United_States.

53    Author's name withheld, email to Greg Wark, used with permission.

54    Bryan Doerries, *The Theater of War: What Ancient Greek Tragedies Can Teach Us Today* (New York: Vintage Books, 2016), 60–61.

55    Doerries, *The Theater of War*.

56    *Troy*, directed by Wolfgang Petersen (2004; Burbank: Warner Bros. Pictures, 2005), DVD, 163 min.

57    "The Plays of Sophocles," *Britannica*, accessed October 26, 2020, https://www.britannica.com/biography/Sophocles/The-plays.

58    Bryan Doerries, "How the Secrets of the Ancient Greeks Can Heal Our Wounded Warriors," *Observer*, November 10, 2015, https://observer.com/2015/11/ptsd-is-from-b-c/.

59    *Forrest Gump*, directed by Robert Zemeckis (1994; Hollywood: Paramount, 1995), DVD, 142 min., https://www.imdb.com/title/tt0109830/?ref_=nv_sr_srsg_0.

60    "Our Impact by the Numbers," Gary Sinise Foundation, accessed July 31, 2021, https://www.garysinisefoundation.org/by-the-numbers/.

61   "Gary Sinise Foundation: Our Mission," Gary Sinise Foundation, accessed July 31, 2021, https://www.garysinisefoundation.org/mission/.

62   Roger P. Watts, "How the Addicted Brain Hijacks the Mind," MentalHelp.net, accessed July 31, 2021, https://www.mentalhelp.net/blogs/how-the-addicted-brain-hijacks-the-mind/.

63   J. Douglas Bremner, "Traumatic Stress: Effects on the Brain," National Library of Medicine, accessed July 31, 2021, https://pubmed.ncbi.nlm.nih.gov/17290802/.

64   Sarah Klein, "Adrenaline, Cortisol, Norepinephrine: The Three Major Stress Hormones, Explained," *HuffPost*, April 19, 2013, https://www.huffpost.com/entry/adrenaline-cortisol-stress-hormones_n_3112800.

65   Franz Calvo et al., "Diagnoses, Syndromes, and Diseases: A Knowledge Representation Problem," US National Library of Medicine National Institutes of Health, 2003, https://www.ncbi.nlm.nih.gov/pmc/articles/PMC1480257/.

66   "Chronic Pain Syndrome," Columbia University Department of Neurology, August 18, 2020, found at the Library of the US Courts of the Seventh Circuit, http://www.lb7.uscourts.gov/documents/18c75181.pdf.

67   Neil Romano et al., "The Danger of Assisted Suicide Laws," National Council on Disability, October 9, 2019, https://ncd.gov/sites/default/files/NCD_Assisted_Suicide_Report_508.pdf.

68   In reference to Myers-Briggs personality type indicators of competitive, driven, multitaskers.

69   Wikipedia, s.v. "Survivor Guilt," last modified June 2, 2021, https://en.wikipedia.org/wiki/Survivor_guilt.

# ENDNOTES

70    Jayne Leonard, "What Is Survivor's Guilt?" *Medical News Today*, June 27, 2019, https://www.medicalnewstoday.com/articles/325578.

71    Ed Darack, "Extortion 17, Seal Team Six and What Really Happened on the Deadliest Day in the History of Naval Special Warfare and the US War in Afghanistan," *Newsweek*, August 31, 2017, https://www.newsweek.com/extortion-17-seal-team-six-navy-seals-afghanistan-conspiracy-theories-names-657841.

72    Jayne Leonard, "What Is Trauma? What to Know," *Medical News Today*, June 3, 2020, https://www.medicalnewstoday.com/articles/trauma.

73    Jon Davis, "What Does War Smell like, Whether on Land, in Cockpits, in Submarines or Elsewhere?" Quora, February 6, 2017, https://www.quora.com/What-does-war-smell-like-whether-on-land-in-cockpits-in-submarines-or-elsewhere.

74    Melissa Brymer et al., *Psychological First Aid: Field Operations Guide*, 2nd ed. (Los Angeles: National Child Traumatic Stress Network, 2006).

75    "Psychological First Aid: Field Operations Guide," US Department of Veterans Affairs, April 13, 2006, https://www.ptsd.va.gov/professional/treat/type/psych_firstaid_manual.asp.

76    Lynn K. Hall, *Counseling Military Families: What Mental Health Professionals Need to Know* (New York: Routledge, Taylor and Francis Group, 2008), 45.

77    Hall, *Counseling*, 45.

78    *U-571*, directed by Jonathan Mostow (2000; Universal City, CA: Universal Pictures, 2000), DVD, 116 min.

79    U-571.

80    *U*-571.

81    Krnel, "Great Ideas? Average Events? Small People?" *Steemit*, accessed June 30, 2021, https://steemit.com/psychology/@krnel/great-ideas-average-events-small-people.

82    *The Hurt Locker*, directed by Kathryn Bigelow (2008; Universal City, CA: Summit Entertainment, 2012), DVD, 131 min.

83    Wikipedia, s.v. "Tap Code," last modified May 21, 2021, https://en.wikipedia.org/wiki/Tap_code.

84    Adam Greene, "Suicidal Language," *Science in Our World: Certainty and Controversy*, September 14, 2014, https://sites.psu.edu/siowfa14/tag/body-language/.

85    Sarita Robinson, "Isolation Has Profound Effects on the Human Body and Brain. Here's What Happens," *Science Alert*, February 3, 2019, https://www.sciencealert.com/isolation-has-profound-effects-on-the-human-body-and-brain-here-s-what-happens.

86    Robinson, "Isolation."

87    "The Body Language of Depression," *Exploring Your Mind*, updated February 21, 2020, https://exploringyourmind.com/the-body-language-of-depression/.

88    Jill Suttie, "Why the World Needs an Empathy Revolution," *Greater Good Magazine*, February 1, 2019, https://greatergood.berkeley.edu/article/item/why_the_world_needs_an_empathy_revolution.

89    Rabbi Corey Helfand, "Why Did It Take 40 Years to Reach the Promised Land?" *Jewish News of Northern California*, January 25, 2013, https://www.jweekly.com/2013/01/25/torah-why-did-it-take-40-years-to-reach-the-promised-land/.

# ENDNOTES

90    Gordon Rayner, Lexi Finnigan, and Henry Bodkin, "Girl, 14, Who Died of Cancer Cryogenically Frozen after Telling Judge She Wanted to Be Brought Back to Life 'in Hundreds of Years,'" *The Telegraph*, November 18, 2016, https://www.telegraph.co.uk/news/2016/11/18/cancer-girl-14-is-cryogenically-frozen-after-telling-judge-she-w/.

91    "Depression," World Health Organization, January 30, 2020, https://www.who.int/news-room/fact-sheets/detail/depression.

92    Richard F. Shepard, "Overcoming the Holocaust with Success," *New York Times*, December 20, 1992, https://www.nytimes.com/1992/12/20/nyregion/overcoming-the-holocaust-with-success.html.

93    John Maxwell, "Changing Your Beliefs Starts with Changing Your Thinking," *Houston Business Journal*, February 22, 2004, https://www.bizjournals.com/houston/stories/2004/02/23/smallb4.html.

94    *Cast Away*, directed by Robert Zemeckis (2000; Los Angeles, CA: 20th Century Fox, 2000), DVD, 144 min.

95    Boulder Crest Foundation, https://www.facebook.com/BoulderCrestFoundation/photos/a.2653801634917 55/3046942592002151/?type=3.

96    For more information on these conferences, go to https://www.lifeofvalor.com.

97    Szabolcs Szecsei, "20 Statistics on Fatherless Homeless and the Importance of Dads," *Modern Gentlemen*, January 7, 2021, https://moderngentlemen.net/statistics-on-fatherless-homes/.

98    Wikipedia, s.v. "John Gotti," accessed July 24, 2021, https://en.wikipedia.org/wiki/John_Gotti.

99    US Department of Health and Human Services, as reported by The Center for Family Justice, "Statistics," https://centerforfamilyjustice.org/community-education/statistics/.

100   W. Wynn Westcott, *A Social Science Treatise Suicide: Its History, Literature, Jurisprudence, Causation, and Prevention* (London: H. K. Lewis, 1885).

101   Westcott, *Social Science*, 1.

102   Westcott, *Social Science*, 73.

103   Sun Tzu, *Art of War*, https://suntzusaid.com/book/11.

104   Peggy Sanders, "Rules and Common Sense," *Fence Post*, May 29, 2020, https://www.thefencepost.com/opinion/peggy-sanders/rules-and-common-sense/.

105   Lyttle, *If I Should Die before I Wake*, 54.

106   *Lexico*, s.v. "Mind," accessed August 7, 2020, https://www.lexico.com/definition/mind.

107   *Lexico*, s.v. "Soul," accessed August 1, 2020, https://www.lexico.com/definition/soul.

108   Adam Zeman, "Consciousness," *Brain: A Journal of Neurology* 124, no. 7 (July 1, 2001): 1263–89, https://doi.org/10.1093/brain/124.7.1263, 1283.

109   Robert Van Gulick, "Consciousness," *Stanford Encyclopedia of Philosophy Archive*, June 18, 2004, https://plato.stanford.edu/archives/spr2018/entries/consciousness/.

# ENDNOTES

110    *Lexico*, s.v. "Spirit," accessed August 7, 2020, https://www.lexico.com/definition/spirit.

111    *Lexico*, s.v. "Conscience," accessed August 7, 2020, https://www.lexico.com/definition/conscience.

112    "Conscience," *Online Etymology Dictionary*, accessed August 7, 2020, https://www.etymonline.com/word/conscience.

113    *Lexico*, s.v. "Common Sense," accessed August 7, 2020, https://www.lexico.com/definition/common_sense.

114    Thomas Paine, *Common Sense* (New York: Fall River Press, 2013), 3, https://www.ushistory.org/paine/commonsense/sense2.htm.

115    *Lexico*, s.v. "Belief," accessed August 7, 2020, https://www.lexico.com/definition/belief.

116    *Lexico*, s.v. "Faith," accessed August 8, 2020, https://www.lexico.com/definition/faith.

117    David A. Bell, *The First Total War: Napoleon's Europe and the Birth of Warfare as We Know It* (Boston: Mariner Books, 2008), 1.

118    "Norman Schwarzkopf," *Biography*, January 14, 2015, https://www.biography.com/military-figure/norman-schwarzkopf.

119    "Geneva Convention," *History*, November 17, 2017, https://www.history.com/topics/world-war-ii/geneva-convention.

120    "1st Battalion, 6th Marines: 2nd Marine Division," Marines, accessed November 28, 2020, https://www.6thmarines.marines.mil/Units/1st-Battalion/History/.

121    Alfred Lord Tennyson, "The Charge of the Light Brigade," accessed June 28, 2021, https://www.poetryfoundation.org/poems/45319/the-charge-of-the-light-brigade.

122    Michael Moore, "Causation in the Law," *Stanford Encyclopedia of Philosophy*, October 3, 2019, https://plato.stanford.edu/entries/causation-law/.

123    "Nicole Brown Simpson and Ron Goldman Murdered," *History*, November 13, 2009, https://www.history.com/this-day-in-history/nicole-brown-simpson-and-ron-goldman-murdered.

124    "What's the Difference between a Civil Judgment and a Criminal Conviction?," NOLO, accessed July 31, 2021, https://www.nolo.com/legal-encyclopedia/question-civil-judgment-versus-criminal-conviction-28300.html.

125    Terry Skolnik, "Hot Bench: A Theory of Appellate Adjudication," *Boston College Law Review*, 2020, https://lawdigitalcommons.bc.edu/cgi/viewcontent.cgi?article=3867&context=bclr, 1274.

126    "Suicide: 9 Deadliest Myths," CBS News, August 4, 2011, https://www.cbsnews.com/pictures/suicide-9-deadliest-myths/.

127    M. A. Oquendo, M. M. Perez-Rodriguez et al., "Life Events: a Complex Role in the Timing of Suicidal Behavior among Depressed Patients." *Molecular Psychiatry* 19, no. 8 (October 15, 2013): 902–909, https://doi.org/10.1038/mp.2013.128.

128    "Fifth Amendment," Legal Information Institute, accessed October 11, 2020, https://www.law.cornell.edu/constitution/fifth_amendment.

129    "Double Jeopardy," Legal Information Institute, accessed October 11, 2020, https://www.law.cornell.edu/wex/double_jeopardy.

# ENDNOTES

130     "Sixth Amendment," Legal Information Institute, accessed October 11, 2020, https://www.law.cornell.edu/constitution/sixth_amendment.

131     "Stress and Your Health," MedlinePlus, accessed on September 6, 2020, https://medlineplus.gov/ency/article/003211.htm.

132     "Types of Stressors (Eustress vs. Distress)," MentalHelp.net, accessed July 31, 2021, https://www.mentalhelp.net/stress/types-of-stressors-eustress-vs-distress/.

133     "Types of Stressors."

134     "Types of Stressors."

135     "Stress and Your Health," MedlinePlus, accessed July 31, 2021, https://medlineplus.gov/ency/article/003211.htm.

136     "Stress and Your Health."

137     *Lexico*, s.v. "Anxiety," accessed September 20, 2020, https://www.lexico.com/en/definition/anxiety.

138     "Depression," Anxiety and Depression Association of America, accessed July 31, 2021, https://adaa.org/understanding-anxiety/depression.

139     Jonathan I. Bisson et al., "Psychological Therapies for Chronic Post-Traumatic Stress Disorder (PTSD) in Adults," Cochrane Library, December 13, 2013, https://doi.org/10.1002/14651858.cd003388.pub4.

140     "Oldest Person Living (Female)," *Guinness World Records*, accessed on August 22, 2020, https://www.guinnessworldrecords.com/world-records/67477-oldest-person-living-female.

141   "Oldest Person Ever," *Guinness World Records*, accessed on August 22, 2020, https://www.guinnessworldrecords.com/world-records/oldest-person.

142   "Oldest Person."

143   "Life Expectancy of the World Population," Worldometer, accessed on August 22, 2020, https://www.worldometers.info/demographics/life-expectancy/.

144   Rajita Sinha, "Chronic Stress, Drug Use, and Vulnerability to Addiction," US National Library of Medicine National Institutes of Health, August 26, 2009, https://www.ncbi.nlm.nih.gov/pmc/articles/PMC2732004/.

145   Sinha, "Chronic Stress."

146   "Suicide and Suicidal Thoughts," Mayo Clinic, accessed on September 3, 2020, https://www.mayoclinic.org/diseases-conditions/suicide/symptoms-causes/syc-20378048..

147   Jonathon D. Brown and Keith A. Dutton, "The Thrill of Victory, the Complexity of Defeat: Self-Esteem and People's Emotional Reactions to Success and Failure," *Journal of Personality and Social Psychology* 68, no. 4 (1995): 712–722, https://doi.org/10.1037/0022-3514.68.4.712.

148   Oscar Wilde, "The Decay of Lying," *Intentions* (New York: Brentano, 1905 [1889]), https://www.sscnet.ucla.edu/comm/steen/cogweb/Abstracts/Wilde_1889.html.

149   "7 Types of Conflict in Literature," Scribendi, accessed September 6, 2020, https://www.scribendi.com/academy/articles/types_of_conflict_in_literature.en.html.

# ENDNOTES

150   Cheryl E. Rodriguez, *What's Your Story?*, 2nd ed. (Scotts Valley, CA: CreateSpace Independent Publishing, 2013), 105.

151   Celeste Friend, "Social Contract Theory," *Internet Encyclopedia of Philosophy*, accessed October 17, 2020, https://iep.utm.edu/soc-cont/.

152   Katie Shonk, "Elements of Conflict: Diagnose What's Gone Wrong," Harvard Law School Daily Blog, April 1, 2021, https://www.pon. harvard.edu/daily/conflict-resolution/elements-conflict-diagnose-whats-gone-wrong/.

153   Carl von Clausewitz, *On War*, ed. Michael Howard and Peter Paret (Princeton, NJ: Princeton University Press, 1984), 75–76.

154   Clausewitz, *On War*, 80.

155   Mark Grimsley, *The Hard Hand of War* (New York: Cambridge University Press, 1995), 143.

156   "William Tecumseh Sherman," Wikiquote, last modified May 18, 2021, https://en.wikiquote.org/wiki/William_Tecumseh_Sherman.

157   Grimsley, *Hard Hand*, 149.

158   Bernard Gert and Joshua Gert, "The Definition of Morality," *Stanford Encyclopedia of Philosophy* Archive, April 17, 2002, https://plato. stanford.edu/archives/fall2020/entries/morality-definition/.

159   Thomas Jefferson et al, "The Declaration of Independence," National Archives, accessed July 31, 2021, https://www.archives.gov/founding-docs/declaration.

160   "Jean Piaget," *Britannica*, accessed on September 16, 2020, https://www. britannica.com/biography/Jean-Piaget.

161    Jean Piaget, *The Moral Judgment of the Child*, trans. Marjorie Gabain (New York: Free Press, 1997), 13.

162    Piaget, *Moral Judgment*, 14.

163    Dave Grossman, *On Killing* (Boston, MA: Little, Brown, 1996), 3.

164    Grossman, *On Killing*, 253.

165    Wikipedia, s.v. "Erik Erikson," last modified May 11, 2021, https://en.wikipedia.org/wiki/Erik_Erikson.

166    Erik H. Erikson, *Identity and the Life Cycle* (New York, NY: Norton, 1980), 65.

167    Erikson, *Identity and the Life Cycle*, 65.

168    "Daniel 5," Bible Study Tools, accessed on August 27, 2020, https://www.biblestudytools.com/nkjv/daniel/5.html.

# BIBLIOGRAPHY

"7 Types of Conflict in Literature." Scribendi. Accessed September 6, 2020. https://www.scribendi.com/academy/articles/types_of_conflict_in_literature.en.html.

"America Has Been at War 93% of the Time—222 out of 239 Years—Since 1776." *Washington's Blog*. Global Research: Center for Research on Globalization. January 20, 2019. https://www.globalresearch.ca/america-has-been-at-war-93-of-the-time-222-out-of-239-years-since-1776/5565946.

ARMY.MIL Features. "Oath of Commissioned Officers." US Army. Accessed November 1, 2020. https://www.army.mil/values/officers.html.

_____ "Oath of Enlistment." US Army. Accessed November 1, 2020. https://www.army.mil/values/oath.html.

Bell, David A. *The First Total War: Napoleon's Europe and the Birth of Warfare as We Know It*. Boston, MA: Mariner Books, 2008.

Berger, Fred K., and David Zieve. "Stress and Your Health." *MedlinePlus Medical Encyclopedia*. National Library of Medicine. Last modified May 10, 2020. https://medlineplus.gov/ency/article/003211.htm.

"Biography of Walter Cronkite." Walter Cronkite School of Journalism and Mass Communication. March 8, 2021. https://cronkite.asu.edu/about/walter-cronkite-and-asu/walter-cronkite-biography.

"The Biology of Stress." Mental Help.net: An American Addiction Centers Resource. Accessed October 12, 2021. https://www.mentalhelp.net/stress/the-biology-of-stress/.

Bisson, Jonathan I., Neil P. Roberts, Martin Andrew, Rosalind Cooper, and Catrin Lewis. "Psychological Therapies for Chronic Post-Traumatic Stress Disorder (PTSD) in Adults." *Cochrane Database of Systematic Reviews*, December 13, 2013. https://doi.org/10.1002/14651858.cd003388.pub4.

Black, Henry Campbell, Joseph R. Nolan, and Michael J. Connolly. *Black's Law Dictionary: Definitions of the Terms and Phrases of American and English Jurisprudence, Ancient and Modern*. Sixth ed. St. Paul, MN: West Pub. Co., 1990.

"The Body Language of Depression." *Exploring Your Mind*. February 21, 2020. https://exploringyourmind.com/the-body-language-of-depression/.

Bremner, Dr. J. Douglas. "Traumatic Stress: Effects on the Brain." *Dialogues in Clinical Neuroscience*. US National Library of Medicine. 2006. https://pubmed.ncbi.nlm.nih.gov/17290802/.

Briquelet, Kate. "Feds Are Asking Epstein Victims about Sex-Trafficking Crimes." *Daily Beast*. June 3, 2019. https://www.thedailybeast.com/feds-are-asking-jeffrey-epsteins-victims-about-sex-trafficking-crimes.

Brown, Eric. "Plato's Ethics and Politics in The Republic." *Stanford Encyclopedia of Philosophy*. Stanford University, September 12, 2017. https://plato.stanford.edu/archives/fall2017/entries/plato-ethics-politics/.

Brown, Jonathon D., and Keith A. Dutton. "The Thrill of Victory, the Complexity of Defeat: Self-Esteem and People's Emotional Reactions to Success and Failure." *Journal of Personality and Social Psychology* 68, no. 4 (1995): 712–22. https://doi.org/10.1037/0022-3514.68.4.712.

Brymer, Melissa, Christopher Layne, Anne Jacobs, Robert Pynoos, Josef Ruzek, Alan Steinburg, Eric Vernberg, and Patricia Watson. *Psychological First Aid: Field Operations Guide*. Second edition. Los Angeles: National Child Traumatic Stress Network, 2006.

# BIBLIOGRAPHY

"By The Numbers." Gary Sinise Foundation. Accessed October 26, 2020. https://www.garysinisefoundation.org/by-the-numbers/.

Calvo, Franz, Bryant T Karras, Richard Phillips, Ann Marie Kimball, and Fred Wolf. "Diagnoses, Syndromes, and Diseases: A Knowledge Representation Problem." AMIA Symposium. American Medical Informatics Association, 2003. https://www.ncbi.nlm.nih.gov/pmc/articles/PMC1480257/.

Cascio, Christopher. "Types of Conflict That Can Be Found in a Narrative." *Seattle PI* (website). November 21, 2017. https://education.seattlepi.com/types-conflict-can-found-narrative-3739.html.

"The Causes and Effects of Drug Addiction." Alta Mira Recovery. Accessed September 6, 2020. https://www.altamirarecovery.com/drug-addiction/causes-effects-drug-addiction/.

Charlton, James. *The Military Quotation Book: More than 1,200 of the Best Quotations about War, Leadership, Courage, Victory, and Defeat.* New York: St. Martin's Press, 2002.

"Child Trafficking Statistics: U.S. and International." Ark of Hope for Children. April 9, 2019. https://arkofhopeforchildren.org/child-trafficking/child-trafficking-statistics.

"Chronic Pain Syndrome." Department of Neurology. Columbia University. August 18, 2020. https://www.columbianeurology.org/neurology/staywell/chronic-pain-syndrome.

"Classification of Burns." *Health Encyclopedia.* University of Rochester Medical Center. Accessed October 1, 2020. https://www.urmc.rochester.edu/encyclopedia/content.aspx?ContentTypeID=90.

Clausewitz, Carl von. *On War.* Princeton, NJ: Princeton University Press, 1984.

"Conscience." Etymonline.com. Accessed August 7, 2020. https://www.etymonline.com/word/conscience.

Cowan, Kristina. "Suicide and Its Unrelenting Stigma." *Huffington*

*Post*. December 7, 2017. https://www.huffpost.com/entry/
suicide-and-its-unrelenti_b_6543364.

Dale, Edwin L. "What Vietnam Did to the American Economy." *New York Times*. January 28, 1973. https://www.nytimes.com/1973/01/28/
archives/what-vietnam-did-to-the-american-economy-worsening-
payments-deficit.html.

Darack, Ed. "Extortion 17, Seal Team Six and What Really Happened on the Deadliest Day in the History of Naval Special Warfare and the US War in Afghanistan." *Newsweek*. August 31, 2017. https://
www.newsweek.com/extortion-17-seal-team-six-navy-seals-
afghanistan-conspiracy-theories-names-657841.

Davis, Jon. "What Does War Smell like, Whether on Land, in Cockpits, in Submarines or Elsewhere?" Quora.com. February 6, 2017. https://
www.quora.com/What-does-war-smell-like-whether-on-land-in-
cockpits-in-submarines-or-elsewhere.

"Depression." Anxiety and Depression Association of America. 2020. https://adaa.org/understanding-anxiety/depression.

"Depression." World Health Organization. World Health Organization, January 30, 2020. https://www.who.int/news-room/fact-sheets/
detail/depression.

Doerries, Bryan. "How the Secrets of the Ancient Greeks Can Heal Our Wounded Warriors." *Observer*. November 2, 2016. https://observer.
com/2015/11/ptsd-is-from-b-c/.

_____ *The Theater of War: What Ancient Greek Tragedies Can Teach Us Today*. New York, NY: Vintage Books, a division of Penguin Random House LLC, 2016.

"Double Jeopardy." Legal Information Institute. Cornell Law School. Accessed October 11, 2020. https://www.law.cornell.edu/wex/
double_jeopardy.

"Drug Addiction (Substance Use Disorder)." Mayo Clinic. Mayo Foundation for Medical Education and Research. October 26, 2017.

# BIBLIOGRAPHY

https://www.mayoclinic.org/diseases-conditions/drug-addiction/ symptoms-causes/syc-20365112.

Edwards, Lee. "Three Nations That Tried Socialism and Rejected It." The Heritage Foundation. October 16, 2019. https://www.heritage.org/progressivism/commentary/ three-nations-tried-socialism-and-rejected-it.

Emery, Lea Rose. "15 Crazy Stories of People Who Survived Unsurvivable Situations." Ranker.com. December 20, 2019. https:// www.ranker.com/list/crazy-survival-stories/lea-rose-emery.

*Encyclopaedia Britannica*. "Jean Piaget." September 16, 2020. https:// www.britannica.com/biography/Jean-Piaget.

_____ "The Plays." Accessed October 26, 2020. https://www.britannica. com/biography/Sophocles/The-plays.

_____ "Quantum Mechanics." Accessed October 13, 2021. https://www. britannica.com/science/quantum-mechanics-physics.

Erikson, Erik H. *Identity and the Life Cycle*. New York, NY: Norton, 1980.

"Fifth Amendment." Legal Information Institute. Cornell Law School. Accessed October 11, 2020. https://www.law.cornell.edu/ constitution/fifth_amendment.

Folk, Jim. "Are There Good and Bad Stress Hormones?" Anxietycentre. com. June 2, 2020. https://www.anxietycentre.com/FAQ/are-there- good-and-bad-stress-hormones.shtml.

"Frequently Asked Questions about Suicide." National Institute of Mental Health. US Department of Health and Human Services. Accessed September 6, 2020. https://www.nimh.nih.gov/health/ publications/suicide-faq/index.shtml.

Friedkin, William, dir. *The Exorcist*. 1973. Los Angeles: Warner Brothers, 1998. DVD. 121 minutes.

Friend, Celeste. "Social Contract Theory." *Internet Encyclopedia of Philosophy*. Hamilton College. Accessed October 17, 2020. https:// iep.utm.edu/soc-cont/.

Furton, Edward J. "Is a Soul Conscious after Death?" *Legatus*. Accessed August 7, 2020. https://legatus.org/news/ is-a-soul-conscious-after-death.

Gert, Bernard, and Joshua Gert. "The Definition of Morality." *Stanford Encyclopedia of Philosophy*. Stanford University. September 8, 2020. https://plato.stanford.edu/archives/fall2020/entries/ morality-definition/.

Grant, R. G. *Battle: A Visual Journey through 5,000 Years of Combat*. London: Dorling Kindersley, 2005.

Greene, Adam. "Suicidal Language." *Science in Our World: Certainty and Controversy* (blog). Penn State University. September 14, 2014. https://sites.psu.edu/siowfa14/tag/body-language/.

Grimsley, Mark. *The Hard Hand of War*. New York: Cambridge University Press, 1995.

Grossman, Dave. *On Killing*. Boston, MA: Little, Brown, 1996.

Hall, Lynn K. *Counseling Military Families: What Mental Health Professionals Need to Know*. New York, NY: Routledge, Taylor and Francis Group, 2008.

Hamilton, Bernard. "'God Wills It': Signs of Divine Approval in the Crusade Movement." *Studies in Church History* 41 (2005): 88–98. https://doi.org/10.1017/s0424208400000140.

Hautzinger, Sarah, Catherine Lutz, Robert Miller, and Jean Scandlyn. "US & Allied Wounded." *Costs of War*. The Watson Institute for International and Public Affairs at Brown University. February 2015. https://watson.brown.edu/costsofwar/costs/human/military/ wounded.

Helfand, Rabbi Corey. "Why Did It Take 40 Years to Reach the Promised Land?" *Jewish News of Northern California*. March 7, 2017. https://www.jweekly.com/2013/01/25/ torah-why-did-it-take-40-years-to-reach-the-promised-land/.

Helgeland, Brian, dir. *A Knight's Tale*. 2001. Culver City, CA: Sony Pictures, 2002. DVD. 132 minutes.

# BIBLIOGRAPHY

Hilgevoord, Jan, and Jos Uffink. "The Uncertainty Principle." *Stanford Encyclopedia of Philosophy*. Stanford University. October 8, 2001. https://plato.stanford.edu/archives/win2016/entries/qt-uncertainty.

History.com. "Geneva Convention." November 17, 2017. https://www.history.com/topics/world-war-ii/geneva-convention.

_____ "Nicole Brown Simpson and Ron Goldman Murdered." November 13, 2009. https://www.history.com/this-day-in-history/nicole-brown-simpson-and-ron-goldman-murdered.

_____ "Woodstock." March 9, 2018. https://www.history.com/topics/1960s/woodstock.

"How Is TBI Diagnosed?" BrainLine: All About Brain Injury and PTSD. WETA Public Television. August 9, 2018. https://www.brainline.org/article/how-tbi-diagnosed.

"How Much Cargo Can the Largest Shipping Container Ship Really Hold?" Universal Cargo. July 17, 2018. https://www.universalcargo.com/how-much-cargo-can-the-largest-shipping-container-ship-really-hold/.

"Increase in Armed Forces Suicides over Last Five Years, MOD Figures Show." Forces Network. British Forces Broadcasting Service. March 26, 2020. https://www.forces.net/news/increase-armed-forces-suicides-over-last-five-years-mod-figures-show.

Jefferson, Thomas, and et al. "The Declaration of Independence." National Archives and Records Administration. July 4, 1776. https://www.archives.gov/founding-docs/declaration.

Johnson, Captain Charles. *A General History of the Pyrates*. London: T. Warner, at the Black-Boy, 1724. https://archive.org/details/generalhistoryof00defo/page/n3/mode/2up?q=The+articles+for+Captain+Bartholomew++Roberts.

Johnstone, Ainsilie. "The Amazing Phenomenon of Muscle Memory." Medium.com. Oxford University. December 14, 2017. https://medium.com/oxford-university/the-amazing-phenomenon-of-muscle-memory-fb1cc4c4726.

Kemp, Janet, and Robert Bossarte. "Suicide Data Report—2012—Veterans Affairs." VA Office of Public and Intergovernmental Affairs. US Department of Veteran Affairs. 2012. https://www.va.gov/opa/docs/Suicide-Data-Report-2012-final.pdf.

Keneally, Meghan. "The 11 Mass Deadly School Shootings That Happened since Columbine." ABC News. April 19, 2019. https://abcnews.go.com/US/11-mass-deadly-school-shootings-happened-columbine/story?id=62494128.

Kime, Patricia. "Active-Duty Military Suicides at Record Highs in 2018." Military.com. January 30, 2019. https://www.military.com/daily-news/2019/01/30/active-duty-military-suicides-near-record-highs-2018.html.

Klein, Sarah. "The 3 Major Stress Hormones, Explained." *Huffington Post*. April 19, 2013. https://www.huffpost.com/entry/adrenaline-cortisol-stress-hormones_n_3112800.

Krnel. "Great Ideas? Average Events? Small People?" *Steemit*. Accessed June 30, 2021. https://steemit.com/psychology/@krnel/great-ideas-average-events-small-people.

Landis, John, dir. *National Lampoon's Animal House*. 1978. Universal City, CA: Universal Studios, 1998. DVD. 109 minutes.

Lanza, Robert. "Does the Soul Exist? Evidence Says 'Yes.'" *Psychology Today*. Sussex Publishers. December 21, 2011. https://www.psychologytoday.com/us/blog/biocentrism/201112/does-the-soul-exist-evidence-says-yes.

Leonard, Jayne. "Survivor's Guilt: What Is It, Symptoms, and How to Cope." In *Medical News Today*, edited by Timothy J. Legg. MediLexicon International. June 27, 2019. https://www.medicalnewstoday.com/articles/325578.

_____ "What Is Trauma? Types, Symptoms, and Treatments." *Medical News Today*, edited by Timothy J. Legg. MediLexicon International. June 3, 2020. https://www.medicalnewstoday.com/articles/trauma.

# BIBLIOGRAPHY

Li, Johanna. "Navy SEAL Donates Liver to Stranger across the Country: 'That Was a No-Brainer for Me.'" *Inside Edition*. February 2, 2018. https://www.insideedition.com/navy-seal-donates-liver-stranger-across-country-was-no-brainer-me-40392.

Lloyd, Sharon A, and Susanne Sreedhar. "Hobbes's Moral and Political Philosophy." *Stanford Encyclopedia of Philosophy*. Stanford University. April 30, 2018. https://plato.stanford.edu/entries/hobbes-moral/.

Longley, Robert. "Differences between Communism and Socialism." ThoughtCo. March 3, 2020. https://www.thoughtco.com/difference-between-communism-and-socialism-195448.

Lyttle, John B. *If I Should Die before I Wake: One Marine's Experience on Iwo Jima*. New York, NY: Vantage Press, 2007.

Maxwell, John. "Changing Your Beliefs Starts with Changing Your Thinking." *Houston Business Journal*. February 22, 2004. https://www.bizjournals.com/houston/stories/2004/02/23/smallb4.html.

McConnell, Terrance. "Moral Dilemmas." *Stanford Encyclopedia of Philosophy*. Stanford University. June 16, 2018. https://plato.stanford.edu/entries/moral-dilemmas/.

Mcnaughton, Neil, and Luke D. Smillie. "Some Metatheoretical Principles for Personality Neuroscience." *Personality Neuroscience* 1 (2018). https://doi.org/10.1017/pen.2018.9.

"Mental Health Disorders Common Following Mild Head Injury." National Institutes of Health. US Department of Health and Human Services. January 30, 2019. https://www.nih.gov/news-events/news-releases/mental-health-disorders-common-following-mild-head-injury.

Minster, Christopher. "Biography of 'Black Bart' Roberts, Highly Successful Pirate." ThoughtCo. July 21, 2019. https://www.thoughtco.com/bartholomew-black-bart-roberts-2136212.

Moore, Michael. "Causation in the Law." *Stanford Encyclopedia of*

*Philosophy*. Stanford University. October 3, 2019. https://plato. stanford.edu/entries/causation-law/.

Mostow, Jonathan, dir. *U-571*. 2000. Universal City, CA: Universal Pictures, 2000. DVD. 116 minutes.

*National Veteran Suicide Prevention Annual Report 2020*. Office of Mental Health and Suicide Prevention. US Department of Veterans Affairs. Accessed October 15, 2021. https://www.mentalhealth. va.gov/docs/data-sheets/2020/2020-National-Veteran-Suicide-Prevention-Annual-Report-11-2020-508.pdf.

Najdowski, Cynthia J, and Catherine L Bonventre. "Deception in the Interrogation Room." *Monitor on Psychology*. American Psychological Association, May 2014. https://www.apa.org/ monitor/2014/05/jn.

"Norman Schwarzkopf." Biography.com. A&E Networks Television, July 16, 2020. https://www.biography.com/military-figure/ norman-schwarzkopf.

Oord, Christian. "Believe It or Not: Since Its Birth the USA Has Only Had 17 Years of Peace." War History Online. May 19, 2019. https:// www.warhistoryonline.com/instant-articles/usa-only-17-years-of-peace.html.

Oquendo, M. A., et al. "Life Events: a Complex Role in the Timing of Suicidal Behavior among Depressed Patients." *Molecular Psychiatry* 19, no. 8 (October 15, 2013): 902–9. https://doi.org/10.1038/ mp.2013.128.

O'Toole, Garson. "Better to Remain Silent and Be Thought a Fool than to Speak and Remove All Doubt." Quote Investigator, July 4, 2019. https://quoteinvestigator.com/2010/05/17/remain-silent/.

Paine, Thomas. *Common Sense*. New York: Fall River Press, 2013.

Paridon, Seth. "The Highest and Purest Democracy: Rabbi Roland Gittelsohn's Iwo Jima Eulogy to His Fallen Comrades." The National WWII Museum: New Orleans. February 18, 2020. https://www.nationalww2museum.org/war/articles/

highest-and-purest-democracy-rabbi-roland-gittelsohns-iwo-jima-eulogy-his-fallen.

Petersen, Wolfgang, dir. *Troy*. 2004. Burbank, CA: Warner Brothers, 2007. DVD. 163 minutes.

Piaget, Jean. *The Moral Judgment of the Child*. Translated by Marjorie Gabain. New York, NY: Free Press Paperbacks, 1997.

"Protect Your Brain from Stress." Harvard Health Publishing. August 2018. https://www.health.harvard.edu/mind-and-mood/protect-your-brain-from-stress.

"Psychological First Aid: Field Operations Guide." PTSD: National Center for PTSD. U.S. Department of Veterans Affairs. April 13, 2006. https://www.ptsd.va.gov/professional/treat/type/psych_firstaid_manual.asp.

Rayner, Gordon, Lexi Finnigan, and Henry Bodkin. "Girl, 14, Who Died of Cancer Cryogenically Frozen after Telling Judge She Wanted to Be Brought Back to Life 'in Hundreds of Years.'" *The Telegraph*. November 18, 2016. https://www.telegraph.co.uk/news/2016/11/18/cancer-girl-14-is-cryogenically-frozen-after-telling-judge-she-w/.

Robinson, Sarita. "Isolation Has Profound Effects on the Human Body and Brain. Here's What Happens." *Science Alert*. September 14, 2014. https://www.sciencealert.com/isolation-has-profound-effects-on-the-human-body-and-brain-here-s-what-happens.

Rodriguez, Cheryl E. *What's Your Story?* Scotts Valley, CA: CreateSpace Independent Publishing, 2013.

Romano, Neil, et al. *The Danger of Assisted Suicide Laws*. National Council on Disability. October 9, 2019. https://ncd.gov/sites/default/files/NCD_Assisted_Suicide_Report_508.pdf.

Rummel, R. J. "The Elements of Social Conflict." *Understanding Conflict and War: Volume 2, The Conflict Helix*. Los Angeles: Sage Publishing, 1976. https://www.hawaii.edu/powerkills/TCH.CHAP28.HTM.

Sanders, Peggy. "Rules and Common Sense." *Fence Post*, May 29,

2020. https://www.thefencepost.com/opinion/peggy-sanders/
rules-and-common-sense/.

Sapolsky, Robert M. "Stress Hormones: Good and Bad." *Neurobiology
of Disease* 7, no. 5 (2000): 540–42. https://doi.org/10.1006/
nbdi.2000.0350.

Shakespeare, William. *King Henry V*. In *The Complete Works of William
Shakespeare*, "Introduction," by Michael A. Cramer, 532–69. San
Diego, CA: Canterbury Classics, 2014.

Shane, Leo III. "VA: Suicide Rate for Younger Veterans Increased by
More Than 10 Percent." *Military Times*. September 26, 2018. https://
www.militarytimes.com/news/pentagon-congress/2018/09/26/
suicide-rate-spikes-among-younger-veterans/.

Shepard, Richard F. "Overcoming the Holocaust with Success."
*New York Times*. December 20, 1992. https://www.nytimes.
com/1992/12/20/nyregion/overcoming-the-holocaust-with-success.
html.

Shonk, Katie. "3 Types of Conflict and How to Address Them." Program
On Negotiation. Harvard Law School. February 28, 2020. https://
www.pon.harvard.edu/daily/conflict-resolution/types-conflict/.

_____ "Elements of Conflict: Diagnose What's Gone Wrong."
Program On Negotiation. Harvard Law School. March 12,
2020. https://www.pon.harvard.edu/daily/conflict-resolution/
elements-conflict-diagnose-whats-gone-wrong/.

Sinha, Rajita. "Chronic Stress, Drug Use, and Vulnerability to
Addiction." *Annals of the New York Academy of Sciences*. US
National Library of Medicine. October 2008. https://www.ncbi.nlm.
nih.gov/pmc/articles/PMC2732004/.

Sinise, Gary. "Our Mission." Gary Sinise Foundation. Accessed October
26, 2020. https://www.garysinisefoundation.org/mission/.

"Sixth Amendment." Legal Information Institute. Cornell Law
School. Accessed October 11, 2020. https://www.law.cornell.edu/
constitution/sixth_amendment.

Skolnik, Terry. "Hot Bench: A Theory of Appellate Adjudication." *Boston College Law Review*. Boston College Law School. April 30, 2020. https://lawdigitalcommons.bc.edu/bclr/vol61/iss4/2/.

Smith, Sylvia. "The Five Elements of Conflict." Marriage.com. May 8, 2020. https://www.marriage.com/advice/relationship/elements-of-conflict/.

Smith-MacDonald, Lorraine, Jill M. Norris, Shelley Raffin-Bouchal, and Shane Sinclair. "Spirituality and Mental Well-Being in Combat Veterans: A Systematic Review." OUP Academic. Oxford University Press. November 1, 2017. https://academic.oup.com/milmed/article/182/11-12/e1920/4661639.

Starr, Barbara. "US Special Ops Suicides Tripled in 2018." CNN. Cable News Network. February 2, 2019. https://www.cnn.com/2019/02/02/politics/socom-military-suicide-spike-2018/index.html.

"Suicide: 9 Deadliest Myths." CBS News. August 10, 2011. https://www.cbsnews.com/pictures/suicide-9-deadliest-myths/2/.

"Suicide Rate Estimates, Crude Estimates by Country." World Health Organization. April 5, 2018. http://apps.who.int/gho/data/node.main.MHSUICIDE.

Suttie, Jill. "Why the World Needs an Empathy Revolution." *Greater Good Magazine*. Berkley University of California. February 1, 2019. https://greatergood.berkeley.edu/article/item/why_the_world_needs_an_empathy_revolution.

Szecsei, Szabolcs. "20 Statistics on Fatherless Homeless and the Importance of Dads." *Modern Gentlemen*. January 7, 2021. https://moderngentlemen.net/statistics-on-fatherless-homes/.

Tilghman, Andrew. "The Pentagon Keeps Data on Millennials. This Is What It Says." *Military Times*. July 9, 2016. https://www.militarytimes.com/news/your-military/2016/07/09/the-pentagon-keeps-data-on-millennials-this-is-what-it-says/.

"Tom Brokaw Explains the Origins of 'The Greatest Generation.'" NBCNews.com. NBCUniversal News Group. June 5, 2014. https://

www.nbcnews.com/video/tom-brokaw-explains-the-origins-of-the-greatest-generation-273640003752.

"Types of Stressors (Eustress vs. Distress)." Mentalhealth.net. American Addiction Centers. Accessed October 1, 2021. https://www.mentalhelp.net/stress/types-of-stressors-eustress-vs-distress/.

Tzu, Sun. *The Art of War*. Translated by Thomas F. Cleary. Boston and London: Shambhala Publications, Inc., 2003.

"Understanding the Stress Response." Harvard Health Publishing. Harvard Medical School. July 6, 2020. https://www.health.harvard.edu/staying-healthy/understanding-the-stress-response.

The United States Department of Justice. "About DOJ." October 14, 2020. https://www.justice.gov/about.

United States Marine Corps. "6th Marine Regiment: 1st Battalion History." Accessed November 28, 2020. https://www.6thmarines.marines.mil/Units/1st-Battalion/History/.

"Updates to DSM–5 Criteria, Text and ICD-10 Codes." American Psychiatric Association. Accessed November 6, 2020. https://www.psychiatry.org/psychiatrists/practice/dsm/updates-to-dsm-5.

Van Gulick, Robert. "Consciousness." *Stanford Encyclopedia of Philosophy*. Edited by Edward N Zalta. 2018. https://plato.stanford.edu/archives/spr2018/entries/consciousness/.

Vance, Erik. "Unlocking the Healing Power of You." *National Geographic*. June 3, 2020. https://www.nationalgeographic.com/magazine/2016/12/healing-science-belief-placebo/.

Verbinski, Gore, dir. *Pirates of the Caribbean: The Curse of the Black Pearl*. 2003. Burbank: Walt Disney Pictures, 2004. DVD. 143 minutes.

Watts, Roger P. "How the Addicted Brain Hijacks the Mind." MentalHelp.net. An American Addictions Center Resource. Accessed October 17, 2021. https://www.mentalhelp.net/blogs/how-the-addicted-brain-hijacks-the-mind/.

Westcott, W. Wynn. *A Social Science Treatise Suicide: Its History,*

# BIBLIOGRAPHY

*Literature, Jurisprudence, Causation, and Prevention.* London: H. K. Lewis, 1885.

"What's the Difference between a Civil Judgment and a Criminal Conviction?" Nolo. Accessed on October 15, 2021. https://www.nolo.com/legal-encyclopedia/question-civil-judgment-versus-criminal-conviction-28300.html.

Wikipedia. "Conscription in the United States." Last modified November 1, 2020. https://en.wikipedia.org/wiki/Conscription_in_the_United_States.

_____ "Erik Erikson." Last modified May 11, 2021. https://en.wikipedia.org/wiki/Erik_Erikson.

_____ "John Gotti." Last modified October 12, 2021. https://en.wikipedia.org/wiki/John_Gotti.

_____ "Jonathan Shay." Last modified April 19, 2020. https://en.wikipedia.org/wiki/Jonathan_Shay.

_____ "Survivor Guilt." Last modified June 2, 2021. https://en.wikipedia.org/wiki/Survivor_guilt.

_____ "Tap Code." Last modified May 21, 2021. https://en.wikipedia.org/wiki/Tap_code.

Wilde, Oscar. "The Decay of Lying." In *Intentions*. New York: Brentano's, 1905. Online at https://www.sscnet.ucla.edu/comm/steen/cogweb/Abstracts/Wilde_1889.html.

Wilmot, William W., and Joyce L. Hocker. "Key Elements of Conflict: Conflict and Interdependence." From *Interpersonal Conflict*, fifth edition. New York, NY: McGraw-Hill, 1998. Available at Conflict Management (website). http://www.cios.org/encyclopedia/conflict/BKeyelements2_interdependence.htm.

World Population Review. "Suicide Rate by Country 2020," 2020. https://worldpopulationreview.com/countries/suicide-rate-by-country/.

Zahn, Timothy. *Star Wars: Thrawn.* New York, NY: Del Rey, Random House, 2017.

Zeman, Adam. "Consciousness." *Brain: A Journal of Neurology* 124, no. 7 (July 1, 2001): 1263–89. https://doi.org/10.1093/brain/124.7.1263.

Zemeckis, Robert, dir. *Cast Away*. 2000. Los Angeles: 20th Century Fox, 2001. DVD. 114 minutes.

Zemeckis, Robert, dir. *Forrest Gump*. 1994. Hollywood: Paramount Pictures, 2001. DVD. 142 minutes.

# ABOUT THE AUTHORS

 **Greg Wark** founded Mission Force in 1996 and currently serves as president. Prior to starting Force, Greg served as lead pastor of a congregation in Southern California, which had a large percentage of military personnel. This experience drove him to concentrate on the unique moral needs of those who serve in America's armed forces. Several years later, he began to work full time developing leaders among military and law enforcement personnel. Greg holds several postgraduate degrees, including a master's degree in theology and a Doctor of Ministry degree. His experience, education, and drive make him an excellent fit for this task.

Greg continues to be a pastor, counselor, mentor, and friend to a large group of military and law enforcement personnel spread across the United States. He also serves as a chaplain for a federal law enforcement agency. As such, Greg devotes his time, energy, and knowledge to developing positive and influential leaders who work in high-pressure environments. He also mentors military and law enforcement personnel to help them and their families cope with the emotional difficulties of their service. For Greg, the work of Mission Force is a continuation of his passion to create dynamic, positive leaders who defend the vulnerable and fulfill their civic responsibilities with excellence.

Currently, Greg is the executive vice president of Atlas Aegis LLC, a premier security firm based in Nashville, Tennessee. Greg's main responsibilities are business development and customer relations.

Greg has authored three books: *A Prophets Reward*, *A Good Death*, and *The Warfighter's Soul*. Greg and Amber have been married for forty years and have five children, nineteen grandchildren, and one great granddaughter. They currently reside in Nashville, Tennessee.

**R. T. Rodriguez (Dr. Ray)** has dedicated his life to helping people in crisis while continuing to maintain a successful career as an engineer and remaining a lifelong student. Ray was born and raised in Texas among a loving family. His father, a farmer, a lifelong student himself, and a Korean war combat veteran, instilled in him a love for children and the importance of a caring environment. His father witnessed the suffering of young men enduring trauma born out their warfare experience. During the Vietnam War, Ray himself noticed a phenomenon that has driven him to seek answers to this day: *Why do two seemingly equal veterans return from war with one leading a hope-filled life and the other suffering with lifelong trauma?*

While attending Texas Tech University, Ray was convinced to join the US Marine Corp. While there he learned about and found a knack for writing computer code. This career path allowed him to become a business entrepreneur with extensive experience in encoding and encryption systems engineering. His job has allowed him to work and live in multiple countries. Ray and his wife, Cheryl, have raised four children of their own and now have six grandchildren. While raising their children, they volunteered as directors of the children and youth departments at their local church. At the same time, Ray finished up his undergraduate degree in preparation for law school and possibly entering a career in politics. After he received his juris doctorate degree, he changed course and earned a master's degree in military history and became certified as a crisis counselor.